Macroeconomics at the Service of Public Policy

Macroeconomics at the Service of Public Policy

Edited by

Thomas J. Sargent
Jouko Vilmunen

OXFORD
UNIVERSITY PRESS

OXFORD
UNIVERSITY PRESS

Great Clarendon Street, Oxford, OX2 6DP,
United Kingdom

Oxford University Press is a department of the University of Oxford. It furthers the University's objective of excellence in research, scholarship, and education by publishing worldwide. Oxford is a registered trade mark of Oxford University Press in the UK and in certain other countries

First published 2013
First published in paperback 2015

Published in the United States of America by Oxford University Press
198 Madison Avenue, New York, NY 10016, United States of America

British Library Cataloguing in Publication Data
Data available

Library of Congress Cataloging in Publication Data
Data available

ISBN 978–0–19–966612–6 (Hbk.)
ISBN 978–0–19–874376–7 (Pbk.)

Dedicated to Seppo Honkapohja

Acknowledgements

This book containing a collection of contributions from well-known academic researchers would not have been possible without very significant effort from several people. First of all, we are grateful to all the authors, whose research papers are published as separate chapters of this book. The value of their effort is further enhanced by the fact that they contributed by producing new papers with novel results. We are particularly grateful to Martin Ellison, who in addition to contributing a chapter also provided valuable editorial help in parts of the book. Erkki Koskela, also one of the contributors to this book, initially introduced us to the idea of publishing a *festschrift* celebrating Seppo Honkapohja's 60th birthday. His help is gratefully acknowledged. We are also grateful to Ms Päivi Nietosvaara, who produced the initial manuscript. Having seen all the contributions collected in a single manuscript convinced us that instead of publishing a *festschrift*, we should opt for a commercial publication with a well-known international publisher. Finally, the extremely positive feedback provided by the three referees that Oxford University Press selected to review the manuscript is gratefully acknowledged.

25 June 2012

Thomas J. Sargent
Jouko Vilmunen

Contents

List of Figures

List of Tables

List of Contributors

Kenneth J. Arrow, Stanford University

Jess Benhabib, New York University and Paris School of Economics

William Branch, University of California, Irvine

In-Koo Cho, University of Illinois

Martin Ellison, University of Oxford and Bank of Finland

David Evans, New York University

George W. Evans, University of Oregon and University of St. Andrews

Chryssi Giannitsarou, University of Cambridge and CEPR

Seppo Honkapohja, Bank of Finland

Kenneth Kasa, Simon Fraser University

Erkki Koskela, Helsinki University

Bruce McGough, Oregon State University

Kaushik Mitra, University of St. Andrews

Thomas J. Sargent, New York University and Hoover Institution

Hans-Werner Sinn, Ifo Institute for Economic Research

Jouko Vilmunen, Bank of Finland

Noah Williams, University of Wisconsin, Madison

Introduction

Thomas J. Sargent and Jouko Vilmunen

Modern macroeconomics can hold its head high because so much of it is research directed at informing important public policy decisions. It is a noble aspiration to seek better rules for our central banks and fiscal authorities and this is what attracted the contributors to this volume into macroeconomics.

The logical structures that emerge from striving to put economic theory at the service of public policy are intrinsically beautiful in their internal structures and also useful in their applications. The contributors to this volume are leaders in patiently creating models and pushing forward technical frontiers. Revealed preferences show that they love equilibrium stochastic processes that are determined by Euler equations for modelling people's decisions about working, saving, investing, and learning, set within contexts designed to enlighten monetary and fiscal policy-makers. Their papers focus on forces that can help us to understand macroeconomic outcomes, including learning, multiple equilibria, moral hazard, asymmetric information, heterogeneity, and constraints on commitment technologies.

The papers follow modern macroeconomics in using mathematics and statistics to understand behaviour in situations where there is uncertainty about how the future unfolds from the past. They are thus united in a belief that the more dynamic, uncertain, and ambiguous the economic environment they seek to understand is, the more we have to roll up our sleeves and figure out how to apply mathematics in new ways.

The contributions to this volume cover a wide range of issues in macroeconomics and macroeconomic policy. They also testify to a high research intensity in many areas of macroeconomics. They form the basis for warning against interpreting the scope of macroeconomics too narrowly. For example, a subfield of macroeconomics, namely the line of modern business cycle research culminating in the dynamic stochastic general equilibrium (DSGE) models now widely used in central banks and treasuries, has been criticized for not predicting the recent financial crisis and for providing imperfect policies for managing its consequences. There is a grain of truth in this criticism when applied to a particular subclass of models within macroeconomics. But it is also misleading because it is inaccurate and shortsighted in missing the diversity of macroeconomic research on financial, information, learning, and other types of imperfections that long before the recent crisis were actively being studied in other parts of macroeconomics, and that had not yet made their way into many of the pre-crisis DSGE models because practical econometric versions of those models were mainly designed to fit data periods that did not include financial crises. A major constructive scientific response to the limitations of those older DSGE models is an active research programme within central banks and at universities to bring big financial shocks and various kinds of financial, learning, and labour market frictions into a new generation of DSGE models for guiding policy. DSGE modelling today is a vigorous adaptive process that learns from past mistakes in a continuing struggle to understand macroeconomic outcomes.

In Chapter 1 Kenneth Arrow poses the fundamental question of 'Is the Market System an Efficient Bearer of Risk?' and focuses on deficiencies in models that combine risk aversion and general equilibrium. As Arrow aptly notes, the title of his chapter poses a vexing question and leads to many further questions. A new conceptual basis for future research may be needed for the economics profession to provide a more definite answer.

Arrow notes that the market system is ideally efficient in allocating resources in two ways. Firstly, given the stock of resources and technological knowledge in the economy, the competitive market economy is efficient in the sense of Pareto. Secondly, the market economy economizes on information. In the simplest general equilibrium formulations, agents need know only prices and information to which they are naturally privy. Arrow argues that these usual characterizations of the efficiency of the market system are problematic, even under certainty. At a logical level, for the market economy to find an equilibrium may require more information than what the usual characterization implies.

After noting that the concept of information is already contained in the economic problem, with information meaningless without the presence of uncertainty and uncertainty inherent to the concept of a dispersed economic system, Arrow raises the more general issue of uncertainty and how it is addressed by the market system. The natural starting point is his work with Gerard Debreu, which demonstrates how general equilibrium modelling can be extended to cover uncertainty.

State-contingent quantities, prices, and securities lie at the core of the Arrow–Debreu general equilibrium paradigm. With sufficiently many securities with uncorrelated returns, existence and Pareto efficiency of the competitive equilibrium is theoretically assured. In this Arrow–Debreu world, where the behaviour of individual expected utility maximizers is governed by risk aversion, there are generally gains from trade in risk. However, Arrow argues that the complete risk shifting implied by the general equilibrium model does not necessarily take place, for example if there is asymmetric information. Moreover, he focuses on other failures in the spreading of market risk and on deficiencies in the model that combines risk aversion and general equilibrium—the RAGE model as he calls it.

Arrow discusses a series of factual examples of risk-spreading to highlight the extent to which they represent deviations from the RAGE model, including classical insurance markets, futures markets, leveraged loans, and stock markets. Indeed, from the perspective of applying the RAGE model many important questions can be asked. Why impose legal restrictions and regulations on insurance companies? Why should an insured have an insurable interest in the property insured? Why do speculators sell protection even though they could earn as much in other activities? Why are transactions so much higher, relative to the amount of trade, in foreign exchange markets? Why is the stock market so volatile? Is the volume of transactions on the stock market too high to be explained by smooth risk-spreading? Why do lenders lend money to highly leveraged hedge funds on terms that appear, relative to the risks involved, too favourable to the borrowers?

Although Arrow makes reference to behavioural economics and psychological biases, he offers a different explanation as to why the RAGE model fails. Because of the lack of private information on general equilibrium effects of a state of nature, an individual is not able to buy protection against any realization of an uncertainty. To be able to predict the general equilibrium effects of the resolution of uncertainty, an individual would have to know the preferences and production possibility sets of all other agents.

The US financial crisis of 2008 precipitated a global recession and a sovereign debt crisis in Europe in late April 2010, when EU leaders agreed on an €80 billion Greek rescue package, supplemented by €30 billion from the IMF. Just over a week after agreeing the Greek rescue package, EU leaders decided on a €500 billion rescue package for member countries at risk, on the assumption that the IMF would provide additional support of €250 billion. In his critical essay, Hans-Werner Sinn (Chapter 2) reviews the rescue measures and offers an explanation for the crisis that differs from the mainstream thinking prevailing in 2010. He is very critical of the measures taken because of the moral hazard problems they potentially give rise to.

According to Sinn, the bail-out measures of May 2010 that threw the Maastricht Treaty overboard in a mere 48 hours were overly hasty and ill-designed. The situation in his opinion was not as dangerous at that point in time as politicians claimed, so that there would have been ample time to come up with a more carefully constructed rescue operation. In particular, it was wrong to set up rescue operations that did not involve haircuts to ensure that investors bore the risks they incurred and that would provide an incentive to avoid them in the future. The risk of haircuts generates interest spreads, and interest spreads are necessary to discipline borrowing countries. Sinn argues that the crisis resulted from excessive capital flows that lead to overheating economies in the euro area's periphery and to huge trade deficits. Markets are basically right in trying to correct this, although they act too aggressively and need to be reined in. Rescue operations without haircuts would again result in excessive capital movements and would preserve the trade imbalances currently affecting Europe.

Sinn counters the view that countries with a current account surplus such as Germany were the beneficiaries of the euro, since its current account surplus resulted from capital flight at the expense of domestic investment. In fact, during the years preceding the crisis, Germany had the lowest net investment share of all OECD countries, suffered from mass unemployment, and experienced the second-lowest growth rate in Europe. The widening of interest spreads resulting from the crisis, on the other hand, has been the main driver of Germany's new economic vigour. Investors are now shying away from foreign investment and turning their attention to the German market. Sinn predicts that this will reduce the current account imbalances in the eurozone.

Sinn thus sees a chance for the euro area to self-correct some of these imbalances, but argues that this would only happen if the rescue measures are not overly generous. In particular he argues that haircuts are necessary to ensure that the capital market can perform its allocative function. As an alternative to the measures taken in the spring of 2010, Sinn endorses the ten-point plan for a more stable institutional framework in the euro area that he and his co-authors proposed.[1] The list covers various aspects of conditional help for distressed economies, and proposes that countries be allowed voluntary exit from the euro area.

[1] Wolfgang Franz, Von Clemens Fuest, Martin Hellwig and Hans-Werner Sinn, 'Zehn Regeln zur Rettung des Euro', *Frankfurter Allgemeine Zeitung*, 18 June 2010.

The importance of expectations in generating a liquidity trap at the zero lower bound of interest rates, where conventional monetary policy loses its ability to stimulate the economy, is well understood. Indeed, the possibility of multiple equilibria with a continuum of dynamic paths to an unintended low inflation equilibrium is an established result. The data from Japan and the USA for 2002–10 suggest that a Japanese-style deflation may be a real possibility for the US economy in the coming years. George Evans notes in Chapter 3 that the learning approach provides a perspective on this issue that is quite different from the established wisdom based on fully rational expectations. Although we know that the targeted steady state is locally stable when expectations are formed by adaptive learning, it is not globally stable and there is potentially a serious problem with unstable trajectories. The unintended low-inflation steady state is not even locally stable, and it lies on the boundary of a deflation trap region in which there are divergent paths under learning. More specifically, the danger is that inflation and output decline beyond the low inflation equilibrium if expectations of future inflation, output, and consumption are sufficiently pessimistic. These unstable paths are self-reinforcing, pushing the economy to falling output and deflation. The learning perspective takes these divergent paths seriously. It is more alarmist than the related literature, which is more concerned with the possibility of simple policy rules not preventing the economy converging to the unintended low inflation steady state.

If a pessimistic expectations shock is small then aggressive monetary policy that immediately reduces interest rates close to zero may prevent the economy from falling into a deflation trap. For larger pessimistic expectations shocks, increases in public expenditure may also be needed to spring the deflation trap. Evans notes that policy responses in the USA, UK and Europe are consistent with this line of thinking. However, as Evans also notes, even if the US economy seemed to stabilize after these policy measures, it did so with a weak recovery in 2010 and unemployment that has remained high. At the same time, inflation was low and hovering on the brink of deflation.

Naturally, the data can be interpreted in different ways and there is a case for asking whether and under what conditions the outcomes reflected in macroeconomic data can be generated under learning. To explore this issue, Evans constructs a New Keynesian model featuring asymmetric price adjustment costs. He reports that a deflation trap remains a distinct possibility if there is a large pessimistic shock in the model, with trajectories now converging to a stagnation regime. The stagnation regime is characterized by low steady deflation, zero net interest rates, and a continuum of below normal consumption and output levels. Government expenditure is an important policy tool in the stagnation regime, with the economy exiting the trap only after government spending increases above a certain threshold level.

The macroeconomic learning literature has progressed in a number of stages. Early contributions focused on convergence and stability questions, and were followed by research into learning as a way of selecting between multiple rational expectations equilibria. Empirical applications followed once theoretical issues were resolved. The most recent phase of the learning literature has turned its attention to optimal policy design and more general normative questions.

Infinite-horizon representative agent models with adaptive learning and Euler equation-based behaviour may appear to be potentially inconsistent in their intertemporal accounting, since under 'Euler equation learning' agents do not explicitly account for their intertemporal budget constraint in their behavioural rules. Another criticism that has been made of Euler-equation learning is that it is not natural in the way it postulates agents making forecasts of their future consumption, which is their own choice variable. A final issue sometimes raised is whether temporary equilibrium equations based on Euler equations with subjective expectations may be subject to inconsistency when used in equilibrium equations derived under rational expectations. The alternative 'infinite horizon learning' approach reformulates the problem by assuming that agents incorporate a subjective version of their intertemporal budget constraint when deciding on their behaviour under learning.

Seppo Honkapohja, Kaushik Mitra, and George Evans (Chapter 4) clarify the relationship between the Euler-equation and infinite-horizon approaches to agents' intertemporal behaviour under adaptive learning. They show that intertemporal accounting consistency and the transversality condition hold in an ex post sense along the sequence of temporary equilibria under Euler-equation learning in a dynamic consumption-saving model. The key step in formulating Euler-equation learning is the law of iterated expectations at the individual level. Finally, when learning dynamics are stable the decision rules used by agents are asymptotically optimal. Thus they conclude that Euler-equation and infinite-horizon learning models are alternative, consistent models of decision-making under learning. An advantage of Euler-equation learning is that it does not require agents to base decisions on forecasts of variables far into the future.

Honkapohja et al. emphasize that the convergence conditions for the dynamics of the Euler-equation and infinite-horizon approaches are in general not identical, but show that they are the same in the case of the consumption-saving model and in a New Keynesian model of monetary policy under an interest rate rule. These results are striking, since the Euler-equation and infinite-horizon approaches in general lead to different paths of learning dynamics and there is no general guarantee that the convergence conditions of the two dynamics are identical. Furthermore, there may be differences in the convergence of learning dynamics under Euler-equation and infinite-horizon approaches if there are different informational assumptions, for example whether agents know the central bank's interest rate rule in the infinite-horizon approach. This reflects a more general property of dynamics under adaptive learning, namely that conditions for stability depend crucially on the form of the perceived law of motion used by the economic agents.

It is surprising, as In-Koo Cho and Kenneth Kasa note in Chapter 5, that the learning literature has typically assumed agents are endowed with a *given* model. Whereas the early literature, with its focus on learnability, assumed that this model conformed to the rational expectations equilibrium, more recent approaches have explored the implications of model misspecification by agents. Agents and modellers are though treated asymmetrically in that agents are not allowed to question their model and so never detect any misspecification. One of the main objectives of the learning literature has been to treat agents and their modellers symmetrically, so although it is a step in the right direction to allow agents to revise their statistical forecasting model, Cho and Kasa argue that it is more important for them to model agents as searching for better models rather than refining estimates of a given model.

Cho and Kasa take the next natural step in the learning literature by allowing agents to test the specification of their models. They extend the learning approach by assuming that agents entertain a fixed *set* of models instead of a fixed *single* model. The models contained in the set are potentially misspecified and non-nested, with each model containing a collection of unknown parameters. The agent is assumed to run his current model through a specification test each period. If the current model survives the test then it is used to formulate a policy function, assuming provisionally that the model will not change in the future. If the test indicates rejection then the agent randomly chooses a new model. The approach therefore combines estimation, testing, and selection. Cho and Kasa provide such a model validation exercise for one of the most well-known models, the cobweb model. One of the advantages of their approach is that it can be analysed by large deviations methods, which enables Cho and Kasa to provide explicit predictions about which models will survive repeated specification tests.

The choice between competing forecasting models is also the subject of George Evans, Seppo Honkapohja, Thomas Sargent, and Noah Williams (Chapter 6). As the authors note, most of the research on adaptive learning in macroeconomics assumes that agents update the parameters of a single fixed forecasting model over time. There is no inherent uncertainty about the model or parameters, so agents do not need to choose or average across multiple forecasting models. Evans et al. instead postulate that agents have two alternative forecasting models, using them to form expectations over economic outcomes by a combination of Bayesian estimation and model averaging techniques. The first forecasting model is consistent with the unique rational expectations equilibrium in the usual way under adaptive learning. The second forecasting model has a time-varying parameter structure, which it is argued is likely to better describe dynamics in the transition to rational expectations equilibrium. Private agents assign and update probabilities on the two models through Bayesian learning.

The first question in Evans et al. is whether learning with multiple forecasting models still converges in the limit to the rational expectations equilibrium. They show that convergence obtains provided that expectations have either a negative or a positive but not too strong influence on current outcomes. The range of structural parameters for which learning converges is generally found to be smaller than in the case with a single fixed forecasting model, but Bayesian learning does usually lead to model selection. Most interestingly, the authors show that agents may converge on the time-varying forecasting model, even though they initially place at least some probability mass on the alternative model consistent with rational expectations equilibrium. This can occur when expectations have a strong positive, but less than one-to-one, influence on current outcomes. Evans et al. apply their setup to a cobweb model and a Lucas islands model. The analysis of multiple forecasting models extends the literature on adaptive learning in a way that should stimulate future research.

A lot of work in recent decades has been devoted to understanding how policy-makers should conduct policy. A common argument is that private sector expectations are an important channel through which policy operates, so issues of time consistency are a legitimate and material policy concern. Such concerns feature prominently in the optimal policy design literature, which emphasises the distinction between commitment and discretion by asking whether society has access to commitment technologies that can tie the hands of future governments and policy-makers. The existence of such commitment technologies potentially contributes to better management of expectations. However, precommitment often suffers from time-consistency problems. Even though commitment policies are ex ante welfare improving, they may not survive incentives to reoptimize and deviate from the precommited policy path. Much of the literature views these strategic interactions between policy-makers and the private sector through the lens of dynamic games, so timing conventions matter a great deal. By implication, the meaning of the term 'optimal policy' critically depends on the timing conventions and protocols of the model.

To analyse history-dependent policies and clarify the nature of optimal policies under two timing protocols, David Evans and Thomas Sargent (Chapter 7) study a model of a benevolent policymaker imposing a distortionary flat tax rate on the output of a competitive firm to finance a given present value of public expenditure. The firm faces adjustment costs and operates in a competitive equilibrium, which act as constraints on the policy-maker.

Evans and Sargent consider two timing protocols. In the first, a benevolent policy-maker chooses an infinite sequence of distortionary tax rates in the initial period. More technically, this policy-maker acts as a leader in an underlying Ramsey problem, taking the response of the private sector as follower as given. Furthermore, this timing convention models the policy-maker as able to precommit, hence the notion of a commitment solution found in the literature. In the second timing protocol, the tax rate is chosen sequentially such that in each period the policy-maker reoptimizes the tax rate. Alternatively, the authors interpret the second timing protocol as describing a sequence of policy-makers, each choosing only a time t tax rate. Evans and Sargent use the notion of a sustainable plan or credible public policy to characterize the optimal policy under this timing protocol. The basic idea is that history-dependent policies can be designed so that, when regarded as a representative firm's forecasting functions, they create the right incentives for policy-makers not to deviate.

Evans and Sargent show that the optimal tax policy under both timing protocols is history-dependent. The key difference is that history dependence reflects different economic forces across the two timing conventions. In both cases the authors represent history-dependent tax policies recursively.

One of the challenges of implementing adaptive learning in macroeconomic models is deciding how agents incorporate their forecasts into decision making. In Chapter 8 William Branch, George Evans, and Bruce McGough develop a new theory of bounded rationality that generalises the two existing benchmarks in the literature, namely Euler-equation learning and infinite-horizon learning. Under Euler-equation learning, agents are identified as two-period planners who make decisions in the current period based on their forecast of what will happen in the next period. More specifically, agents forecast prices and their own behaviour and use these to make decisions that satisfy their perceived Euler equation. The Euler equation itself is taken as a behavioural primitive that summarises individual decision making. Infinite-horizon learning, in contrast, posits that agents make decisions that satisfy their lifetime budget constraint, i.e. their current and all future Euler equations. As the authors note, this requires that agents a priori account for a transversality condition. In this way they make optimal decisions, given the beliefs captured by their forecasting model.

The new theory of finite-horizon learning developed by Branch et al. rests on the plausible idea that agents know that their beliefs may be incorrect and likely to change in the future. If agents acknowledge that the parameter estimates in their forecasting models may evolve then it is no longer obvious that optimal decisions are determined as the full solution to their dynamic programming problem *given their current beliefs*. Although this observation also holds for short-horizon learning, it is more pertinent in the context of infinite-horizon learning because the infinite horizon places considerable weight on distant forecasts. Hence, agents may do best with finite-horizon learning models that look ahead more than one period but not as far as the infinite horizon.

Branch et al. ground their analysis of finite-horizon learning in a simple dynamic general equilibrium model, the Ramsey model. The approach allows agents to make dynamic decisions based on a planning horizon of a given finite length N. In this context, the generalization of Euler-equation learning to N-step Euler-equation learning involves iterating the Euler equation forward N periods. Agents are assumed to make consumption decisions in the current period, based on forecasts of consumption and interest rates N periods in the future. Although the N-step Euler-equation learning is a generalization of the Euler-equation learning mechanism, Branch et al. discuss why it is not possible to provide an interpretation of N-step Euler-equation learning at an infinite horizon. They argue that a distinct learning mechanism—N-step optimal learning—is required to provide a finite horizon analog to infinite-horizon learning.

Stability analyses based on the E-stability properties of the Ramsey model under finite-horizon learning show numerically that the unique rational expectations equilibrium (REE) is E-stable for a range of parameter combinations and planning horizons under both N-step Euler-equation learning and N-step optimal learning. Furthermore, the authors argue that longer horizons provide more rapid convergence to the REE, with N-step Euler-equation learning converging faster than N-step optimal learning. This latter result is due to stronger negative feedback for the N-step Euler-equation learning mechanism. However, the authors show that the time path of beliefs during convergence to REE involve dramatically different variations in feedback across planning horizon. Transition dynamics thus vary across both planning horizon and the learning mechanism.

The results on transition dynamics have potentially important implications. The internal propagation mechanisms and empirical fit of more realistic dynamic stochastic general equilibrium models may well be improved by assuming finite-horizon learning and constant-gain recursive updating. There may also be less need for modellers to assume exogenous shocks with unmodelled time series properties. If Branch et al.'s result holds in more realistic models then the planning horizon is a key parameter that needs estimating when fitting DSGE models incorporating learning agents.

Price level determinacy has been studied extensively in simple New Keynesian models of monetary policy, so the conditions under which monetary policy can lead to indeterminacy in these simple settings are well understood. Active rules that satisfy the Taylor principle and imply a procyclical real interest rate generate determinacy, whereas passive rules that are insufficiently aggressive generate countercyclical movements in the real interest rate and indeterminacy. However, matters become more complex if monetary policy is subject to regime shifts, as argued by Jess Benhabib in Chapter 9. Such regime shifts may come from a number of underlying causes, for example the dependence of a monetary policy regime on changing economic conditions and fundamentals such as employment and output growth. Whatever the underlying reason, asserting that a model is determinate in a switching environment involves more complex calculations because policy can be active in one regime and inactive in another.

Using a simple linear model of inflation determination incorporating flexible prices, the Fisher equation and an interest rate rule with a time-varying coefficient on the deviation of inflation from its steady state level, Benhabib uses recent results for stochastic processes to show that price level determinacy can obtain, even if the Taylor rule is passive on average. More specifically, if the coefficient on inflation deviations in the Taylor rule is fixed then indeterminacy requires that this coefficient is below 1, implying a less aggressive interest rate response of the central bank to inflation deviations. If, on the other hand, the inflation coefficient is stochastic then one would naturally like to extend the deterministic case by assuming that a condition for indeterminacy is that the expected value of the inflation coefficient is less than 1, where the expectation is taken with respect to the stationary distribution of the inflation coefficient. Benhabib shows, however, that if the expected value of the inflation coefficient is below 1, then the model admits solutions to the inflation dynamics other than the minimum state variable solution. These other solutions may not have finite first, second, and higher moments. If the first moment fails to exist, they imply that the relevant transversality conditions associated with agents' optimizing problems may be violated, generating unbounded asset value dynamics. Benhabib discusses several extension of his results.

In the recent financial crisis, much has been made of unsatisfactory underwriting standards in the sub-prime mortgage sector and shortcomings in risk management by financial institutions. An additional issue was the lack of due diligence of some key market players such as investors and financial advisers. Individual investors dealt directly with risky complex financial instruments that may have been beyond their comprehension, and institutional investors arguably did not exercise sufficient due diligence before investing. In the case of financial advisers, one would have thought that they would exercise due diligence on every investment project they proposed. This of course assumes that the contractual arrangements between investors and financial advisers provided sufficiently strong incentives for financial advisers to do due diligence.

In Chapter 10, Martin Ellison and Chryssi Giannitsarou examine the incentives for due diligence in the run up to the most recent financial crisis. In motivating their analysis, the authors draw on the reality television series *Dragons' Den,* in which entrepreneurs pitch their business ideas to a panel of venture capitalists—the eponymous dragons—in the hope of securing investment finance. Once the entrepreneur has presented the business idea, the dragons ask a series of probing questions aimed at uncovering any lack of preparation or fundamental flaws in the business proposition. In return for investing, the dragons negotiate an equity stake in the entrepreneur's company.

The way the rules of *Dragons' Den* are set makes it formally a principal–agent game with endogenous effort and costly state verification. In the game, the dragons as the principal must provide incentives for the entrepreneur as the agent to exercise effort by performing due diligence on the business proposal. As effort is unobservable, the principal can provide incentives for the agent to do due diligence by spending time asking about the agent's proposal, a form of costly state verification. Alternatively, the principal can strengthen the incentives for the agent to do due diligence by only requiring a small equity stake in the entrepreneur's company. Ellison and Giannitsarou show that entrepreneurs perform due diligence provided that there is sufficient monitoring and that they receive a sufficiently large equity share. The combinations of monitoring intensity and equity shares that guarantee due diligence are summarized by a **due diligence condition** (DDC).

This condition gives a lower bound on the entrepreneur's equity share, above which the entrepreneur exercises due diligence. The lower bound depends on the features of the venture capital market, in particular the number of dragons offering venture capital relative to the number of entrepreneurs seeking venture capital. In the context of the most recent financial crisis, the economics of the *Dragons' Den* suggests that a global savings glut fuelled by new capital from Chinese dragons potentially weakens the incentives for entrepreneurs to do due diligence. The resulting increase in credit supply from China presumably funds more business ventures, but too many dragons relative to entrepreneurs makes it difficult for the dragons to ensure that their financial advisers are doing due diligence because there are many competing sources of venture capital. The nature of the trade-off needs to be studied further, particularly by financial market regulators and supervisors, as it has the potential to increase the systemic fragility of financial markets.

The shock-absorbing capabilities of Western economies have been severely put to test by globalization and the re-division of labour between countries. The rising importance in world trade of Asian and ex-socialist economies has meant that almost a third of the world's population has emerged from behind the Iron Curtain and Chinese Wall to participate in markets. Adding India, with more than a billion new players who want to join the market, takes the share of new entrants up to 45% of the world's population. There will be gains from trade for most countries involved, but also problems and challenges to the developed Western economies. Outsourcing jobs to low-cost emerging markets forces developed economies to innovate in the use of the labour resources that it frees up and makes available. The implied re-allocation process is costly and potentially involves major changes in relative wages and other prices. Skill mismatch may worsen, deepening the dual nature of labour markets as low- and high-skill labour are not affected equally. What happens to the labour tax base? What are the effects of changes in the structure of taxation on the relative wage of low-skill workers? How does progressivity of the tax system affect employment?

Erkki Koskela (Chapter 11) presents a comprehensive analysis of these issues by looking at the effects of tax reforms in a heterogenous labour market model under flexible outsourcing. In the model, division of the labour force into low- and high-skilled gives rise to a dual labour market. Low-skilled labour is unionized, while high-skilled workers face more competitive pressure on wage formation because they negotiate their wages individually. Outsourcing decisions concern low-skilled labour, with domestic and outsourced labour input perfect substitutes in a decreasing returns-to-scale production function of competitive, profit-maximizing firms. Under *flexible* outsourcing firms decide on outsourcing at the same time as labour demand, after the wage have been set by the union. This is distinct from *strategic* outsourcing, where firms make outsourcing decisions before wages have been set. The wages of high-skilled labour adjust to equilibrate their demand and supply. High-skilled workers maximize their utility over consumption and leisure to derive their labour supply, subject to a constraint that real net labour income equals consumption. Low- and high-skilled labour enjoy different tax exemptions and are therefore taxed at different rates. The tax base is income net of tax exemption. Tax policy, exemptions, rates, and progressiveness are determined before unions set the wages of low-skilled workers.

Koskela derives a number of results for the labour market effects of government tax policies. He assumes that the average tax rate of either low- or high-skilled labour is kept constant, but varies progressivity by simultaneously raising both the marginal tax rate and tax exemptions. Koskela shows that greater progressivity in taxes on low-skilled labour reduces the optimal wage set for them by the union in the model. Consequently, employment of low-skilled labour will increase. The implied employment effects on high-skilled labour depend on the elasticity of substitution between consumption and leisure in the utility function of a representative high-skilled worker. The effects of an increase in tax progressivity is asymmetric in that an increase in the progression of taxation of the wages for high-skilled workers, given their average tax rate, does not affect the wage and hence employment of high-skilled workers. Whether these theoretical results are robust to changes in functional forms needs to be established with further research. Koskela also discusses extensions of his analysis, including allowing for spillover effects between countries from spending resources on outsourcing, which implies that there may be arguments for international coordination of outsourcing policy. Koskela also notes that the nature of optimal monetary policy under outsourcing and heterogenous, imperfectly competitive labour markets needs to be explored.

Part I
Financial Crisis and Recovery

1

Is the Market System an Efficient Bearer of Risk?

Kenneth J. Arrow

These observations are intended as an essay, not a true research paper. They are based on recollections of research by others over many years, not documented here. These loose notes can be regarded as constituting a conceptual basis for future research (by someone); a nagging question which contains many subquestions.

The market system, ideally, is efficient in allocating resources, and, in fact, in two ways. One is the one usually characterized as the workings of the invisible hand. Given the stock of resources in the economy and given the technological knowledge, the competitive market allocation is efficient in the sense of Pareto: there is no other feasible allocation which could make everyone better off.

The other sense in which the market is efficient is that, in some sense, it economizes on information. In the simplest general equilibrium formulations, each individual controls certain decisions, specifically, his or her consumption bundle, sales of initial holdings of goods, and production decisions. (Consumption here includes supplies of different kinds of labour, thought of as choosing different kinds of leisure.) The information needed is his or her own preferences, holdings of goods, and production possibilities, and, in addition, some publicly available pieces of information, namely, the prices of all goods. In brief, the individual need know only information to which he or she is naturally privy (since it relates to the individual's own special aspects) plus the knowledge of prices.

These characterizations are of course already problematic, even in a world of certainty. The consistency demanded of individuals is excessive according to cognitive psychologists and the behavioural economists who have followed and developed their work. Even at a logical level, the process of coming into equilibrium, the problem of stability, as it is termed, seems to demand more information than that asked for above. Interest in these issues was generated by the twentieth-century debate whether a socialist economic system could function at all and, if it did, could it be at all efficient? The discussion was started by Enrico Barone (under Vilfredo Pareto's influence) and continued especially by Oskar Lange and Friedrich von Hayek, the latter especially in his 1945 paper which raised (though hardly settled) the question how any economic system could convey relevant information among the extended participants. It was Leonid Hurwicz who gave the sharpest abstract formulation of the problem of assembling dispersed information to produce economically efficient outcomes while minimizing communication costs.

The economic problem then already contains the concept of information. Information is meaningless except in the presence of uncertainty. In this case, it means that individuals are uncertain about the preferences, endowments, and production possibilities of other individuals. If everyone knew all the private information of everyone else, then each individual could compute the general equilibrium allocation and go directly to his or her own decisions which are part of it. Hence, uncertainty is already built into the concept of a dispersed economic system, though in certain ideal situations only a small amount of summary information about aggregates (the prices) need be determined.

In this chapter, I want to raise the impact of uncertainties more generally and ask how the market system addresses it. In the simplest case, we must consider that there are matters which are uncertain to all participants. Most obviously, there are acts of nature: storms, earthquakes, industrial and other accidents (may I instance oil well spills), and the accidents of mortality and morbidity which affect all of us. There are also political disturbances, wars, foreign and civil, taxes, and government expenditures. Most interesting and important of all are technological innovations, which change the technological possibilities.

Many years ago, I pointed out that the framework of general equilibrium theory could be extended to cover uncertainty. My own model was over-simplified in several dimensions (only one time period, pure exchange economy) but was subsequently extended to the general case by Gerard Debreu. The idea was to consider all the possible uncertainties as defining a state of nature (i.e., a given state of nature would be a particular realization of all the uncertainties). Then assume that all commodities were distinguished according to the state of nature in which they were bought or sold. This could be reduced to transactions in commodities conditional given that it was known what state of nature prevailed plus a set of securities defining money payments for each possible state of nature.

I interpreted an actual security as a promise to pay a amount varying with the state of nature. This interpretation clearly included the usual insurance policies (life, fire, automobile accidents, and so forth). It also included common stocks, where the payment clearly depends on various factors that are random from point of view of both the issuing companies and the stockholders. Without going into more details, it was shown that if there are sufficiently many securities with differing payoffs under the various states of nature, then competitive equilibrium exists and is Pareto efficient.

The behaviour of individuals in this world and according to the standard models in the literature is governed by risk aversion, the maximization of expected utility, where the utility function is concave. This hypothesis originated in Daniel Bernoulli's justly famous paper of 1738. In it, he not only discussed behaviour at games of chance, as in the St. Petersburg paradox raised by one of his uncles, but also insurance, specifically, marine insurance. The basic assumption of the paper was that an individual would not take a bet unless it was actuarially favourable to him or her. Yet shippers took out insurance against the loss of their cargo even though the insurers had a positive expected gain. This was, of course, because the insurance offset the loss of the cargo. What was shown was the gain from trade in risks. The expected utility of both insured and insurer was higher than in the absence of insurance. It is therefore a prototype of the spreading of risks through the operation of a market and demonstrates the potential for considerable welfare gain.

These two strands have had an influence on the economic analysis of risk bearing. It is easy to see that the complete shifting of risk implied by the general equilibrium model does not take place. One explanation was soon found, that of asymmetric information, as developed by many authors. We can have contracts contingent on the realization of a state of nature only if both parties can verify that that state occurred. But this is not usually the case. The insurance companies had realized this difficulty earlier, under the headings of moral hazard and adverse selection, and limited the range of their insurance coverage accordingly. There has been a rich literature developing contractual relations which depart in one way or another from competitive markets and which reduce the welfare loss due to asymmetric information.

In this chapter, I want to direct attention to other failures of market risk-spreading. Before asking what deficiencies there are in the model combining risk aversion and general equilibrium (let's call it RAGE) and therefore permitting the spreading of risks, I will review some factual examples of risk-spreading and examine the extent to which they display departures from what would be predicted by the RAGE model. I am doing this from memory and do not give citations.

Let me start with classical insurance (life, fire, and so forth). Here, the model works best. For example, since insurance is always actuarially unfair, no rational person will insure his or her house for more than its value. Also, one does not buy insurance against damage to someone else's house. The insurance companies can be counted on to pay the insurance claim without question.

But it must be observed that much of this compliance with the model occurs not because of the individually rational decisions but because of legal regulation and restrictions imposed by the insurance companies. Insured are required by the companies to have an insurable interest in the property insured. If the insured were following the RAGE assumptions, there would be no need to impose these conditions. Similarly, the fact that insurance companies pay their obligations is due in good measure to legal regulation, which requires the maintenance of adequate reserves.

The force of these observations can be observed in the contracts called credit default swaps, which played such an important role in the genesis of the current Great Recession (at least in the United States). This is simply insurance against default. Yet the insured were not required to have an insurable interest, and the insurers were not required to maintain adequate reserves. The resulting collapse displayed how even an insurance market does not work to spread risks in an appropriate way.

Let me turn to another set of examples, futures markets. These are highly organized and have strong protections against default. Let us first consider the wheat futures markets. The textbook explanation for their function is that the millers (those who buy the grain to make flour) are risk-averters. They buy long, that is they pay for commitments to deliver the wheat at a fixed price. We do not find farmers on the other side of the market. Instead, we have speculators who are betting that the spot price at the time of delivery will be below the agreed delivery price. According to the RAGE model, the millers should on the average lose money (compared buying at the spot price), and the speculators gain. The millers are paying for certainty. In fact, the millers do lose, as predicted.[1] But the speculators can be divided into two parts, those who are themselves brokers (members of the exchange) and outsiders. It turns out that the outsiders lose on the average. The brokers do indeed profit, but their incomes are roughly what they could make at reasonable alternative occupations, such as banking.

Let us now consider another futures (or forward) market, that for foreign exchange. What is the buying firm protecting itself against? For instance, suppose that an American firm sells to a firm in Europe, with payment in euros and delivery in sixty days. The firm is concerned that the exchange rate between euros and dollars may change by the delivery date. This would explain, then, a demand for foreign exchange at most equal to the volume of trade. In fact, the transactions on the foreign exchange markets are, I understand, about 300 times as much.

I understand that similar or even more extreme conditions hold in the futures markets for metals.

The stock market is in many ways the best functioning of all risk-spreading markets, partly indeed because of severe regulation, especially after the collapse of the market in the Great Depression. High margin requirements reduce the possibility of extreme collapses, though they have not prevented some spectacular rises and falls. But there are at least two empirical manifestations that give one pause.

1. In an ideal RAGE model, the value of a stock at any given moment should be an estimate of the issuing firm's discounted stream of future profits, adjusted for risk. How can such an estimate change abruptly? For any given firm, there may of course be special new information which would account for the change. But one would not expect the market as a whole to change. In fact, a change of 1% in total market value in one day happens very frequently, yet what news could possibly account for it? Larger changes are not infrequent. Hence, the volatility of the market seems grossly excessive under RAGE assumptions.
2. As with the futures markets, the volume of transactions on the stock market seems much too high to be explained by smooth risk-spreading through the market. Individuals may buy and sell in order to meet fluctuations in other sources of income, as in the case

[1] In fact this prediction is somewhat problematic. The millers are large corporations. Their stockholders should, in accordance with risk aversion, be holding diversified portfolios and hence have only a small part of their wealth invested in the miller. Therefore, their utilities are approximately linear, and they not want the milling firm to be a risk-averter.

of retirement. But such transactions could not possibly explain the actual volume and especially not explain the great variations from day to day. It has been shown that even asymmetric information cannot explain transactions under a RAGE model. Changes in one person's information (news) will change prices and so reveal the information to everyone.

Consider now still another example of risk-spreading, that involved in highly leveraged loans. A hedge fund, for example, generally makes money on very small profit margins and can only be really profitable by a high degree of leveraging, that is, borrowing the needed money. That may well be thoroughly rational for the hedge fund. But how can one explain the behaviour of the lenders? In the absence of fraud, they are fully aware of the degree of leveraging. No doubt, they charge a somewhat higher rate of interest than they would on safer loans, but it is clear that they must have high confidence in the hedge fund's predictive capacity. The lending and the speculations of the investment bankers on their own accounts were so dangerous to the bankers themselves as to bring both themselves and the world economy to the edge of collapse.

One can easily give other examples where risk-spreading seems to have failed even though engaged in by presumably rational individuals and firms seeking their own welfare. Indeed, it is striking how many of those involved are in the business of managing risks and so should be more capable of handling them.

There are of course a variety of possible answers, even at a systematic level. One is the rising branch of studies called behavioural economics. In this context, what is meant is that the assembling of large amounts of information is subject to important biases based on the inability of the human mind to handle them. Hence, rules of thumb, which have worked reasonably well in the past, dominate behaviour in new situations.

Indeed, it is not at all clear what a rational inference about uncertainties means. The Bayesian approach starts with arbitrary priors. Inferences about the knowledge held by others depends on assumptions about their priors and what they can have been expected to observe, neither of which can be at all well known.

Let me conclude with an internal explanation why the RAGE model fails. It presumes the possibility of buying protection against any realization of an uncertainty that might affect one. But in a general equilibrium world, one may not have private information about the possible effects of a state of nature. A coastal storm directly affects those with houses on the beach. But it may cause a decline in tourism, which in turn may affect the demand for some products produced elsewhere, or it may cause an increase in the demand for rebuilding supplies, again produced elsewhere.

Many people bought ordinary stocks, not mortgage-based securities. Yet the collapse of the latter strongly affected the former.

The problem is that, in a general equilibrium world, the resolution of any uncertainty has effects throughout the system. But no individual can predict these effects, even in principle, without knowing everyone's utility functions and production possibility sets. Obviously, the most important examples are those arising from technological innovations. An oil producer in 1880 selling only for illumination would not have recognized the effects on the value of its investments due to the competition from electric lights and the increased demand from automobiles.

I intended here only to raise issues, both empirical and theoretical. I certainly do not see any obvious way of resolving them, but they do rest on analysis of the formation of beliefs in a social environment with many means of communication, both explicit and implicit in actions.

2

The European Debt Crisis*

Hans-Werner Sinn

2.1 The European crisis

During the night of 9–10 May 2010 in Brussels, the EU countries agreed a €500 billion rescue package for member countries at risk, assuming that supplementary help, to the order of €250 billion, would come from the IMF.[1] The pact came in addition to the €80 billion rescue plan for Greece, topped by €30 billion from the IMF that had been agreed previously.[2] In addition to these measures, the ECB also allowed itself to be included in the new rescue programme. Making use of a loophole in the Maastricht Treaty, it decided on 12 May 2010 to buy government securities for the first time in its history, instead of only accepting them as collateral.[3] Literally overnight, the EU turned the no-bail-out philosophy of the Maastricht Treaty on its head. Though, at the time of writing, in October 2010 the crisis has not yet been overcome.

In this chapter I criticize the rescue measures because of the moral hazard effects they generate and I offer an explanation for the crisis that is quite different from the mainstream line of thinking. I do not want to be misunderstood. I am not against rescue measures, but I opt for different ones that also make the creditors responsible for some of the problems faced by the debtors. Neither do I wish to dispose of the

* The analysis in this chapter reflects the state of affairs at the time of writing in 2010.

[1] *The European Stabilization Mechanism*, Council Regulation (EU) 407/2010 of 11 May 2010 establishing a European financial stabilization mechanism, online at <http://www.eur-lex.europa.eu>, 7 July 2010; *EFSF Framework Agreement*, 7 June 2010, online at <http://www.bundesfinanzministerium.de>, 5 July 2010.

[2] *Statement by the Eurogroup*, Brussels, 2 May 2010, and *IMF Reaches Staff-level Agreement with Greece on €30 Billion Stand-By Arrangement*, IMF Press Release 10/176.

[3] *ECB Decides on Measures to Address Severe Tensions in Financial Markets*, ECB Press Release of 10 May 2010 (<http://www.ecb.int/press/pr/date/2010/html/pr100510.en.html>).

euro. The euro has given Europe stability amidst the financial turmoil of recent years, and it is an important vehicle for further European integration. However, I will argue that the euro has not been as beneficial for all European countries as has often been claimed. The euro has shifted Europe's growth forces from the centre to the periphery. It has not been particularly beneficial for Germany, for example, and because of a lack of proper private and public debt constraints, it has stimulated the periphery of Europe up to the point of overheating, with ultimately dangerous consequences for European cohesion. Obviously, the construction of the eurozone, in particular the rules of conduct for the participating countries, needs to be reconsidered. So at the end of this chapter I propose a new political design for a more prosperous and stable development of the eurozone.

2.2 Was the euro really at risk?

Politicians claimed and obviously believed that the bail-outs were necessary because the euro was at risk. There was no alternative to a bail-out over the weekend of 8 and 9 May, it was argued, for the financial markets were in such disarray that Europe's financial system, if not the Western world's, would have collapsed had the rescue packages not been agreed immediately, before the stock market in Tokyo was to open on Monday morning at 2 a.m. Brussels time. The similarity to the collapse of the interbank market after the insolvency of Lehman Brothers on 15 September 2008 seemed all too obvious.

The question, however, is whether the euro was really at risk and what could possibly have been meant by such statements. A possible hypothesis is that the euro was in danger of losing much of its internal and external value in this crisis. However, there is little empirical evidence for such a view. On Friday, 7 May 2010, the last trading day before the agreement, €1 cost $1.27. This was indeed less than in previous months but much more than the $0.88 which was the average of January and February 2002, when the euro currency was physically introduced. It was also more than the OECD purchasing power parity, which stood at $1.17. Amidst the crisis the euro was overvalued, not undervalued.

Neither were there indications of an unexpectedly strong decline in domestic purchasing power because of inflation. Most recently, in September 2010, the inflation rate in the euro area amounted to 1.8 per cent. That was one of the lowest rates since the introduction of the euro. It was also much lower than the inflation rate of the deutschmark during its 50 years of existence, which averaged 2.7 per cent between 1948 and 1998.

In this respect as well there was no evident danger. In danger was not the euro, but the ability of the countries of Europe's periphery to continue financing themselves as cheaply in the capital markets as had been possible in the initial years of the euro. The next section will try to shed some light on this issue.

2.3 The true problem: Widening interest spreads

The decline in the market value of government bonds during the crisis was equivalent to an increase in the effective interest rates on these bonds. In Figure 2.1 the development of interest rates is plotted for ten-year government bonds since 1994. Evidently, the interest rate spreads were widening rapidly during the financial crisis, as shown on the

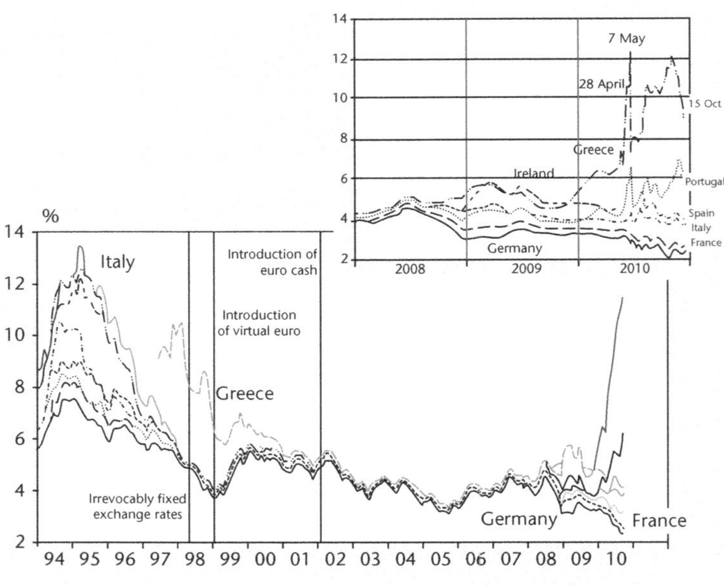

Figure 2.1 Interest rates for ten-year government bonds.

Source: Reuters Ecowin, *Government Benchmarks, Bid, 10 year, yield close*, 18 October 2010.

right-hand side of the diagram. No doubt, there was some danger, but it was a danger to very specific countries rather than a systemic danger to the euro system as such. Apart from France, which was indirectly affected via its banks' ownership of problematic state bonds, the countries at risk included Greece, Ireland, Portugal, Spain, and Italy (and to a limited extent Belgium), if the criterion was the increase in interest rates in the preceding months. The countries that were not at risk in terms of rising interest rates included Germany, the Netherlands, Austria, and Finland.

However, apart from Greece, even for the countries directly affected, the risk was limited. As the figure shows, interest spreads relative to Germany had been much more problematic before the euro was introduced. In 1995, Italy, Portugal, and Spain on average had had to pay 5.0 percentage points higher interest rates on ten-year government bonds than Germany.

The current crisis is characterized by a new divergence of interest rates. While the risk of implicit default via inflation and devaluation has disappeared under the euro regime, investors began to fear the explicit default of countries suffering from the consequences of the world financial crisis, demanding compensation by higher interest rates. Not only for Greece, but also for Ireland, Portugal, and Spain, and to some extent even for Italy, interest rates rose up to 7 May 2010, the day before the bail-out decisions of the EU countries were taken. After this agreement, the interest rate spreads did narrow for a while compared to the German benchmark, but after only a few weeks they were again on the rise with some easing in the weeks before the European summer holiday season.

Figure 2.1 shows why France and many other countries regarded the interest rate development as alarming. Before the introduction of the euro, they had suffered very much from the high interest rates that they had to offer to skeptical international investors. At that time, the interest premia on government debt that the investors demanded was the main reason these countries wanted to introduce the euro. They wanted to enjoy the same low interest rates with which Germany was able to satisfy its creditors. The calculation seemed to have paid off, because by 1998 the interest rate premia over German rates had in fact nearly disappeared. Nevertheless, now with the European debt crisis, the former circumstances threatened to return. The advantages promised by the euro, and which it had also delivered for some time, dwindled. This was the reason for the crisis atmosphere in the debtor countries, which was shared by the creditor countries' banks, fearing corresponding write-off losses on their assets.

2.4 The alternatives

Politicians claim that there was no alternative to the measures taken on 9 and 10 May 2010. This is, of course, not true. There are always alternatives, and it is a matter of choosing which one to take.

One alternative to the policy chosen by the EU could have been the American solution. As a rule, federal states in trouble in the United States are not bailed out. In US history, some states were even allowed to go bankrupt without receiving any help from the federal government. In light of the fact that Europe is a confederation of independent states rather than a union of federal states like the United States, it was not particularly plausible to organize a more extensive and generous bail-out than the USA would have done in similar circumstances.

Another, probably better, alternative would have been a bail-out procedure similar to the kind agreed, but preceded by a debt moratorium or haircut at the expense of the creditors. In private bankruptcy law, restructuring funds are not available unless a well-defined reduction of the creditor's claims is negotiated beforehand, so as to ensure that the help will benefit the troubled company rather than its creditors and induce the necessary caution in investment decisions. The risk of losing at least part of one's capital is essential for investors' prudence and for minimizing the risk of bankruptcy in the first place.

2.5 Trade imbalances

Many observers who have pointed to the imbalances in European development in recent years have obviously different theories in mind regarding the effects caused by the euro. They focus their attention on the goods markets rather than the capital markets and argue that countries that developed a trade surplus under the euro were winners of the European development. Germany, in particular, is seen to have profited from the euro. This view is often expressed outside Germany, but even inside the country it is shared by many politicians.

Recently, critics of the German development have even argued that the country should take active measures to increase its domestic demand instead of living on other countries' demand. French Finance Minister Christine Lagarde suggested that Germany increase its wages to reduce its competitiveness, because 'it takes two to tango',[4] and

[4] 'Lagarde Criticises Berlin Policy', *Financial Times Online*, 14 March 2010, <http://www.ft.com>.

IMF president Dominique Strauss-Kahn argued that in economies with persistent current account surpluses, domestic demand must go up, including by boosting consumption.[5] US Secretary of the Treasury Timothy Geithner wrote a letter to the G20 countries in which he proposed a rule, according to which countries with a current account surplus of more than 4 per cent of GDP (such as Germany and China) should take policy actions to increase their imports by boosting domestic demand.[6] While these statements are understandable, they only scratch the surface of the problem, demonstrating a misunderstanding of the forces that have produced the current account imbalances.

It is true that Germany has developed a large trade surplus that mirrored the trade deficit of other euro countries. This is confirmed by Figure 2.2 that compares the GANL countries, i.e., the former effective deutschmark zone consisting of Germany, Austria, and the Netherlands, with the rest of the euro countries. The GANL countries

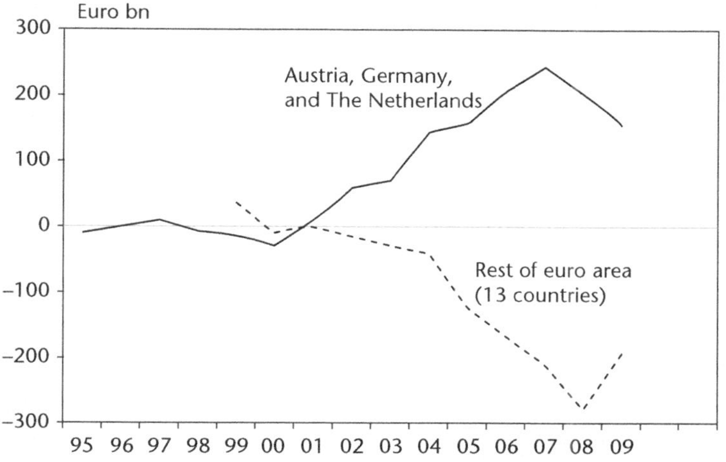

Figure 2.2 Current account surplus = net capital exports.

Sources: Eurostat, Database, *Economy and Finance, Balance of Payments—International Transactions*; Ifo Institute calculations.

[5] *Closer Policy Coordination Needed in Europe*, IMF Survey online, 17 March 2010, <http://www.imf.org>.

[6] Reuters, 22 October 2010.

developed a current account surplus that culminated at a value of €244 billion in 2007, of which €185 billion was accounted for by Germany alone. By contrast, the rest of the euro countries accumulated current account deficits that peaked at €280 billion in 2008.

However, it is not true that this trade surplus has benefited Germany, at least not for reasons that have to do with demand effects. A trade surplus is basically the same as a capital export. Apart from a flow of money balances, a country's capital export equals its current account surplus, and the current account surplus is defined as the trade surplus minus regular gifts the country may make to other countries, for example via one of the EU's transfer systems. The terms 'current account surplus' and 'capital export' have different semantic connotations that tend to confuse politicians and the media, but for all practical purposes they mean the same thing.

Germany lost a huge amount of capital under the euro regime even though it urgently needed the capital to rebuild its ex-communist East. In fact, in recent years, Germany was the world's second biggest capital exporter after China and ahead of Japan. The outflow of capital has benefited other countries, including the USA and the countries of Europe's south-western periphery, all of which were sucking in capital to finance their investment and to enjoy a good life. The opposite happened in Germany. Except for Italy, Germany had the lowest growth rate of all EU countries from 1995 to 2009, and in fact, it had the second-lowest growth rate of all European countries regardless of how Europe is defined. The comparison with a selection of EU countries shown in Figure 2.3 illustrates Germany's meager growth performance.

In terms of GDP per capita in the period 1995 to 2009 Germany fell from third to tenth place among the EU15 countries. Even west Germany alone fell below France, for example.

Germany's low growth rate resulted from low investment. Over the period from 1995 to 2009, Germany had the lowest net investment share in net domestic product among all OECD countries, ranking very close to Switzerland that faced similar problems. No country spent a smaller share of its output on the enlargement of its private and public capital stock than Germany, after it was clear that a currency union would come and interest rates started to converge (see Figure 2.1).

Germany exported its savings instead of using them as loans for investment in the domestic economy. In the period from 1995 to 2009, Germans on average exported three-quarters of their current savings and invested only one-quarter. And once again, by definition, this was also identical to the surplus in the German current account.

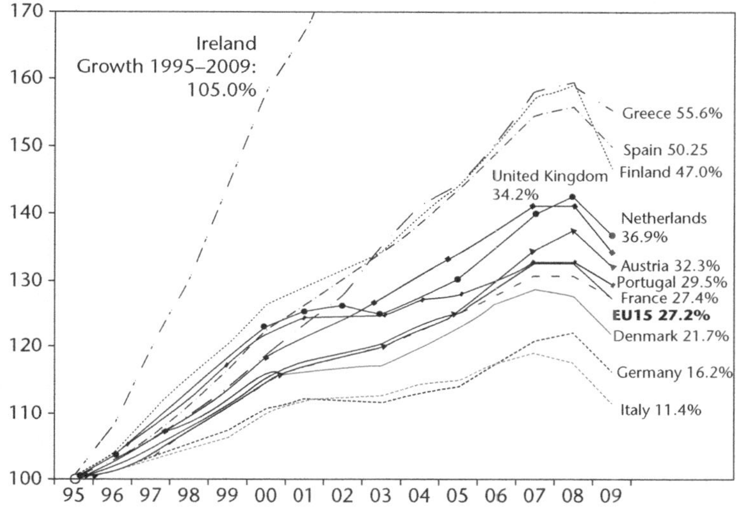

Figure 2.3 Economic growth in selected EU countries. Chain-linked volumes at prices, 1995 = 100.

Sources: Eurostat, Database, *Economy and Finance, National Accounts*; Ifo Institute calculations.

If Germany is to reduce its current account surplus, it should take action not to export so much capital abroad but to use more of its savings at home. However, this would not be particularly good news for the countries of Europe's south-western periphery nor for the USA, whose living standard has relied to such a large extent on borrowed funds.

2.6 The future of the euro economy and the economic implications of the rescue programmes

Currently, the market seems to self-correct the current account imbalances. The previously booming countries of Europe's south-western periphery are caught in a deep economic crisis, and Europe is struggling to find a new equilibrium that fits the new reality of country risk. All of a sudden investors have given up their prior stance that country risks are only exchange rate risks. Investors now anticipate events they had previously thought close to impossible, and they want to be compensated for the perceived risk with corresponding interest premiums. The increasing interest spreads for ten-year government bonds reflect this effect, although it has a much wider relevance, also applying to a large variety of private investment categories, such as company debt, private equity, shares, and direct investment.

In this light, the EU rescue measures must be regarded with suspicion. The €920 billion rescue packages agreed in early May 2010 have reduced the risk of country defaults and were designed to narrow the interest spreads and thus to soften the budget constraints in Europe once again. They have the potential of recreating the capital flows and refueling the overheating on Europe's periphery. If things go very wrong, the result could be an aggregate default risk for the entire system, pulling all euro countries into the vortex. What today is the default risk for a few smaller countries could end up in a default of the major European countries, with unpredictable consequences for the political stability of Europe.

Fortunately, however, the rescue packages were limited to only three years. This is the main reason for the persistence of the interest spreads. A month after the rescue measures were agreed, the interest spreads were even larger than on 10 May, the first day of the decision on the European rescue measures (Figure 2.1), and even in September 2010 there were many days with larger spreads.

If the rescue measures are not prolonged, this means that once again a toggle switch will have been flipped in Europe's development that will lead to a more balanced growth pattern, revitalizing the previously sluggish centre. The most plausible scenario for the Continent's future, from today's perspective (at the time of writing in October 2010), looks like this: Investors from the former deutschmark zone, including their banks, increasingly hesitate to send the national savings abroad, as they had done in the past to such an enormous extent. Due to the lack of suitable investment opportunities and heightened risk awareness, banks will seek alternative investment possibilities. They may try to invest in natural resources or new energies, but they will surely also offer better credit terms to domestic homeowners and firms. This will touch off a domestic boom in construction activity that will resemble that in Europe's south-western periphery during the previous fifteen years, if on a smaller scale. The two curves shown in Figure 2.2 will again be converging. This is what French officials and the US Secretary of the Treasury demanded so vigorously, but it comes endogenously as a result of the reallocation of savings flows and the resulting economic boom rather than exogenously through government-imposed measures.

2.7 A rescue plan for Europe

At the time of writing (October 2010), there are strong forces in Europe that press for a prolongation and strengthening of the rescue plan in order to complete the socialization of the country default risk and enforce a reduction in interest spreads in order to reduce the interest burden on public budgets in the countries of Europe's south-western periphery. Some even advocate going all the way to the issuance of eurobonds, i.e., replacing regular national issues of government bonds by Community bonds. However, this would be the end of European fiscal discipline and open a dangerous road where the debtors and their creditors could continue to speculate on being bailed out should problems arise. The European debt bubble would expand further and the damage caused by its bursting would be even greater. The risk of sovereign default would be extended to all the major countries of Europe.

Moreover, the current account imbalances would continue unabated. Thus, if the imbalances are to shrink, the rescue measures should not be prolonged unchanged, as many politicians demand.

This does not mean that Europe should fully return to the Maastricht Treaty without any rescue plan. But it does mean that the creditors would also have to bear some responsibility when sending capital to other countries, implying smaller capital flows and hence lower current account imbalances. A group of fellow economists and myself formulated a ten-point plan for a more stable institutional framework for the eurozone.[7] The following largely coincides with this plan.

1. Distressed countries can expect help only if an imminent insolvency or quasi-insolvency is unanimously confirmed by all helping countries and if the IMF helps, too.
2. Assistance can be provided in exchange for interest-bearing covered bonds collateralized with privatizable state assets, or by loans, the yield of which must be set at a reasonable amount (possibly 3.5 percentage points) above the European average. The accumulated credit thus provided must not exceed a given maximum percentage of the distressed country's GDP, say 20 per cent.
3. Before assistance is granted, the original creditors must waive a portion of their claims through a so-called haircut or debt moratorium. The maximum percentage to be waived must be

[7] W. Franz, C. Fuest, M. Hellwig, and H.-W. Sinn, 'A Euro Rescue Plan', *CESifo Forum*, 11(2) (2010), 101–4.

clearly defined beforehand in order to prevent a panic-fuelled intensification of the crisis. A reasonable haircut could be 5 per cent per year since the issuance of the respective government bond. This would limit the interest premium demanded upfront by the creditors to a maximum of around 5 percentage points.

4. The budget of the state facing quasi-insolvency must be placed under the control of the European Commission. Together with the country in question, the Commission would work out a programme to overhaul the state's finances, including reforms aimed at strengthening economic growth. Disbursement of rescue funds must be contingent on compliance with the conditions set forth by the rescue programme.
5. This quasi-insolvency process must in no circumstances be undermined by other assistance systems that could provide incentives for opportunistic behaviour, in particular by such mechanisms as eurobonds. A particular risk in the coming negotiations is that the capital exporting countries will be pressured to accept eurobonds in return for a quasi-insolvency procedure.
6. The deficit limit set by the Stability and Growth Pact should be modified in accordance with each country's debt-to-GDP ratio, in order to demand greater debt discipline early enough from the highly indebted countries. For example, the limit could be tightened by 1 percentage point for every 10 percentage points that the debt-to-GDP ratio exceeds the 60 per cent limit. A country with an 80 per cent debt-to-GDP ratio, for instance, would be allowed a maximum deficit of 1 per cent of GDP, while a country with a 110 per cent debt-to-GDP ratio would be required to have a budget surplus of at least 2 per cent.[8]
7. Penalties for exceeding the debt limits must apply automatically, without any further political decisions, once Eurostat has formally ascertained the deficits. The penalties can take the form of covered bonds collateralized by privatizable state assets, and they can also contain non-pecuniary elements such as the withdrawal of voting rights.
8. In order to ascertain deficit and debt-to-GDP ratios, Eurostat must be given the right to directly request information from every

[8] A similar proposal was made by the EEAG. See European Economic Advisory Group at CESifo, 'Fiscal Policy and Macroeconomic Stabilisation in the Euro Area: Possible Reforms of the Stability and Growth Pact and National Decision-Making Processes', *Report on the European Economy* (2003), pp. 46–75.

level of the national statistics offices and to conduct independent controls of the data-gathering procedures on site.

9. Finally, in case all the above assistance and control systems fail and insolvency approaches, the country in question may be asked to leave the eurozone by a majority of the eurozone members.
10. A voluntary exit from the eurozone must be possible at any time.

If these rules are respected, stability and prosperity of the eurozone will be strengthened, capital flows and current account imbalances will diminish, and the chances will improve that the European dream we have dreamt all our lives will become reality.

3

The Stagnation Regime of the New Keynesian Model and Recent US Policy*

George W. Evans

3.1 Introduction

The economic experiences of 2008–10 have highlighted the issue of appropriate macroeconomic policy in deep recessions. A particular concern is what macroeconomic policies should be used when slow growth and high unemployment persist even after the monetary policy interest rate instrument has been at or close to the zero net interest rate lower bound for a sustained period of time. In Evans et al. (2008) and Evans and Honkapohja (2010), using a New Keynesian model with learning, we argued that if the economy is subject to a large negative expectational shock, such as plausibly arose in response to the financial crisis of 2008–9, then it may be necessary, in order to return the economy to the targeted steady state, to supplement monetary policy with fiscal policy, in particular with temporary increases in government spending.

The importance of expectations in generating a 'liquidity trap' at the zero-lower bound is now widely understood. For example, Benhabib et al. (2001a,b) show the possibility of multiple equilibria under perfect foresight, with a continuum of paths to an unintended low or negative inflation steady state.[1] Recently, Bullard (2010) has argued that data

* I am indebted to the University of Oregon Macro workshop for comments on the first draft of this chapter, to Mark Thoma for several further discussions and to James Bullard, Seppo Honkapohja, Frank Smets, Jacek Suda, and George Waters for comments. Of course, the views expressed in this chapter remain my own. Financial support from National Science Foundation Grant SES-1025011 is gratefully acknowledged.

[1] See Krugman (1998) for a seminal discussion and Eggertsson and Woodford (2003) for a recent analysis and references.

from Japan and the USA over 2002–10 suggest that we should take seriously the possibility that 'the US economy may become enmeshed in a Japanese-style deflationary outcome within the next several years'.

The learning approach provides a perspective on this issue that is quite different from the rational expectations results.[2] As shown in Evans et al. (2008) and Evans and Honkapohja (2010), when expectations are formed using adaptive learning, the targeted steady state is locally stable under standard policy, but it is not globally stable. However, the potential problem is not convergence to the deflation steady state, but instead unstable trajectories. The danger is that sufficiently pessimistic expectations of future inflation, output, and consumption can become self-reinforcing, leading to a deflationary process accompanied by declining inflation and output. These unstable paths arise when expectations are pessimistic enough to fall into what we call the 'deflation trap'. Thus, while in Bullard (2010) the local stability results of the learning approach to expectations is characterized as one of the forms of denial of 'the peril', the learning perspective is actually more alarmist in that it takes seriously these divergent paths.

As we showed in Evans et al. (2008), in this deflation trap region aggressive monetary policy, i.e., immediate reductions on interest rates to close to 0, will in some cases avoid the deflationary spiral and return the economy to the intended steady state. However, if the pessimistic expectation shock is too large then temporary increases in government spending may be needed. The policy response in the USA, UK, and Europe has to some extent followed the policies advocated in Evans et al. (2008). Monetary policy was quick, decisive, and aggressive, with, for example, the US federal funds rate reduced to near zero levels by the end of 2008. In the USA, in addition to a variety of less conventional interventions in the financial markets by the Treasury and the Federal Reserve, including the TARP measures in late 2008 and a large-scale expansion of the Fed balance sheet designed to stabilize the banking system, there was the $727 billion ARRA stimulus package passed in February 2009.

While the US economy then stabilized, the recovery through 2010 was weak and the unemployment rate remained both very high and roughly constant for the year through November 2010. At the same time, although inflation was low, and hovering on the brink of deflation, we did not see the economy recording large and increasing deflation rates.[3] From the viewpoint of Evans et al. (2008), various

[2] For a closely related argument see Reifschneider and Williams (2000).

[3] However, the CPI 12-month inflation measure, excluding food and energy, did show a downward trend over 2007–10, and in December 2010 was at 0.6%.

interpretations of the data are possible, depending on one's view of the severity of the initial negative expectations shock and the strength of the monetary and fiscal policy impacts. However, since recent US (and Japanese) data may also be consistent with convergence to a deflation steady state, it is worth revisiting the issue of whether this outcome can in some circumstances arise under learning.

In this chapter I develop a modification of the model of Evans et al. (2008) that generates a new outcome under adaptive learning. Introducing asymmetric adjustment costs into the Rotemberg model of price setting leads to the possibility of convergence to a stagnation regime following a large pessimistic shock. In the stagnation regime, inflation is trapped at a low steady deflation level, consistent with zero net interest rates, and there is a continuum of consumption and output levels that may emerge. Thus, once again, the learning approach raises the alarm concerning the evolution of the economy when faced with a large shock, since the outcome may be persistently inefficiently low levels of output. This is in contrast to the rational expectations approach of Benhabib et al. (2001b), in which the deflation steady state has output levels that are not greatly different from the targeted steady state.

In the stagnation regime, fiscal policy taking the form of temporary increases in government spending is important as a policy tool. Increased government spending raises output, but leaves the economy within the stagnation regime until raised to the point at which a critical level of output is reached. Once output exceeds the critical level, the usual stabilizing mechanisms of the economy resume, pushing consumption, output, and inflation back to the targeted steady state, and permitting a scaling back of government expenditure.

After introducing the model, and exploring its principal policy implications, I discuss the policy options more generally for the US economy.

3.2 The model

We use the model of Evans et al. (2008), itself a discrete-time version of Benhabib et al. (2001b), but with rational expectations replaced by adaptive learning. The model is a stylized 'New Keynesian' model of the type that underlies widely used DSGE models. For simplicity we use the version without capital and with consolidated household-firms. As in Benhabib et al. (2001b), the pricing friction is modelled as a cost of adjusting prices, in the spirit of Rotemberg (1982), rather than a Calvo-type friction. An important advantage of the Rotemberg pricing friction is that the resulting model does not need to be linearized, making global analysis possible.

Details of the model are given in the Appendix. For simplicity I use a nonstochastic version of the model. The dynamic first-order Euler conditions, satisfied by optimal decision-making, lead to aggregate equations of the form

$$\pi_t = H_\pi(\pi^e_{t+1}, c_t, g_t) \tag{3.1}$$

$$c_t = H_c(\pi^e_{t+1}, c^e_{t+1}, R_t), \tag{3.2}$$

where c_t is consumption at time t, π_t is the inflation factor, g_t is government purchases of goods and services, and $R_t \geq 1$ is the interest rate factor on one-period debt. Equation (3.1) is the 'Phillips equation' for this model, and Eq. (3.2) is the 'IS equation'. The functions H_π and H_c are determined by Eqs. (3.7) and (3.8) in the Appendix. When linearized at a steady state both equations take the standard form. Because this is a model without capital, aggregate output satisfies $y_t = c_t + g_t$.

Under the learning approach followed here, we treat Eqs. (3.1) and (3.2) as arising from aggregations of the corresponding behavioural equations of individual agents, and assume that they hold whether or not the expectations held by agents are fully 'rational'. Put differently, Eqs. (3.1) and (3.2) are temporary equilibrium equations that determine π_t and c_t, given government purchases g_t, the interest rate R_t, and expectation c^e_{t+1} and π^e_{t+1}.[4]

The particular form of the Phillips equation arises from a quadratic inflation adjustment cost $k(\pi_{t,j}) = 0.5(\pi_{t,j} - 1)^2$, where $\pi_{t,j} = \frac{P_{t,j}}{P_{t-1,j}}$ is the inflation factor for agent j's good. The IS equation (3.2) is simply the standard consumption Euler equation obtained from $u'(c_{t,j}) = \beta(R_t/\pi^e_{t+1})u'(c^e_{t+1,j})$, where $u(c)$ is the utility of consumption and $0 < \beta < 1$ is the discount factor. Note that because π_t measures the gross inflation rate (or inflation factor), $\pi_t - 1$ is the usual net inflation rate. Similarly $\beta^{-1} - 1$ is the net discount rate, $R_t - 1$ is the net interest rate, and $R_t = 1$ corresponds to the zero lower bound on interest rates. The variables c^e_{t+1} and π^e_{t+1} denote the time t expectations of the values of these variables in $t + 1$.

We next discuss fiscal and monetary policy. We assume that in normal times government spending is constant over time, i.e., $g_t = g > 0$.

[4] In the learning literature the formulation (3.1)–(3.2) is sometimes called the Euler-learning approach. This approach emphasizes short planning horizons, in contrast to the infinite-horizon approach emphasized, for example, in Preston (2006). In Evans and Honkapohja (2010) we found that the main qualitative results obtained in Evans et al. (2008) carried over to an infinite-horizon learning formulation.

The government's flow budget constraint is that government spending plus interest must be financed by taxes, debt, and seigniorage. Taxes are treated as lump sum and are assumed to follow a feedback rule with respect to government debt, with a feedback parameter that ensures convergence to a specified finite debt level in a steady-state equilibrium.

Monetary policy is assumed to follow a continuous nondecreasing interest rate rule[5]

$$R_t = f\left(\pi^e_{t+1}\right). \tag{3.3}$$

We assume the monetary authorities have an inflation target $\pi^* > 1$. For example, if the inflation target is 2 per cent p.a. then $\pi^* = 1.02$. From the consumption Euler equation it can be seen that at a steady state $c_t = c^e_{t+1} = c$, $\pi_t = \pi^e_{t+1} = \pi$, and $R_t = R$, the Fisher equation

$$R = \pi/\beta$$

must be satisfied, and the steady-state real interest rate factor is β^{-1}. The function $f(\pi)$ is assumed to be consistent at π^* with the Fisher equation, i.e., $f\left(\pi^*\right) = \pi^*/\beta$. In addition we assume that $f'(\pi^*) > \beta^{-1}$, so that the Taylor principle is satisfied at π^*. Because of the ZLB (zero lower bound on net interest rates) there will also be another steady state at a lower inflation rate, and if (3.3) is such that $R_t = 1$ at low π^e_{t+1} then the other steady state is one of deflation, corresponding to inflation factor $\pi = \beta < 1$. For simplicity I will assume a linear spline rule of the form shown in Figure 3.1. Figure 3.1, which graphs this interest rate rule combined with the steady-state Fisher equation, shows that there are two steady states that arise in this model, the targeted steady state at π^* and the unintended steady state at $\pi = \beta$, which corresponds to a deflation rate at the net discount rate.

Finally we need to specify how expectations are updated over time. Since we have omitted all exogenous random shocks in the model we can choose a particularly simple form of adaptive learning rule, namely

$$\pi^e_{t+1} = \pi^e_t + \phi(\pi_{t-1} - \pi^e_t) \tag{3.4}$$

$$c^e_{t+1} = c^e_t + \phi(c_{t-1} - c^e_t), \tag{3.5}$$

where $0 < \phi < 1$ parameterizes the response of expectations to the most recent data point and is usually assumed to be small. If there

[5] Here for convenience we assume R_t is set on the basis of π^e_{t+1} instead of π_t as in Evans et al. (2008).

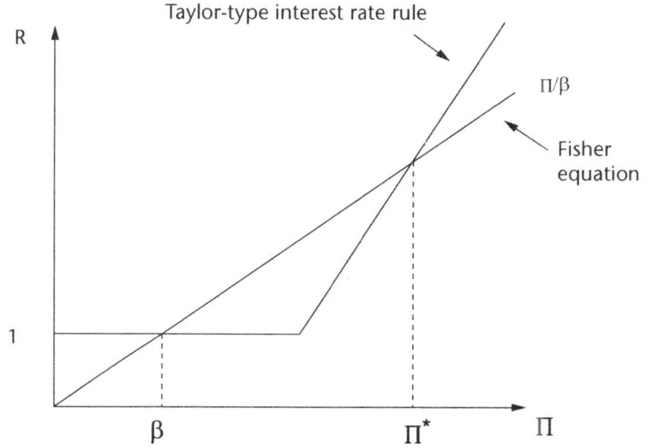

Figure 3.1 The Taylor rule and Fisher equation. Here $R = 1$ is an interest rate of 0 and $\beta = 0.99$ (or 0.97) corresponds to a deflation rate of about 1% p.a. (or 3% p.a.). $\pi^* = 1.02$ means an inflation target of 2% p.a.

were observable random shocks in the model, then a more general formulation would be a form of least-squares learning in which the variables to be forecasted are regressed on the exogenous observables and an intercept.[6] This would not alter the qualitative results. The crucial assumption of adaptive learning is that expectations are driven by the evolution of observed data. This might be thought of as the 'Missouri' view of expectations, since Missouri's state nickname is the 'Show Me State'. On the adaptive learning approach, agents are unlikely to increase or decrease their forecasts, say, of inflation unless they have data-based reasons for doing so.[7]

This completes the description of the model. In summary the dynamics of the model is determined by (i) a temporary equilibrium map (3.1)–(3.2), the interest rate rule (3.3), and government spending $g_t = g$; and (ii) the expectations updating rules (3.4)–(3.5). As is well known (e.g. see Evans and Honkapohja 2001) for small ϕ the dynamics are well approximated by a corresponding ordinary differential equation

[6] If habit persistence, indexation, lags, and/or serially correlated exogenous shocks were present, then least-squares-type learning using vector autoregessions would be appropriate.

[7] The adaptive learning approach can be extended to incorporate credible expected future interest rate policy, as announced by the Fed. See Evans et al. (2009) for a general discussion of incorporating forward-looking structural information into adaptive learning frameworks. In Evans and Honkapohja (2010) we assume that private agents know the policy rule used by the central bank in setting interest rates.

and hence, for the case at hand, by a two-dimensional phase diagram. This is illustrated by Figure 3.A1 in the Appendix. Corresponding phase diagrams were given in Evans et al. (2008) for an interest rate rule $R_t = f(\pi_t)$ with f a smooth, increasing, convex function. Qualitatively the results are as described in Section 3.1: the π^* steady state is locally stable, while the deflation steady state is locally unstable, taking the form of a saddle, with a deflation trap region in the southwest part of the space. In the deflation trap region trajectories are unstable and follow divergent trajectories under learning.

The model, of course, is very simple and highly stylized. More realistic versions would incorporate various elements standard in DSGE models, such as habit persistence, partial indexation, separate wage and price dynamics, capital and costs of adjusting the capital stock, and explicit models of job search and unemployment, as well as a model of financial intermediation. Thus the model here is very simple and incomplete. Nonetheless it provides a story of some key mechanisms that are of great concern to policy-makers.

3.3 A modified model

We now come to the modification mentioned in Section 3.1. To motivate this we briefly reflect on the experience of the USA in the 1930s, the Japanese economy since the mid-1990s, and the experience of the USA over 2007–10, as well as the data summary in Figure 1 of Bullard (2010). According to Evans et al. (2008), if we are in the unstable region then we will eventually see a deflationary spiral, with eventually falling deflation rates. However, we have not seen this yet in the USA, and this has not happened in Japan, despite an expended period of deflation. Similarly, in the USA in the 1930s, after two or three years of marked deflation, the inflation rate stabilized at near zero rates.[8] At the same time, output was greatly depressed, and unemployment much higher, in the USA in the 1930s, and low output growth and elevated unemployment rates have also been seen since the mid-1990s in Japan.

There are a number of avenues within the model that could explain these outcomes. As noted by Evans et al. (2008), if policy-makers do use aggressive fiscal policy to prevent inflation falling below a threshold, but that threshold is too low, then this can lead to another locally

[8] The initial significant deflation in 1931 and 1932 can perhaps be explained as due to reverse bottleneck effects (as in Evans 1985), i.e., reductions in prices when demand falls for goods that had been at capacity production in the prior years.

stable unintended steady state. This situation might arise if policy-makers are unwilling to pursue an aggressive increase in government spending, e.g., because of concerns about the size of government debt, unless deflation is unmistakable and significant. This is one possible explanation for Japan's experience.

An alternative avenue, which may perhaps be appealing for the recent US experience, is that the initial negative expectational shock may have placed us very close to the saddle path. We would then move towards the low-inflation steady state, where the economy could hover for an extended period of time, before 'declaring' itself, i.e., beginning a long path back to the targeted steady state at π^* or falling into a deflationary spiral. An extension of this line of thought is that after the initial expectational shock the economy may have been in the deflation trap region, and that the fiscal stimulus measures then pushed the economy close to the saddle path, with a weak recovery.

For the USA in the 1930s, one might argue, along the lines of Eggertsson (2008), that the New Deal policies to stabilize prices had both direct and expectational effects that prevented deflation and assisted in initiating a fragile recovery, which finally became robust when a large fiscal stimulus, taking the form of war-time expenditures, pushed the economy back to full employment.

However, we now set aside these possible explanations and pursue an alternative (and in a sense complementary) approach that modifies the model to incorporate an asymmetry in the adjustment of wages and prices. To do this we modify the quadratic functional form $k(\pi_{t,j}) = 0.5(\pi_{t,j} - 1)^2$ for price adjustment costs, which was made only because it is standard and analytically convenient. There is a long tradition of arguing that agents are subject to money illusion, which is manifested mainly in a strong resistance to reductions in nominal wages.[9] To incorporate this one can introduce an asymmetry in $k(\pi_{t,j})$, with agents being more averse to reductions in $\pi_{t,j}$ than to equal increases in $\pi_{t,j}$. For convenience we adopt an extreme form of this asymmetry,

$$k(\pi_{t,j}) = \begin{cases} 0.5(\pi_{t,j} - 1)^2 \text{ for } \pi_{t,j} \geq \underline{\pi} \\ +\infty \text{ for } \pi_{t,j} < \underline{\pi} \end{cases}.$$

This, in effect, places a lower bound of $\underline{\pi}$ on $\pi_{t,j}$. The result is that $\pi_t = H_\pi(\pi^e_{t+1}, c^e_{t+1}, g_t)$, Eq. (3.1), is replaced by

[9] For a recent argument that people strongly resist reductions in wages, see Akerlof and Shiller (2009), Ch. 9.

$$\pi_t = \begin{cases} H_\pi(\pi^e_{t+1}, c_t, g_t) \text{ if } H_\pi(\pi^e_{t+1}, c_t, g_t) \geq \underline{\pi} \\ \underline{\pi}, \text{ otherwise.} \end{cases}$$

The qualitative features of the phase diagram depend critically on the value of $\underline{\pi}$, and I focus on one possible value that leads to particularly interesting results, namely

$$\underline{\pi} = \beta. \tag{3.6}$$

Quantitatively, this choice is perhaps not implausible. If in most sectors there is great resistance to deflation, but decreases in prices cannot be prevented in some markets, then an inflation floor at a low rate of deflation might arise.[10] The assumption $\underline{\pi} = \beta$ is obviously special,[11] but the results for this case will informative also for values $\underline{\pi} \approx \beta$.

The resulting phase diagram, shown in Figure 3.2, is very revealing. It can be seen that the deflation trap region of divergent paths has been replaced by a region that converges to a continuum of stationary states at $\pi_t = \pi^e = \underline{\pi}$ and $c_t = c^e = c$ for $0 \leq c \leq c_L$, where c_L is the level of

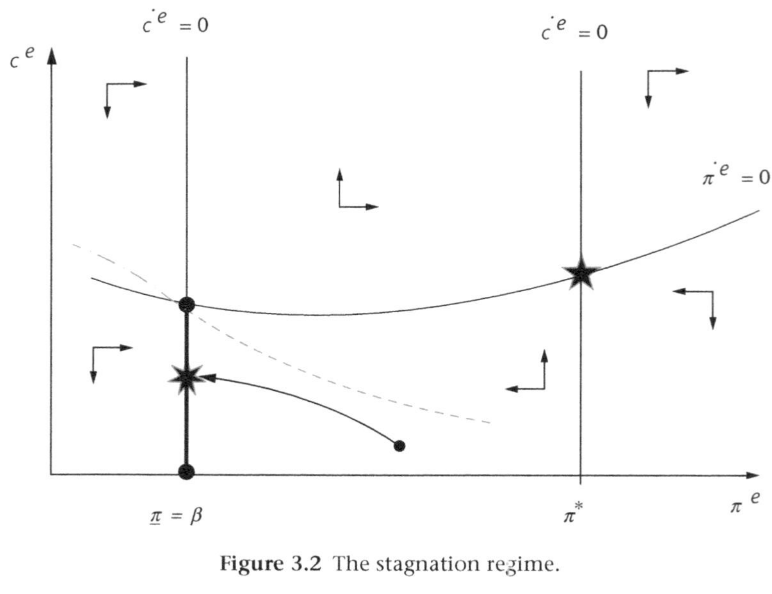

Figure 3.2 The stagnation regime.

[10] Depending on assumptions about the CRRA parameter, a low rate of deflation might also arise as a result of zero wage inflation combined with technical progress.

[11] And one at which a bifurcation of the system occurs.

c such that $H_\pi(\beta, c_L, g) = \underline{\pi}$. The pessimistic expectations shock that in Figure 3.A1 leads to a divergent trajectory culminating in continually falling inflation and consumption now converges to $\pi = \underline{\pi} = \beta$, i.e., a deflation rate equal to the negative of the discount rate, and a low level of consumption and output. This set of stationary states constitutes the *stagnation regime* of the model. This is a very Keynesian regime, in that it is one in which output is constrained by the aggregate demand for goods. In contrast to the rational expectations analysis of Benhabib et al. (2001a), in which the unintended low deflation steady state has levels of output and consumption that are not much different from their levels in the intended steady state, in the stagnation regime consumption and welfare can be much lower than at the π^* steady state.

The stagnation regime has interesting comparative statics. A small increase in government spending g raises output by an equal amount, i.e., the government spending multiplier is 1. Government spending does not stimulate increases in consumption, but it also does not crowd out consumption. Evans and Honkapohja (2010) noted this result in the temporary equilibrium, for given expectations, and in the stagnation regime the result holds for the continuum of stagnation regime stationary states. In this regime, an increase in g increases output y but has no effect on either c_t or π_t, provided $H_\pi(\underline{\pi}, c, g) < \underline{\pi}$.

The stagnation regime also has interesting dynamics that result from *sufficiently large* increases in g. Using Lemma 1 of Evans et al. (2008) it follows that there is a critical value $\hat{g}$ such that for $g > \hat{g}$ we have $H_\pi(\underline{\pi}, c, g) > \underline{\pi}$. If g is increased to and held at a value $g > \hat{g}$ then at this point $\pi_t > \underline{\pi}$, leading to increasing π^e, higher c, and higher c^e.[12] This process is self-reinforcing, and once (π^e, c^e) crosses the saddle path boundary it also becomes self-sustaining. That is, at this point the natural stabilizing forces of the economy take over. Government spending can then be reduced back to normal levels, and the economy will follow a path back to (π^*, c^*), the intended steady state.[13] One way to interpret these results is that the temporary increase in g provides enough lift to output and inflation that the economy achieves 'escape velocity' from the stagnation regime.[14] Under a standard 'Leeper-type'

[12] The $\dot{\pi}^e = 0$ curve is obtained by setting $\pi = \pi_t = \pi_t^e$ in Eq. (3.1). An increase in g can be seen as shifting the $\dot{\pi}^e = 0$ curve down. Once it shifts below the stationary value of c in the stagnation regime, π_t and π_t^e will start to rise.

[13] In contrast to traditional Keynesian 'multipliers', the *temporary* increase in government spending here results in a dynamic path leading to a *permanently* higher level of output.

[14] In the 3 April 2010 edition of the *Financial Times*, Lawrence Summers, the Director of the US National Economic Council, was quoted as saying that the economy 'appears to be moving towards escape velocity'.

rule for setting taxes, the temporary increase in g_t leads to a build-up of debt during the period of increased government spending, and is then followed by a period in which debt gradually returns to the original steady-state value, due to the reduction in g_t to normal levels and a period of higher taxes. For an illustrative simulation of all the key variables, including debt, see Evans et al. (2008).

It is important to note that the impact of temporary increases in government spending does not depend on a failure of Ricardian equivalence. In the model of Evans et al. (2008) and the modified model here, the impact of government spending is the same whether it is financed by taxes or by debt. This is also true in the infinite-horizon version of Evans and Honkapohja (2010) in which we explicitly impose Ricardian equivalence on private-agent decision-making. Thus, within our models, the fiscal policy tool is temporary increases in government spending, not reductions in taxes or increases in transfers. However, it is possible, of course, that for a variety of reasons Ricardian equivalence may fail, e.g., because of the presence of liquidity-constrained households, in which case tax cuts financed by bond sales can be effective.[15] Similarly if Ricardian equivalence fails because long-horizon households do not internalize the government's intertemporal budget constraints, then tax reductions can again be effective. However, the most reliable fiscal tool is temporary increases in government spending.

What if the condition $\underline{\pi} = \beta$ does not exactly hold? If $\underline{\pi} \neq \beta$ but $\underline{\pi} \approx \beta$ then the results can be qualitatively similar for long stretches of time. For example, if $\underline{\pi} \approx \beta$ and $\underline{\pi} > \beta$ then the targeted steady state will be globally stable, but the corresponding path followed by the economy once inflation has fallen to $\underline{\pi}$ will include slow increases in c and c^e before eventually inflation increases and the economy returns to the targeted steady state.[16] An interesting feature of the modified model is that, under learning, the inflation floor is not itself a barrier to reaching the targeted steady state. Indeed, it acts to stabilize the economy in the sense that, in the presence of large negative expectation shocks, it prevents the economy from falling into a deflationary spiral and a divergent path. However, although the economy reaches a stable region

[15] The \$858 billion measure, passed by Congress and signed into law in December 2010, includes tax cuts and extended unemployment benefits that will likely have a significant positive effect on aggregate demand and output in 2011 due in part to relaxed liquidity constraints for lower income households.

[16] If instead $\underline{\pi} \approx \beta$ and $\underline{\pi} < \beta$ then the stagnation regime at $\underline{\pi}$ will be accompanied by a slow decline in consumption and output. Such a decline would also result if $\underline{\pi} = \beta$, with the economy in the stagnation regime, and the policy-makers increase the interest rate above the ZLB $R = 1$.

in the stagnation regime, output is persistently depressed below the steady state that policy-makers are aiming to reach.

3.4 Policy

We now discuss at greater length the policy implications when the economy is at risk of becoming trapped in the stagnation regime. Although the discussion is rooted in the model presented, it also will bring in some factors that go beyond our simple model. We have used a closed-economy model without capital, a separate labour market, or an explicit role for financial intermediation and risk. These dimensions provide scope for additional policy levers.[17]

3.4.1 *Fiscal policy*

The basic policy implications of the model are quite clear, and consistent with Evans et al. (2008) and Evans and Honkapohja (2010). If the economy is hit by factors that deliver a shock to expectations that is not too large, then the standard monetary policy response will be satisfactory in the sense that it will ensure the return of the economy to the intended steady state. However, if there is a large negative shock then standard policy will be subject to the zero interest rate lower bound, and for sufficiently large shocks even zero interest rates may be insufficient to return the economy to the targeted steady state. In the modified model of this chapter, the economy may converge instead to the stagnation regime, in which there is deflation at a rate equal to the net discount rate and output is depressed. In this regime consumption is at a low level in line with expectations, which in turn will have adapted to the households' recent experience.

If the economy is trapped in this regime, sufficiently aggressive fiscal policy, taking the form of temporary increases in government spending, will dislodge the economy from the stagnation regime. A relatively small increase will raise output and employment but will not be sufficient to push the economy out of the stagnation regime. However, a large enough temporary increase in government spending will push the economy into the stable region and back to the targeted steady state. This policy would also be indicated if the economy is en route to the

[17] The discussion here is not meant to be exhaustive. Three glaring omissions, from the list of policies considered here, are: dealing with the foreclosure problem in the USA, ensuring that adequate lending is available for small businesses, and moving ahead with the implementation of regulatory reform in the financial sector.

stagnation regime, and may be merited even if the economy is within the stable region, but close enough to the unstable region that it would result in a protracted period of depressed economic activity.

Because of Ricardian equivalence, tax cuts are ineffective unless they are directed towards liquidity constrained households. However, in models with capital a potentially effective policy is investment tax credits. If the investment tax credits are time limited then they work not only by reducing the cost of capital to firms, but also by rescheduling investment from the future to now or the near future, when it is most needed. Investment tax credits could also be made state contingent, in the sense that the tax credit would disappear after explicit macroeconomic goals, e.g., in terms of GDP growth, are reached.

In the USA an effective fiscal stimulus that operates swiftly is federal aid to state and local governments. This was provided on a substantial scale through the ARRA in 2009 and 2010, but (as at the time of writing, October 2012), this money is due to disappear in 2011. Why are states in such difficulties? The central reason is that they fail to smooth their revenues (and expenditures) over the business cycle. States require themselves to balance the budget, and tend to do this year by year (or in some states biennium by biennium). Thus, when there is a recession, state tax revenues decline and they are compelled to reduce expenditures. This is the opposite of what we want: instead of acting as an automatic stabilizer, which is what happens at the federal level, budget balancing by states in recessions acts to intensify the recession. Indeed, in the USA the ARRA fiscal stimulus has largely been offset by reductions in government spending at the state and local level.

3.4.2 *Fiscal policy and rainy day funds*

This does not have to be. States should follow the recommendation that macroeconomists have traditionally given to national economies, which is to balance the budget over the business cycle. This can be done by the states setting up rainy day funds, building up reserves in booms to use in recessions.[18] A common objection to this proposal is that if a state builds up a rainy day fund, then politicians will spend it before the next recession hits. This objection can be dealt with. Setting up the rainy day fund should include a provision that drawing on the fund is

[18] Of course the size of the fund needs to be adequate. The state of Oregon recently started up a rainy day fund, which has turned out to be very useful following the recent recession, but the scale was clearly too small.

prohibited unless specified economic indicators are triggered. The triggers could be based on either national or state data (or a combination). For example, a suitable national indicator would be two successive quarterly declines of real GDP. State-level triggers could be based on the BLS measures of the unemployment rate, e.g., an increase of at least two percentage points in the unemployment rate over the lowest rate most recently achieved. Once triggered the fund would be available for drawing down over a specified period, e.g., three years or until the indicators improved by specified amounts. After that point, the rainy day fund would have to be built up again, until an appropriate level was reached. Obviously there are many provisions that would need to be thought through carefully and specified in detail. However, the basic point seems unassailable that this approach provides a rational basis for managing state and local financing, and that the political objections can be overcome by specifying the rules in advance.

It is also worth emphasizing that the establishment of rainy day funds would act to discipline state spending during expansions. Instead of treating the extra tax revenue generated during booms as free resources, to be used for additional government spending or for distribution to taxpayers, the revenue would go into a fund set aside for use during recessions. This is simply prudent management of state financial resources, which leads to a more efficient response to aggregate fluctuations.[19]

As of late 2010, there appears clearly to be a need for fiscal stimulus taking the form of additional federal aid to states. Politically this is difficult because people are distrustful of politicians and are concerned about deficits and debt. A natural proposal therefore is to provide additional federal money to states during 2011, contingent on the states agreeing to set up adequate rainy day funds, to which contributions would begin as soon as there is a robust recovery. This proposal has the attraction that it provides states with funds that are needed in the short term to avoid impending layoffs of state and local government employees, but in return for changing their institutions in such a way that federal help will be much less likely to be needed during future recessions.

[19] Similar issues arise in the European context. Eurozone countries are committed to the Stability and Growth Pact, which in principle limits deficit and debt levels of member countries. However, these limits have been stressed by recent events and enforcement appears difficult or undesirable in some cases. Reform may therefore be needed. An appropriate way forward would be to require every member country to set up a rainy day fund, during the next expansion, to which contributions are made until a suitable fund level is reached.

3.4.3 *Quantitative easing and the composition of the Fed balance sheet*

Since aggressive fiscal policy in the near term may be politically unpromising, especially in the USA, one must also consider whether more can be done with monetary policy.

In the version of the model used here, agents use short-horizon decision rules, based on Euler equations, and once the monetary authorities have reduced (short) interest rates to 0, there is no scope for further policy easing. In Evans and Honkapohja (2010) we showed that the central qualitative features of the model carry over to infinite-horizon decision rules, and the same would be true of the modified framework here. In this setting there is an additional monetary policy tool, namely policy announcements directed towards influencing expectations of future interest rates. By committing to keep short-term interest rates low for an extended period of time, the Fed can aim to stimulate consumption. An equivalent policy, which in practice is complementary, would be to move out in the maturity structure and purchase longer dated bonds. As Evans and Honkapohja (2010) demonstrate, however, such a policy may still be inadequate: even promising to keep interest rates low forever may be insufficient in the presence of a very large negative expectational shock.

Since financial intermediation and risk have been central to the recent financial crisis, and continue to play a key role in the current economy, there are additional central bank policy interventions that would be natural. One set of policies is being considered by the Federal Reserve Bank under the name of 'quantitative easing' or QE2.[20] Open market purchases of assets at longer maturities can reduce interest rates across the term structure, providing further channels for stimulating demand. More generally the Fed could alter its balance sheet to include bonds with some degree of risk. If expansionary fiscal policy is considered infeasible politically, then quantitative easing or changing the composition of the Federal Reserve balance sheet becomes an attractive option.

In an open economy model, there are additional channels for quantitative easing. If the USA greatly expands its money stock, and other countries do not do so, or do so to a lesser extent, then foreign exchange markets are likely to conclude that there is likely, in the medium or long run, to be a greater increase in prices in the USA than the rest or the world, and therefore a relative depreciation of the dollar. Unlike wages and goods prices, which respond sluggishly to changes in the

[20] As noted in the postscript, QE2 was introduced in November 2010.

money supply, foreign exchange markets often react very quickly to policy changes, and thus quantitative easing could lead to a substantial depreciation of the dollar now.[21] In a more aggressive version of this policy the Fed would directly purchase foreign bonds. This would tend to boost net exports and output and help to stimulate growth in the USA. This policy could, of course, be offset by monetary expansions in other countries, but some countries may be reluctant to do so.[22]

Another set of policies being discussed involve new or more explicit commitments by policy-makers to achieve specified inflation and price level targets. For example, one proposal would commit to returning to a price level path obtained by extrapolating using a target inflation rate of, say, 2 per cent p.a., from an earlier base, followed by a return to inflation targeting after that level is achieved. From the viewpoint of adaptive learning, a basic problem with all of these approaches is that to the extent that expectations are grounded in data, raising π^e may require actual observations of higher inflation rates. As briefly noted above, policy commitments and announcements may indeed have some impact on expectations, but the evolution of data will be decisive.

An additional problem, however, is that there are some distributional consequences that are not benign. Households that are savers, with a portfolio consisting primarily in safe assets like short maturity government bonds, have already been adversely affected by a monetary policy in which the nominal returns on these assets has been pushed down to near zero. A policy commitment at this juncture, which pairs an extended period of continued near zero interest rates with a commitment to use quantitative easing aggressively in order to increase inflation, has a downside of adversely affecting the wealth position of households who are savers aiming for a low risk portfolio.

3.4.4 *A proposal for a mixed fiscal–monetary stimulus*

If political constraints are an impediment to temporary increases in government spending at the federal level in the USA, as they currently appear to be, it may still be possible to use a fiscal–monetary policy mix that is effective. State and local governments are constrained in the United States to balance their budgets, but there is an exception in most states for capital projects. At the same time there is a clear-cut need throughout the United States to increase investment in infras-

[21] This is the mechanism of the Dornbusch (1976) model.

[22] And if all countries engaged in monetary expansion, this might increase inflation expectations.

tructure projects, as the US Society of Civil Engineers has been stressing for some time. In January 2009 the Society gave a grade of D to the nation's infrastructure. Large investments will be required in the nation's bridges, wastewater and sewage treatment, roads, rail, dams, levees, air traffic control, and school buildings. The need for this spending is not particularly controversial. The Society estimates $2.2 trillion over five years as the total amount needed (at all levels of government) to put this infrastructure into a satisfactory state.[23] Thus there is no shortage of useful investment that can be initiated.

The scale of the infrastructure projects needed is appropriate, since a plausible estimate of the cumulative shortfall of GDP relative to potential GDP, as of January 2011, is in excess of $1 trillion.[24,25] The timing and inherent lags in such projects may be acceptable. If we are in the stagnation regime, or heading towards or near the stagnation regime, then it is likely to be some time before we return to the targeted steady state. Projects that take several years may then be quite attractive. The historical evidence of Reinhart and Rogoff (2009) indicate that in the aftermath of recessions associated with banking crises, the recovery is particularly slow.

Furthermore, this area of expenditure appears to be an ideal category for leading a robust recovery. In the stagnation regime, the central problem is deficient aggregate demand. In past US recessions, household consumption and housing construction have often been the sectors that led the economic recovery. But given the excesses of the housing boom and the high indebtedness of households, do we want to rely on, or encourage, a rapid growth of consumption and residential construction in the near future? It would appear much more sensible to stimulate spending in the near term on infrastructure projects that are clearly beneficial, and that do not require us to encourage households to reduce their saving rate. Furthermore, once a robust recovery is underway, these capital investments will raise potential output and growth because of their positive supply-side impact on the nation's capital stock.

[23] For example, see the 28 January 2009 *New York Times* story 'US Infrastructure Is In Dire Straits, Report Says'.

[24] Assuming a 6% natural rate of unemployment and an Okun's law parameter of between 2 and 2.5 gives a range of $1.2 trillion to $1.5 trillion for the GDP shortfall if the unemployment rate, over 2011, 2012, and 2013, averages 8.5, 7.5, and 6.5%, respectively.

[25] For comparison the ARRA stimulus program was estimated by the Congessional Budget Office to have reduced the unemployment rate, relative to what it would otherwise have been, by between 0.7 and 1.8 percentage points. A number of commentators argued in early 2009 that the scale of the ARRA might be inadequate.

How would this be financed? State and local governments can be expected to be well informed about a wide range of needed infrastructure projects, but financing the projects requires issuing state or municipal bonds. Many states and localities are currently hard pressed to balance their budget, and this may make it difficult for them to issue bonds to finance the projects at interest rates that are attractive. Here both the Federal Reserve and the Treasury can play key roles. The Treasury could announce that, up to some stated amount, they would be willing to purchase state and local bonds for qualifying infrastructure projects. The Treasury would provide financing, at relatively low interest rates, for productive investment projects that are widely agreed to be urgently needed. Ideally there would be a federal subsidy to partially match the state or local government expenditure on infrastructure investment, as has often been true in the past. This would both make the investment more attractive and help to orchestrate a coordinated programme over the near term.

The ARRA did include a substantial provision for funding infrastructure through 'Build America Bonds', which has provided a subsidy by the Treasury to state and local governments issuing bonds for infrastructure projects. (Interest on these bonds is not tax-exempt, so the subsidy is partially offset by greater federal taxes received on interest.) The Build America Bonds have been very popular, but there is clearly room for a much larger infrastructure spending at the state and local level.

The Treasury could be involved in vetting and rationing the proposed projects, ensuring geographic diversity as well as quality and feasibility. One possibility would be for the President to announce a plan that encourages states and localities to submit proposals for infrastructure projects, which are then assessed. To finance their purchases of state and municipal bonds, the Treasury would issue bonds with a maturity in line with those acquired. For the Treasury there would be no obvious on-budget implications, since the extra Treasury debt issued by the Treasury to finance purchases of the state and municipal bonds would be offset by holdings of those bonds.

What would be the role of the Federal Reserve? The increase in infrastructure projects would go hand-in-glove with a policy of quantitative easing in which the Fed buys longer dated US Treasuries, extending low interest rates further out the yield curve. In effect, the Fed would provide financing to the Treasury, and the Treasury would provide financing to states and local government, at rates that make investment in infrastructure projects particularly attractive now and in the near future. In principle, the Federal Reserve could also directly purchase the state and municipal bonds. Alternatively they could provide financing indirectly by making purchases in the secondary market for municipal bonds.

Thus this proposal meshes well with the current discussion within the Federal Reserve Bank for quantitative easing, with the additional feature that the injections of money in exchange for longer dated Treasuries would be in part aimed at providing financing for new spending on infrastructure investment projects.

The three proposals discussed above are complementary. Federal aid to states and localities is needed in the near term to reduce current state budget problems and avoid layoffs. A commitment by states to set up rainy day funds during the next expansion will help ensure that state budgeting is put on a secure footing going forward. A large infrastructure programme can provide a major source of demand that will also expand the nation's capital stock and enhance future productivity. Finally, quantitative easing by the Federal Reserve can help provide an environment in which the terms for financing infrastructure projects are attractive.

3.5 Conclusions

In the model of this chapter, if an adverse shock to the economy leads to a large downward shift in consumption and inflation expectations, the resulting path can converge to a stagnation regime, in which output and consumption remain at low levels, accompanied by steady deflation. Small increases in government spending will increase output, but may leave the economy within the stagnation regime. However, a sufficiently large temporary increase in government spending can dislodge the economy from the stagnation regime and restore the natural stabilizing forces of the economy, eventually returning the economy to the targeted steady state.

The aggressive monetary policy response of the Federal Reserve Bank over 2007–9, together with the TARP intervention and the limited ARRA fiscal stimulus, may well have been helped to avert a second Depression in the USA. However, as of late 2010, US data showed continued high levels of unemployment, modest rates of GDP growth, and very low and possibly declining inflation. Although the economy has stabilized, there remains the possibility of either convergence to the stagnation regime or an unusually protracted period before a robust recovery begins.

Although forecasting GDP growth is notoriously difficult, it seems almost certain that in the near-term the economy will continue to have substantial excess capacity and elevated unemployment. In this setting there is a case for further expansionary policies.[26] My suggestions include a combination of additional federal aid to state and local governments, in return for a commitment by states to set up rainy day funds during the next expansion, quantitative easing by the Federal Reserve, and a large-scale infrastructure programme, funded indirectly by the US Treasury and accommodated by the Federal Reserve as part of the programme of quantitative easing.

3.6 Postscript

Between the end of October 2010, when this chapter was initially written, and the beginning of April 2011, when this postscript was added, there were significant changes in the United States in both macroeconomic policy and the trajectory of the economy. The US Federal Reserve Open Market Committee announced in November 2010 a new round of quantitative easing (referred to as QE2, i.e., quantitative easing, round two), which is expected to total $600 billion for purchases of longer dated Treasury bonds over an eight-month period ending in June 2011. In addition, in December 2010 the US Congress passed, and the President signed into law, a new fiscal stimulus measure that included, among other things, temporary reductions in payroll taxes and extended unemployment benefits, as well as continuation of tax reductions introduced in 2001 that would otherwise have expired. Thus, while the specific policies recommended in this chapter were not all adopted, there was shift towards a more expansionary stance in both monetary and fiscal policy.

Over November 2010–March 2011 the US macroeconomic data have also been somewhat more encouraging. The unemployment rate, which had been stuck in the range 9.5–9.8 per cent range, declined over three months to 8.8 per cent in March 2011, while the twelve-month CPI inflation rate, excluding food and energy, which had been in decline and was at 0.6 per cent in October 2010, increased to 1.1 per cent in February 2011. While the unemployment rate is considerably above its pre-crisis levels and the inflation rate remains below the (informal) target of 2 per cent, these data, combined with the recent monetary and fiscal policy stimulus, provide some grounds for hope that we will follow a path back towards the intended steady state and avoid convergence to the stagnation regime. As has been

[26] Additional monetary easing was introduced in November 2010 and expansionary fiscal measures were passed in December 2010.

emphasized in the main text, however, following a large expectational shock, in addition to paths converging to the stagnation regime, there are also paths that converge very slowly to the desired steady state. Under current forecasts of the unemployment rate a case can still be made for additional infrastructure spending over the next few years, especially given the uncertainty attached to macroeconomic forecasts: there remains downside risk as well as upside hope.

The case for a restructuring of US state finances, and of national finances within the euro area, continues to appear compelling. In the USA, states and localities are under pressure to reduce expenditures in the near-term because of the reduced tax revenues, which are the lagged result of the recession, and in several European countries there is still the potential for sovereign debt crises. Establishing rainy day funds during the next expansion, once the recovery is clearly established, would provide the needed fiscal reassurance and flexibility for rational countercyclical fiscal policy, if needed during a future major downturn. A commitment now to establish a rainy day fund in the future should be part of every medium-term financial plan.

Appendix

The framework for the model is from Evans et al. (2008), except that random shocks are omitted and the interest rate rule is modified as discussed in the main text. There is a continuum of household-firms, which produce a differentiated consumption good under monopolistic competition and price-adjustment costs. There is also a government which uses both monetary and fiscal policy and can issue public debt as described below. Agent j's problem is

$$\text{Max } E_0 \sum_{t=0}^{\infty} \beta^t U_{t,j}\left(c_{t,j}, \frac{M_{t-1,j}}{P_t}, h_{t,j}, \pi_{t,j}\right)$$

$$st.\ c_{t,j} + m_{t,j} + b_{t,j} + \Upsilon_{t,j} = m_{t-1,j}\pi_t^{-1} + R_{t-1}\pi_t^{-1}b_{t-1,j} + \frac{P_{t,j}}{P_t}y_{t,j},$$

where $c_{t,j}$ is the Dixit–Stiglitz consumption aggregator, $M_{t,j}$ and $m_{t,j}$ denote nominal and real money balances, $h_{t,j}$ is the labour input into production, $b_{t,j}$ denotes the real quantity of risk-free one-period nominal bonds held by the agent at the end of period t, $\Upsilon_{t,j}$ is the lump-sum tax collected by the government, $P_{t,j}$ is the price of consumption good j, $\pi_{t,j} = \frac{P_{t,j}}{P_{t-1,j}}$, $y_{t,j}$ is output of good j, P_t is the aggregate price level, and the inflation rate is $\pi_t = P_t/P_{t-1}$. The utility function has the parametric form

$$U_{t,j} = \frac{c_{t,j}^{1-\sigma_1}}{1-\sigma_1} + \frac{\chi}{1-\sigma_2}\left(\frac{M_{t-1,j}}{P_t}\right)^{1-\sigma_2} - \frac{h_{t,j}^{1+\varepsilon}}{1+\varepsilon} - \gamma k\left(\pi_{t,j}\right),$$

where $\sigma_1, \sigma_2, \varepsilon, \gamma > 0$. The final term parameterizes the cost of adjusting prices in the spirit of Rotemberg (1982), specifically taking the quadratic form

$$k(\pi_{t,j}) = \frac{1}{2}(\pi_{t,j} - 1)^2.$$

Production function for good j is given by $y_{t,j} = h_{t,j}^{\alpha}$, where $0 < \alpha < 1$. Output is differentiated and firms operate under monopolistic competition. Each firm faces a downward-sloping demand curve given by $P_{t,j} = \left(y_{t,j}/Y_t\right)^{-1/\nu} P_t$. Here $P_{t,j}$ is the profit-maximizing price set by firm j consistent with its production $y_{t,j}$, and $\nu > 1$ is the elasticity of substitution between two goods. Y_t is aggregate output, which is exogenous to the firm.

Using the household-firm's first-order Euler conditions for optimal choices of prices $P_{t,j}$ and consumption $c_{t,j}$, and using the representative agent assumption, we get the equations for the temporary equilibrium at time t:

$$(\pi_t - 1)\,\pi_t = \beta\left(\pi_{t+1}^e - 1\right)\pi_{t+1}^e - \frac{\nu}{\alpha\gamma}(c_t + g_t)^{(1+\varepsilon)/\alpha} \qquad (3.7)$$
$$-\gamma^{-1}(\nu - 1)(c_t + g_t)c_t^{-\sigma_1}$$

and

$$c_t = c_{t+1}^e(\pi_{t+1}^e/\beta R_t)^{\sigma_1}, \qquad (3.8)$$

where we assume $\pi_t > 0.5$.

The government's flow budget constraint is $b_t + m_t + \Upsilon_t = g_t + m_{t-1}\pi_t^{-1} + R_{t-1}\pi_t^{-1}b_{t-1}$, where b_t is the real quantity of government debt, and Υ_t is the real lump-sum tax collected. The rule for lump-sum taxes is $\Upsilon_t = \kappa_0 + \kappa b_{t-1}$, where $\beta^{-1} - 1 < \kappa < 1$ so that fiscal policy is 'passive' in the terminology of Leeper (1991). The interest rate rule, $R_t = f(\pi_{t+1}^e)$, is assumed to be a linear spline

$$f(\pi^e) = \min\{1, (\pi^*/\beta) + \theta(\pi^e - \pi^*)\}$$

where $\theta > \beta^{-1}$.

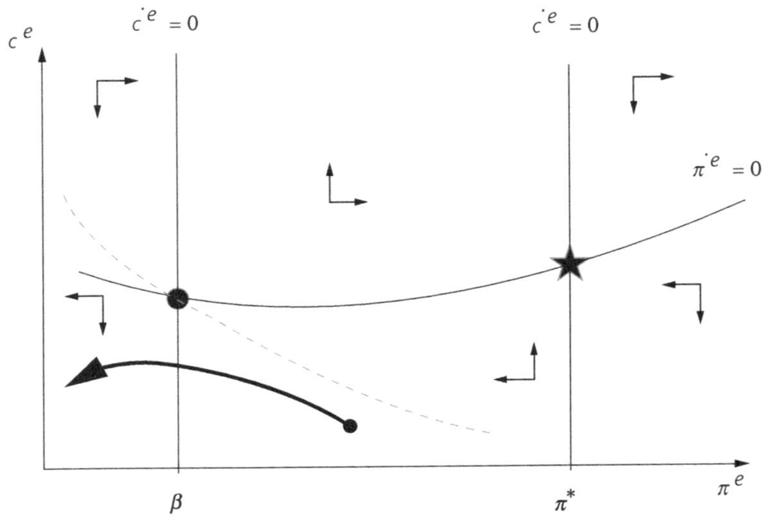

Figure 3.A1 Divergent paths can result from large negative expectation shocks.

Under adaptive learning, for the case without an inflation floor, the phase diagram, giving the dynamics in the small gain case, is shown in Figure 3.A1. Incorporating an inflation floor at $\underline{\pi} = \beta$, as in Section 3.3, leads to the stagnation regime case shown in Figure 3.2 and emphasized in the main text of this chapter.

References

Akerlof, G. A., and R. J. Shiller (2009). *Animal Spirits*. Princeton, NJ: Princeton University Press.

Benhabib, J., S. Schmitt-Grohe, and M. Uribe (2001a). 'Monetary Policy and Multiple Equilibria', *American Economic Review*, 91, 167–86.

——, ——, and —— (2001b). 'The Perils of Taylor Rules', *Journal of Economic Theory*, 96, 40–69.

Bullard, J. (2010). 'Seven Faces of The Peril', *Federal Reserve Bank of St. Louis Review*, 92, 339–52.

Dornbusch, R. (1976). 'Expectations and Exchange Rate Dynamics', *Journal of Political Economy*, 84, 1161–76.

Eggertsson, G. B. (2008). 'Was the New Deal Contractionary?', Working paper.

—— and M. Woodford (2003). 'The Zero Bound on Interest Rates and Optimal Monetary Policy', *Brookings Papers on Economic Activity*, (1), 139–233.

Evans, G. W. (1985). 'Bottlenecks and the Phillips Curve: A Disaggregated Keynesian Model of Inflation, Output and Unemployment', *Economic Journal*, 95, 345–57.

——, E. Guse, and S. Honkapohja (2008). 'Liquidity Traps, Learning and Stagnation', *European Economic Review*, 52, 1438–63.

——and S. Honkapohja (2001). *Learning and Expectations in Macroeconomics*. Princeton, NJ: Princeton University Press.

——and—— (2010): 'Expectations, Deflation Traps and Macroeconomic Policy.' in D. Cobham, Ø. Eitrheim, S. Gerlach, and J. F. Qvigstad (eds), *Twenty Years of Inflation Targeting: Lessons Learned and Future Prospects*. Cambridge: Cambridge University Press, pp. 232–60.

——, ——, and K. Mitra (2009). 'Anticipated Fiscal Policy and Learning', *Journal of Monetary Economics*, 56, 930–53.

Krugman, P. R. (1998). 'It's Baaack: Japan's Slump and the Return of the Liquidity Trap', *Brookings Papers on Economic Activity*, (2), 137–205.

Leeper, E. M. (1991). 'Equilibria under "Active" and "Passive" Monetary and Fiscal Policies', *Journal of Monetary Economics*, 27, 129–47.

Preston, B. (2006). 'Adaptive Learning, Forecast-based Instrument Rules and Monetary Policy', *Journal of Monetary Economics*, 53, 507–35.

Reifschneider, D., and J. C. Williams (2000). 'Three Lessons for Monetary Policy in a Low-Inflation Era', *Journal of Money, Credit and Banking*, 32, 936–66.

Reinhart, C. M., and K. S. Rogoff (2009). *This Time is Different*. Princeton, NJ: Princeton University Press.

Rotemberg, J. J. (1982). 'Sticky Prices in the United States', *Journal of Political Economy*, 90, 1187–211.

Part II

Learning, Incentives, and Public Policies

4

Notes on Agents' Behavioural Rules under Adaptive Learning and Studies of Monetary Policy*

Seppo Honkapohja, Kaushik Mitra, and George W. Evans

4.1 Introduction

In the literature on adaptive learning in infinite-horizon representative agent settings it is often assumed that agents base their behaviour on an Euler equation that is derived under subjective expectations.[1] This formulation has sometimes been criticized in that it does not require that the intertemporal budget constraint be satisfied for the agent since the constraint is not explicitly used when deriving the behavioural rule of the agent.[2]

Another point of criticism has been that the formulation is not natural since it postulates that agents are making forecasts of their future consumption, which is their own choice variable. Preston (2005) has proposed an interesting reformulation of (linearized) intertemporal behaviour under learning in which agents are assumed to incorporate a 'subjective version' of their intertemporal budget constraint in their behaviour under learning. A further issue sometimes raised is whether temporary equilibrium equations based on Euler equations with subjective expectations, such as those used in Bullard and Mitra (2002)

* A preliminary version of this chapter was circulated under the title 'Notes on Agents' Behavioral Rules under Adaptive Learning and Recent Studies of Monetary Policy'.

[1] This is done, e.g., in some of the models of Chapter 10 of Evans and Honkapohja (2001). See also the discussion in Marcet and Sargent (1989) and Sargent (1993).

[2] This point has been made in the context of New Keynesian models of monetary policy. The approach based on Euler equations is used, e.g., in Bullard and Mitra (2002) and Evans and Honkapohja (2003).

and Evans and Honkapohja (2003), are subject to inconsistency when subjective expectations are used in equilibrium equations that have normally been derived under rational expectations.

In these notes we first clarify the relationship between two formulations of intertemporal behaviour under adaptive learning and show that the intertemporal accounting consistency holds in an ex post sense along the sequence of temporary equilibria under 'Euler equation' learning. This is done in the simple context of a consumption-saving model. Second, we consider the Preston (2005) model of monetary policy under learning and show that, under plausible assumptions, the usual system based on Euler equations with subjective expectations can be obtained from Preston's approach and is, therefore, a valid way of analysing learning dynamics under incomplete knowledge.

4.2 A permanent income model

Consider a model in which income follows an exogenous process and there is a representative consumer who makes consumption-saving decisions.[3] The consumer has a standard intertemporal utility function

$$\hat{E}_t \sum_{s=t}^{\infty} \beta^{s-t} U(C_s) \tag{4.1}$$

and the accounting identity for net assets W_s is

$$W_{s+1} = R_s W_s - C_s + Y_s. \tag{4.2}$$

For the initial period of the economy net assets are taken to be zero, i.e., $W_t = 0$.[4] R_s is the one-period real gross rate of return factor for a safe one-period loan, assumed known at s. Because we are in a general equilibrium framework we do not take it to be fixed and its value will be determined by market clearing. Output Y_s follows an exogenous process

$$Y_s = M Y_{s-1}^{\rho} V_s \tag{4.3}$$

or

$$\log Y_s = \mu + \rho \log Y_{s-1} + v_s,$$

[3] The results remain unchanged if it is assumed instead that there is finite (or infinite) number of consumers with identical characteristics, including their forecasts and learning rules.

[4] Note that this is a very simple general equilibrium model of a closed economy. Thus there cannot be any net paper assets (like bonds) before the economy starts.

where $|\rho| < 1$ and v_s is white noise. Expectations are not necessarily rational, which is indicated by ^ in the expectations operator. There is also an intertemporal budget constraint of the form

$$C_t + \sum_{s=t+1}^{\infty} \mathcal{R}_{t+1,s} C_s = Y_t + \sum_{s=t+1}^{\infty} \mathcal{R}_{t+1,s} Y_s, \tag{4.4}$$

where $\mathcal{R}_{t+1,s} = (R_{t+1} \dots R_s)^{-1}$ is the market discount factor.

Maximizing (4.1) subject to (4.4) yields the Euler equation as a necessary condition. It has the familiar form

$$U'(C_t) = \beta R_t \hat{E}_t U'(C_{t+1}) \tag{4.5}$$

and in equilibrium $C_t = Y_t$, as output is assumed to be perishable. In this temporary equilibrium framework, agents' demand for consumption goods C_t depends on their forecast $\hat{E}_t U'(C_{t+1})$ and on the interest rate factor R_t, in accordance with (4.5). Imposing the market clearing condition $C_t = Y_t$ we see that (4.5) determines the interest rate according to

$$R_t^{-1} = \beta(\hat{E}_t U'(C_{t+1}))/U'(Y_t).$$

This gives us the temporary equilibrium at t.

We now log-linearize (4.5) at a non-stochastic steady state. Standard computations yield

$$c_t = \hat{E}_t c_{t+1} - \sigma r_t, \tag{4.6}$$

where $c_t = \log(C_t/\bar{C})$, r_t is the net return, based on the approximation $r_t \approx \log(R_t/\bar{R})$, and $\sigma = -\frac{U'(\bar{C})}{U''(\bar{C})\bar{C}}$ is the coefficient of intertemporal substitution (or risk aversion). Equation (4.6) is the consumer's demand schedule giving current consumption demand as a function of the interest rate r_t and forecasts about the next period.

The log-linearization of the output process gives

$$y_t = \rho y_{t-1} + v_t, \tag{4.7}$$

where $y_t = \log(Y_t/\bar{Y})$. (Bars over the variables denote the non-stochastic steady state.) The rational expectations equilibrium (REE) of the linearized model is given by

$$r_t = -(1-\rho)\sigma^{-1} y_t$$

and for rational forecasts we have

$$E_t c_{t+1} = \rho y_t. \tag{4.8}$$

4.2.1 *Learning based on Euler equations*

To formulate learning in terms of the linearized Euler equation (4.6), which we will call EE approach subsequently, we suppose that agents are learning, using a perceived law of motion (PLM) corresponding to the REE:

$$\hat{E}_t c_{t+1} = m_t + n_t y_t, \tag{4.9}$$

where (m_t, n_t) are obtained using a regression of c_s on y_{s-1} using data $s = 1, \ldots, t-1$. The data are then used to update parameter estimates to (m_{t+1}, n_{t+1}) and we proceed to period $t+1$.

Note that the rational forecast function (4.8) is a particular case of (4.9) and the basic question is whether $(m_t, n_t) \to (0, \rho)$ over time. This can easily be verified, for example using E-stability arguments.[5] Suppose we have (4.9) where the time subscripts are dropped from the parameters, i.e., $\hat{E}_t c_{t+1} = m + n y_t$. Temporary equilibrium, given forecasts $\hat{E}_t c_{t+1}$, in the linearized model is

$$r_t = -\sigma^{-1}(y_t - \hat{E}_t c_{t+1}) = -\sigma^{-1}[y_t(1-n) - m]$$

and the actual law of motion (ALM) is

$$T(m, n) = (0, \rho).$$

The E-stability differential equations are thus

$$\frac{d(m, n)}{d\tau} = (0, \rho) - (m, n),$$

which yields convergence of adaptive learning in this model.

Is this a plausible formulation? One of the necessary conditions for individual optimization is on the margin between today's consumption and tomorrow's consumption, and implementation of this first-order condition (FOC) requires a forecast of that agent's own C_{t+1}. It might seem odd to have an agent forecasting his own behaviour, but it is actually very natural. In the REE future consumption is related to the key exogenous state variable (e.g., income in the model of consumption). In

[5] For the connection between least-squares learning and E-stability see Evans and Honkapohja (2001).

a temporary equilibrium with learning agents are just trying to infer this relationship from past data and in forecasting they use the estimated relationship. The agent needs to plan what level of consumption he will choose in the following period and he also considers the perceived relation of consumption to the key exogenous variable. His best guess, given the AR(1) income process, is plausibly a linear function of current income. Thinking a single step ahead, in this way, appears to us to be one plausible and natural form of bounded rationality.

Note that, at first sight, this formulation of the agent's behaviour rule does not seem to require explicitly the intertemporal life-time budget constraint (4.4) or transversality condition. Yet it is not inconsistent with such a constraint as the agent can be thought to solve the intertemporal problem under subjective expectations. When the behaviour rule of the agent is based on the Euler equation, only the one-step forward margin, the flow budget constraint, and one-step forecasts are explicitly used.[6]

A boundedly rational agent making use only of the current Euler equation and an appropriate forecast function will converge to the household optimum under least-squares learning. It can, moreover, be shown that, along the sequence of temporary equilibria during the convergent learning, ex post consistency in the accounting over the infinite horizon is fulfilled. To see this we note that, iterating the flow accounting identity, we have

$$C_t + \sum_{s=t+1}^{T} \mathcal{R}_{t+1,s} C_s = Y_t + \sum_{s=t+1}^{T} \mathcal{R}_{t+1,s} Y_s + \mathcal{R}_{t+1,T} W_{T+1}.$$

In the sequence of temporary equilibria $C_s = Y_s$ for all s, which implies that $\mathcal{R}_{t+1,T} W_{T+1} = 0$ and so the ex post transversality condition must hold. If learning is convergent, then intertemporal consistency is achieved. Once the Euler equation (EE) learning has reached the REE, the agent has the correct forecast function (4.8) and his behaviour based on the Euler equation generates the REE sequence (c_s^*, r_s^*) of consumptions and interest rates. This type of behaviour by the agent is then consistent with full intertemporal optimization since if he is faced with the sequence of interest rates r_s^* he would choose the consumption sequence c_s^* which does satisfy the transversality condition.[7]

[6] Note also that, in many derivations of the REE, the intertemporal budget constraint is checked only at REE prices. Indeed, there could be problems with existence of solutions to household optimum at arbitrary prices sequences.

[7] EE learning is a special case of shadow-price learning, which can be shown to deliver asymptotically optimal decision-making in general settings. See Evans and McGough (2010).

In other economic models, learning based on Euler equations may fail to be stable. In cases of instability one could argue that if the economy diverges along an explosive path, the household would begin to think through the implications of its lifetime budget constraint and/or transversality condition and eventually alter its behaviour. Of course, in the divergent case the log-linearization is also invalid since the economy will not stay near the steady state.

4.2.2 *Learning with perceptions over an infinite horizon*

A different form of learning behaviour is developed by Preston (2005) in the context of a New Keynesian model of monetary policy.[8] His approach can also be simply presented in the current context. The starting point is to log-linearize the intertemporal budget constraint (4.4) at the non-stochastic steady state, which yields

$$\hat{E}_t \bar{C} c_t + \sum_{s=t+1}^{\infty} \bar{\mathcal{R}}_{t+1,s} \bar{C} \hat{E}_t c_s = \bar{Y} y_t + \sum_{s=t+1}^{\infty} \bar{\mathcal{R}}_{t+1,s} \bar{Y} \hat{E}_t y_s, \tag{4.10}$$

where in fact $\bar{\mathcal{R}}_{t+1,s} = (1/\bar{R})^{s-t} = \beta^{s-t}$ and $\bar{C} = \bar{Y}$ at the steady state. Next, we iterate the linearized Euler equation (4.6) backwards for $s \geq t+1$, giving

$$\hat{E}_t c_s = c_t + \sigma \sum_{j=t}^{s-1} \hat{E}_t r_j. \tag{4.11}$$

Substituting (4.11) into (4.10) leads to

$$c_t + \sum_{s=t+1}^{\infty} \beta^{s-t} [c_t + \sigma \sum_{j=t}^{s-1} \hat{E}_t r_j] = y_t + \sum_{s=t+1}^{\infty} \beta^{s-t} \hat{E}_t y_s.$$

Rearranging the summation and manipulation give a linearized consumption function in the form

$$c_t = \sum_{s=t}^{\infty} \beta^{s-t} [(1-\beta) \hat{E}_t y_s - \sigma \beta \hat{E}_t r_s]. \tag{4.12}$$

We will call this the infinite-horizon (IH) approach to modelling adaptive learning by the agent.

There are several important comments about this formulation.

[8] Infinite-horizon learning based on an iterated Euler equation was applied to the 'investment under uncertainty' example in pp. 122–5 of Sargent (1993).

First, note that if (4.12) is the behavioural rule of the learning agent, then the agent must make forecasts about future income/output and rates of return into the infinite future. The agent is thus assumed to be very far-sighted even though he is boundedly rational.

Second, it can be asked whether the EE approach is consistent with (4.12). This is naturally the case, since the derivation of (4.12) relies in part on (4.6). Moreover, advancing (4.12) and multiplying by β one period gives

$$\beta c_{t+1} = \sum_{s=t+1}^{\infty} \beta^{s-t}[(1-\beta)\hat{E}_{t+1}y_s - \sigma\beta\hat{E}_{t+1}r_s],$$

to which one can apply the subjective expectations $\hat{E}_t(.)$. Once this has been done, it is seen that

$$c_t = (1-\beta)y_t - \sigma\beta r_t + \beta\hat{E}_t c_{t+1},$$

so that by using market clearing $c_t = y_t$ the Euler equation (4.6) also obtains.

This derivation presumes that the law of iterated expectations holds for the subjective expectations of the agent. For standard formulations of adaptive learning this is usually assumed. For example, suppose that agents do not know the relationship between y_t and r_t and assume that the return r_t is a linear function of the key state variable y_t, so that at time t they have the PLM

$$r_t = d_t + f_t y_t. \tag{4.13}$$

For simplicity, we assume that they know the true process of y_t, (4.7). The agents' forecasts are assumed to behave as follows,

$$\hat{E}_t\hat{E}_{t+1}r_s = \hat{E}_t(d_{t+1} + f_{t+1}\hat{E}_{t+1}y_s) = d_t + f_t\hat{E}_t y_s,$$

which says that in iterating expectations back to an earlier period the point estimates of the PLM parameters are shifted back to the earlier values.[9] This is the standard formulation in the adaptive learning literature, and can be viewed as an axiom of the approach.

Third, it is of interest to consider whether learning using the forecasts based on (4.13) converges. We again study this using E-stability, so that the PLM is $r_t = d + fy_t$. Then (4.12) can be written as

[9] More generally, one could have the agents also learn the parameters of the process for y_t. Then they would also have a PLM of the form $y_t = a_t + b_t y_{t-1} + v_t$. In this case the iterated expectations would take the form $\hat{E}_t(a_{t+1} + b_{t+1}\hat{E}_{t+1}y_{s-1}) = a_t + b_t\hat{E}_t y_{s-1}$.

$$c_t = \sum_{s=t}^{\infty} \beta^{s-t}[(1-\beta)\hat{E}_t y_s - \sigma\beta\hat{E}_t r_s]$$

$$= \sum_{s=t}^{\infty} \beta^{s-t}\{[(1-\beta) - \sigma\beta f]\hat{E}_t y_s - \sigma\beta d\}.$$

We have

$$\sum_{s=t}^{\infty} \beta^{s-t}\hat{E}_t y_s = \sum_{s=t}^{\infty} \beta^{s-t}\rho^{s-t} y_t = \frac{1}{1-\beta\rho} y_t$$

and we get

$$c_t = \frac{1-\beta-\sigma\beta f}{1-\beta\rho} y_t - \frac{\sigma\beta d}{1-\beta}.$$

The temporary equilibrium value of the rate of return is determined from the Euler equation (4.6), so that

$$r_t = -\sigma^{-1}(y_t - \hat{E}_t c_{t+1}) = -\sigma^{-1}\left(y_t - \frac{1-\beta-\sigma\beta f}{1-\beta\rho}\rho y_t + \frac{\sigma\beta d}{1-\beta}\right).$$

The T-mapping is thus

$$d \to -\frac{\beta d}{1-\beta}$$

$$f \to -\sigma^{-1}\left(1 - \frac{1-\beta-\sigma\beta f}{1-\beta\rho}\rho\right).$$

The differential equation defining E-stability consists of two independent linear equations with negative coefficients on the variables d and f, respectively, and so we have E-stability.

4.2.3 *Further discussion*

Comparing the two approaches to agent's behaviour under learning we see that the EE approach has the agent making forecasts only one period ahead. It is thus assumed that the agent is relatively short-sighted. In contrast, in the IH approach the agent must make forecasts over the entire infinite future. Thus the agent is very far-sighted. These two approaches represent different ways of modelling agent's behaviour under adaptive, boundedly rational learning.

It should be noted that, quite naturally, the agent forecasts different quantities in the EE and IH approaches. Thus the natural PLM have different parameters and the respective mappings from the PLM to the

ALM are also different. We have seen that the two approaches are not inconsistent in the sense that it is possible to derive the EE formulation from the IH approach under certain plausible conditions. We have convergence of learning for both approaches in this model. In terms of the degree of farsightedness the two approaches represent extreme cases. In the EE approach the boundedly rational agents look ahead only for one period while in the IH approach they look ahead into the infinite future.

Which approach is more plausible (suitable)? This will, of course, depend on the type of situation being analysed in an economic model. There are certainly circumstances where it would be more plausible to assume that agents have long horizons. For instance, assume that future changes in fiscal policy are announced by the government and these changes are viewed as credible by economic agents. The EE approach may not be suitable for this analysis since agents look only one period ahead and would not react to the announcement until the moment the policy change actually takes place! Normally, one would expect agents' current (short-term) decisions to be affected by the possibility of future changes since agents are assumed to be (subjective) dynamic optimizers where the horizon in their utility maximization problem is infinite (in the same spirit as RE). Since the learning analysis based on EE only requires agents to make one-period-ahead forecasts, these forecasts will potentially not be affected by the announcement of future policy changes.[10]

The IH approach is used in Evans et al. (2009) to analyse announced future policy changes; they consider a simple competitive representative-agent endowment economy in which the government purchases output for current consumption and levies lump-sum taxes. The baseline case has balanced-budget spending changes (which agents are assumed to know) and analyses the dynamics arising from credible, permanent anticipated changes in government spending/taxation. Evans et al. (2009) utilize the consumption function of the representative agent which relates current consumption of the household to future (subjective) forecasts of taxes and real interest rates. This allows agents to react to future policy changes (in taxes) through their current consumption/savings choice. Agents need to forecast future real

[10] Note that, under RE, it does not matter whether one conducts the analysis of policy changes using the consumption Euler equation or the consumption function (which involves IH forecasts). However, in the presence of incomplete knowledge of agents, it typically matters whether the analysis is conducted using the consumption EE or the consumption function. For instance, the latter may determine consumption levels based on interest, wage, and tax forecasts, whereas the EE only involves one-period-ahead interest rate (and own consumption) forecasts.

interest rates and taxes to decide their current consumption plans. Since the policy change is credible and announced, agents are endowed with knowledge of the future path of taxes. This announced change in future taxes leads immediately to a change in current consumption. Knowledge of the overall structure of the economy nevertheless remains incomplete, and agents must forecast future interest rates using only the history of interest rate data, revising these forecasts over time in line with standard adaptive learning models.

The results are striking. In line with the agents' forward-looking behaviour under learning, there are immediate changes in the interest rate, with continued evolution over time, and these dynamics are in a sharp contrast to the fully rational path; see Figure 1 of Evans et al. (2009).[11]

In judging the approaches one must perhaps also take note of the empirical observation that in reality public and private forecasting institutions have only a limited time horizon, often at most two years, for detailed business cycle forecasting. Very long-term projections are also made by forecasting institutions but these projections are very broad as they usually show only long-term trends of relatively few variables. Perhaps the 'right' approach is inbetween these two extremes from a practical point of view.[12]

4.3 Learning and monetary policy

The learning viewpoint has been extensively used in the past decade to analyse monetary policy design in the basic New Keynesian model presented in Woodford (2003) (see, e.g., Chapters 2–4) and Woodford (1996). The seminal papers of Bullard and Mitra (2002) and Evans and Honkapohja (2003) examined the performance of various Taylor-type and optimal interest rate policies of the central bank using the Euler equation approach. Preston (2005) considers a model of monetary policy using the IH approach. He shows that if the central bank uses the contemporaneous data Taylor-type rule, then the learning dynamics are E-stable if and only if the Taylor principle is satisfied; see Proposition 2 of the paper. Note that this E-stability result is the same as that in Bullard and Mitra (2002).

We now demonstrate that the EE analysis of Bullard and Mitra (2002) and Evans and Honkapohja (2003) is consistent with the IH analysis of

[11] The EE approach in Evans et al. (2009) for the announced policy change leads to different dynamics of interest rates from the IH approach; see the paper for details.

[12] For a formalization of intermediate approaches, see Branch et al. (2013).

Preston (2005), as in the simple permanent income model of Section 4.2. Consequently, both the EE and IH approaches are valid ways of studying stability under learning in the New Keynesian setting.

4.3.1 *Framework*

We start with the framework presented in Section 2 of Preston which essentially uses a dynamic stochastic equilibrium model of Woodford (2003; Chapters 2–4). Preston (2005) derives an optimal consumption rule for a representative household and an optimal pricing rule for a representative firm.[13] These two equations are, respectively,

$$C_t^i = \hat{E}_t^i \left\{ \sum_{T=t}^{\infty} \beta^{T-t} [(1-\beta)Y_T - \beta\sigma(i_T - \pi_{T+1}) + \beta(g_T - g_{T+1})] \right\}, \quad (4.14)$$

$$p_t^i = \hat{E}_t^i \left\{ \sum_{T=t}^{\infty} (\alpha\beta)^{T-t} \left[\frac{(1-\alpha\beta)(\omega+\sigma^{-1})}{(1+\omega\theta)} x_T + \alpha\beta\pi_{T+1}) \right] \right\}, \quad (4.15)$$

where g_t is an appropriate taste shock. (In some variations of the model g_t represents a government spending shock.)

Under our representative agent assumption agents have identical expectations and thus consumption and price setting (for firms able to set prices) is the same across agents; i.e., for all relevant variables z we have $\hat{E}_t^i z = \hat{E}_t z$ and thus $C_t^i = \int_j C_t^j dj \equiv C_t$ and $p_t^i = \int_j p_t^j dj \equiv p_t$. Given expectations, the temporary equilibrium values of output Y_t and the inflation rate π_t are determined by the market-clearing condition $Y_t = C_t$ and by the relationship between the aggregate price level and prices currently being set, given by $\pi_t = \alpha^{-1}(1-\alpha)p_t$. The equation for Y_t is often reexpressed in terms of the output gap $x_t = Y_t - Y_t^n$, where Y_t^n is the natural rate of output.

Integrating (4.14)–(4.15) over i and using these relationships gives

$$x_t = \hat{E}_t \left\{ \sum_{T=t}^{\infty} \beta^{T-t} [(1-\beta)x_{T+1} - \sigma(i_T - \pi_{T+1}) + r_T^n] \right\} \quad (4.16)$$

where $r_T^n = g_T - g_{T+1} + Y_{T+1}^n - Y_T^n$, and

$$\pi_t = \hat{E}_t \left\{ \sum_{T=t}^{\infty} (\alpha\beta)^{T-t} [\kappa x_T + (1-\alpha)\beta\pi_{T+1})] \right\} \quad (4.17)$$

[13] We refer the reader to Preston (2005) for the details of these derivations.

where

$$\kappa = (1-\alpha)\alpha^{-1}(1-\alpha\beta)(\omega+\sigma^{-1})(1+\omega\theta)^{-1}.$$

Preston (2005) then conducts the analysis using Eqs. (4.16) and (4.17) as the behavioural rule for households and firms.

The analysis in Bullard and Mitra (2002) and Evans and Honkapohja (2003), on the other hand, is based on the EE approach and thus starts from the two equations

$$x_t = \hat{E}_t x_{t+1} - \sigma\left(i_t - \hat{E}_t\pi_{t+1}\right) + r_t^n, \tag{4.18}$$

$$\pi_t = \kappa x_t + \beta\hat{E}_t\pi_{t+1}. \tag{4.19}$$

We now show how to derive (4.18) and (4.19) from (4.14) and (4.15). This implies that (4.18) and (4.19) are an equally valid framework for studying learning.

4.3.2 *Derivation of aggregate Euler equations*

The key assumption that will allow us to derive (4.18) and (4.19) from (4.14) and (4.15) is that the subjective expectations of individual agents obey the law of iterated expectations, i.e., for any variable z

$$\hat{E}_t^i\hat{E}_{t+s}^i z = \hat{E}_t^i z \text{ for } s = 0, 1, 2, \ldots.$$

As indicated above, this is a standard assumption for agents making forecasts from linear laws of motion estimated by least squares.

For example, in Bullard and Mitra (2002), agent i has a PLM of the form[14]

$$x_t = a_{x,t}^i + b_{x,t}^i r_t^n + \epsilon_{xt},$$

$$\pi_t = a_{\pi,t}^i + b_{\pi,t}^i r_t^n + \epsilon_{\pi t},$$

which can be used to form future forecasts for any $T > t$,

$$\hat{E}_t^i x_T = a_{x,t}^i + b_{x,t}^i\hat{E}_t^i r_T^n, \tag{4.20}$$

$$\hat{E}_t^i\pi_T = a_{\pi,t}^i + b_{\pi,t}^i\hat{E}_t^i r_T^n. \tag{4.21}$$

[14] Evans and Honkapohja (2003) allow for an exogenous random shock to the inflation equation (4.19) and consequently they examine a PLM that depends on this shock. Our central points do not depend on the specific PLM, and hold also if the PLM includes lagged endogenous variables, as in Evans and Honkapohja (2006).

Note that if each agent i has identical parameter estimates (and knows the persistence parameter ρ in the process of r_t^n, a simplifying assumption without any loss of generality), then the forecasts of each agent are the same, that is, $\hat{E}_t^i = \hat{E}_t^j$ for all i and j. This, of course, implies that $\hat{E}_t^i = \hat{E}_t$ for all i in the analysis. We emphasize that there is no need for any single agent to make this inference when forming the forecasts needed in his decision-making. In other words, every agent i forms his own forecast independently of the other agents in the economy and uses this forecast in his optimal consumption or pricing rule. It follows that the optimal consumption and pricing rules of each agent given by (4.14) and (4.15) are the same, that is, $C_t^i = C_t$ and $p_t^i = p_t$ for all i. (In principle the rules given by (4.14) and (4.15) could vary across households/firms if the future forecasts are different across them but homogenous forecasts force them to be the same.)

As discussed before, (4.20) implies for $j \geq 1$ that

$$\hat{E}_{t+j}^i x_T = a_{x,t+j}^i + b_{x,t+j}^i \hat{E}_{t+j}^i r_T^n$$

and when we take expectations of the above expression at time t we obtain

$$\hat{E}_t^i \hat{E}_{t+j}^i x_T = a_{x,t}^i + b_{x,t}^i \hat{E}_t^i \hat{E}_{t+j}^i r_T^n = a_{x,t}^i + b_{x,t}^i \hat{E}_t^i r_T^n = \hat{E}_t^i x_T \tag{4.22}$$

In other words, it is assumed that the law of iterated expectations holds at the individual level.[15] With assumption (4.22) and identical expectations across agents, one can show that, for analytical purposes, it is possible to obtain (4.18) from Eq. (4.14). Although there are several ways to obtain the desired results, we give a derivation that focuses on the individual Euler equation. This will reinforce points made earlier in these notes and emphasize the details of individual decision-making.

We begin by taking quasi-differences of (4.14). Advancing (4.14) by one time unit, taking expectations $\hat{E}_t^i$ of both sides, and using the law of iterated expectations, we obtain

$$C_t^i - \beta \hat{E}_t^i C_{t+1}^i = \hat{E}_t^i [(1-\beta) Y_t - \beta\sigma (i_t - \pi_{t+1}) + \beta(g_t - g_{t+1})], \text{ or}$$

$$C_t^i = \beta \hat{E}_t^i C_{t+1}^i + (1-\beta)(x_t + Y_t^n) - \beta\sigma(i_t - \hat{E}_t^i \pi_{t+1}) + \beta(g_t - g_{t+1}), \tag{4.23}$$

where for simplicity we assume that g_t, g_{t+1}, Y_t^n and Y_{t+1}^n are known at t.

[15] We have kept on purpose the superscript i for individuals, though the analysis assumes identical expectations.

To implement (4.23) each agent must forecast their consumption next period. Market clearing and the representative agent assumption imply that $C_t^i = Y_t$ for all i, t; i.e., consumption of each agent is in fact equal to mean/aggregate output in each period. We assume that each agent observes this equality from historical data, and thus forecasts its consumption next period by its forecast of aggregate output.[16] Using also $Y_t = x_t + Y_t^n$, for all t, we obtain

$$\hat{E}_t^i C_{t+1}^i = \hat{E}_t^i x_{t+1} + Y_{t+1}^n.$$

Here we are following the literature in assuming that Y_{t+1}^n is observable at t, in which case it is natural to assume that $\hat{E}_t^i C_{t+1}^i$ would incorporate this information and use least squares to forecast the unknown component x_{t+1}.[17] Hence

$$C_t^i = \beta \hat{E}_t^i x_{t+1} + (1-\beta)x_t + Y_t^n - \beta\sigma(i_t - \hat{E}_t^i \pi_{t+1}) + \beta r_t^n, \qquad (4.24)$$

where $r_t^n = g_t - g_{t+1} + Y_{t+1}^n - Y_t^n$.

Equation (4.24) is our behavioural equation giving consumption demand as a function of interest rates, current income and one-step-ahead forecasts of income and inflation. As discussed earlier, although (4.24) does not explicitly impose the lifetime budget constraint, it is a consistent and plausible way of implementing bounded rationality, which in stable systems will indeed lead to satisfaction of the intertemporal budget constraint. Finally, from market-clearing $C_t^i = Y_t = x_t + Y_t^n$ and using $\hat{E}_t^i x_{t+1} = \hat{E}_t x_{t+1}$ and $\hat{E}_t^i \pi_{t+1} = \hat{E}_t \pi_{t+1}$ we arrive at the aggregate Euler equation (4.18).

The derivation of (4.19) from (4.15) is analogous. Taking quasi-differences of (4.15) and using the law of iterated expectations at the individual level leads to the individual agent Euler equation

$$p_t^i = \alpha\beta \hat{E}_t^i p_{t+1}^i + (1-\alpha\beta)(\omega + \sigma^{-1})(1+\omega\theta)^{-1} x_t + \alpha\beta \hat{E}_t^i \pi_{t+1}.$$

Note that in this Euler equation agent i's expectations of future values of x_T and π_{T+1} are appropriately condensed into $\hat{E}_t^i p_{t+1}^i$, the price the firm expects to set next period if it is again a price setter. Finally, we make use of

[16] Note that we do not need to make any a priori assumption that agents know that all agents are identical, and we do not need to assume that agents make deductions based upon this.

[17] However, nothing hinges on this point. In more general representative agent setups, each agent would forecast its consumption at $t+1$ by a least-squares regression on all relevant information variables.

$$p_t^i = p_t \text{ and } \pi_t = \alpha^{-1}(1-\alpha)p_t \text{ all } t,$$

which implies that[18]

$$\hat{E}_t^i p_{t+1}^i = \alpha(1-\alpha)^{-1}\hat{E}_t^i \pi_{t+1}.$$

It follows that

$$p_t^i = \alpha\beta(1-\alpha)^{-1}\hat{E}_t^i \pi_{t+1} + (1-\alpha\beta)(\omega+\sigma^{-1})(1+\omega\theta)^{-1}x_t. \quad (4.25)$$

Equation (4.25) is our behavioural equation giving individual price setting as a function of the current output gap and the one-step-ahead forecasts of inflation. Integrating over households and using $\pi_t = \alpha^{-1}(1-\alpha)p_t$ we arrive at the aggregate Euler equation (4.19).[19]

Honkapohja and Mitra (2005) have considered cases in which the central bank uses its own forecasts of inflation and output (rather than private sector forecasts) in its interest rate rule. This poses no additional complication for the above derivation of the system (4.18) and (4.19) from (4.14) and (4.15), given the assumption (which we have maintained throughout) that the consumption schedule is conditioned on current interest rates, so that x_t, π_t, and i_t are simultaneously determined in the usual way by market clearing.

4.3.3 *Some final remarks*

The EE and IH approaches to modelling the agent's behaviour rule are not identical and lead to different paths of learning dynamics. Thus there is in general no guarantee that the convergence conditions for the two dynamics are identical, though this happens to be the case in the permanent income model of Section 4.2 and is also the outcome for some interest rate rules in the New Keynesian model of monetary policy considered in Preston (2005).

Preston (2006) analyses optimal monetary policy under commitment from the timeless perspective considered in Chapter 7 of Woodford (2003). Preston (2006) looks at determinate monetary policies capable of implementing the optimal equilibrium under IH learning dynamics as in Preston (2005). He examines variants of monetary policies that

[18] Because there is an exact linear relation between these variables, if agents form expectations using least-squares learning, the expectations $\hat{E}_t^i p_{t+1}^i$ and $\hat{E}_t^i \pi_{t+1}$ will exactly satisfy the stated relationship provided the explanatory variables and sample period are the same for both variables, as we of course assume.

[19] Evans and Honkapohja (2006) derive the Euler equations for the general equilibrium framework of Woodford (1996).

respond to (one-step-ahead) future forecasts of inflation and output gap (capable of implementing the optimal equilibrium), similar to the Taylor-type rules considered in Bullard and Mitra (2002).

The IH approach used in Preston requires agents to forecast all future paths of nominal interest rates (along with the forecasts of inflation and output gap) while the EE approach used in Bullard and Mitra (2002) does not require agents to do so (since no forecasts of interest rates appear in the Euler equations). Another way of interpreting these differences is to assume that agents do not know the policy rule being used by the central bank in Preston (2006) while they have this knowledge in Bullard and Mitra (2002) (say due to the central bank being more transparent about its policy). Preston (2006) claims that the results on convergence of learning dynamics can be different between the IH and EE approaches under these different informational assumptions; see his Proposition 2. On the other hand, if agents have knowledge of the monetary policy rule being used by the central bank (as assumed in Bullard and Mitra 2002), then Preston (2006) continues to find *exactly* the same conditions determining stability under learning dynamics for his IH model; see his Proposition 3.

These results are perhaps not that surprising since it is well known in the adaptive learning literature that the conditions for stability under learning dynamics depend crucially on the form of the PLM used by the economic agents. Stability conditions for the same economic model can vary depending on the nature of the PLMs used by agents (see Evans and Honkapohja 2001 for a number of examples). Depending on whether the agents have knowledge of the monetary policy rule will lead to different PLMs and can affect stability conditions in the monetary model considered above.[20]

References

Branch, W. A., G. W. Evans, and B. McGough (2013). 'Finite Horizon Learning', in T. J. Sargent and J. Vilmunen (eds), *Macroeconomics at the Service of Public Policy*. Oxford: Oxford University Press, 141–63.

Bullard, J., and K. Mitra (2002). 'Learning about Monetary Policy Rules', *Journal of Monetary Economics*, 49, 1105–29.

Evans, G. W., and S. Honkapohja (2001). *Learning and Expectations in Macroeconomics*. Princeton, NJ: Princeton University Press.

[20] Similar remarks apply to the IH approach used in Preston (2002) where he analyses the expectations-based reaction function proposed by Evans and Honkapohja (2006) which uses the EE approach; see Proposition 5 of Preston (2002).

——and—— (2003). 'Expectations and the Stability Problem for Optimal Monetary Policies', *Review of Economic Studies*, 70, 807–24.

——and—— (2006). 'Monetary Policy, Expectations and Commitment', *Scandinavian Journal of Economics*, 108, 15–38.

——, ——, and K. Mitra (2009). 'Anticipated Fiscal Policy and Learning', *Journal of Monetary Economics*, 56, 930–53.

——and B. McGough (2010). 'Learning to Optimize', mimeo.

Honkapohja, S., and K. Mitra (2005). 'Performance of Monetary Policy with Internal Central Bank Forecasting', *Journal of Economic Dynamics and Control*, 29, 627–58.

Marcet, A., and T. J. Sargent (1989). 'Convergence of Least-Squares Learning Mechanisms in Self-Referential Linear Stochastic Models', *Journal of Economic Theory*, 48, 337–68.

Preston, B. (2002). 'Adaptive Learning and the Use of Forecasts in Monetary Policy', mimeo, Princeton University.

——(2005). 'Learning about Monetary Policy Rules when Long-Horizon Expectations Matter', *International Journal of Central Banking*, 1, 81–126.

——(2006). 'Adaptive Learning, Forecast-based Instrument Rules and Monetary Policy', *Journal of Monetary Economics*, 53, 507–35.

Sargent, T. J. (1993). *Bounded Rationality in Macroeconomics*. Oxford: Oxford University Press.

Woodford, M. (1996). 'Control of the Public Debt: A Requirement for Price Stability?', Working paper, NBER WP5684.

——(2003). *Interest and Prices: Foundations of a Theory of Monetary Policy*. Princeton, NJ: Princeton University Press.

5

Learning and Model Validation: An Example*

In-Koo Cho and Kenneth Kasa

5.1 Introduction

The macroeconomic learning literature has progressed through a number of stages. Early contributions focused on convergence questions (Bray 1982, Bray and Savin 1986). Addressing these questions led naturally to issues of stability and selection among multiple rational expectations equilibria (Sargent 1993, Evans and Honkapohja 2001). Once these theoretical issues were resolved, attention shifted to empirical applications. A breakthough came with the work of Sargent (1999), which introduced the idea of 'constant gain' learning. These models feature 'perpetual learning' and stationary equilibria, and are therefore better suited to econometric analysis. Finally, the most recent phase of the learning literature has turned its attention to normative questions, related to optimal policy design (Bullard and Mitra 2002, Evans and Honkapohja 2003).

Looking back on this literature, one is struck by the fact that it always makes one important assumption, namely, that agents are somehow endowed with a *given* model. In the early literature this model conformed to the rational expectations equilibrium, and the question was whether coefficient estimates would converge to their rational expectations counterparts. More recently, researchers have begun to explore the implications of model misspecification (Sargent 1999 and Evans and Honkapohja 2001). Still, even here, agents are not allowed to question their models, so that any misspecification necessarily goes undetected.

* We thank Seppo Honkapohja for suggesting this example to us.

However, from the beginning, one of the main objectives of the learning literature has been to treat agents and their modellers more symmetrically. Although allowing agents to revise coefficient estimates takes a step in this direction, one could argue that economists actually spend *most* of their time searching for better models, not refining estimates of a given model.

This chapter is therefore an attempt to take the next natural step in the learning literature, by allowing agents to *test* the specification of their models. While the existing learning literature has modelled agents who are well acquainted with the first half of a standard econometrics text, which typically focuses on estimation, it has thus far presumed agents never made it to the second half of the book, which discusses inference and specification analysis. Our particular strategy for doing this consists of the following four steps:

(1) We assume an agent is endowed with a fixed *set* of models, each containing a collection of unknown parameters. The models may be misspecified and non-nested;
(2) Each period the agent tests the specification of his current model;
(3) If the current model survives the test, the model is updated and used to formulate a policy function, under the provisional assumption that the model will not change in the future, and
(4) If the model is rejected, a new model is randomly selected.

We refer to this combined process of estimation, testing, and selection as *model validation*. Our goal in this chapter is to provide a detailed analyis of model validation for a simple, widely studied example, i.e., the cobweb model.

The remainder of the chapter is organized as follows. Section 5.2 provides a brief overview of some new issues that arise when combining model uncertainty with adaptive learning. Section 5.3 provides a detailed analyis of model validation in a cobweb model. We show that as the rate of parameter updating decreases, one model comes to dominate, and we identify this model using the tools of large deviations theory. Finally, Section 5.4 offers a few concluding remarks.

5.2 Overview

Incorporating model uncertainty into the learning literature raises a host of new questions and issues. This section briefly outlines our approach to model validation. These issues are discussed in more detail in Cho and Kasa (2010).

5.2.1 *Parameter uncertainty vs model uncertainty*

The existing learning literature focuses on parameter uncertainty. For Bayesians, however, there is no essential difference between parameter uncertainty and model uncertainty. By formulating a single, all-encompassing, 'hypermodel', Bayesians convert model uncertainty into parameter uncertainty. We do not do this. Our agent uses his model to construct a policy function. To make this tractable, models must be relatively simple and parsimonious.[1]

5.2.2 *The model class*

While our agent is not committed to a single model, he is committed to a single set of models, called the *model class*. This set is exogenously specified and fixed over time. Where does it come from? That's an important question we do not address. Although our agent can effectively dispose of (relatively) bad models, he cannot create new models in response to unanticipated events.[2]

5.2.3 *Feedback*

The fact that the data-generating process responds to the agent's own beliefs is of course a crucial issue even without model uncertainty. It means that all the classical econometric results on convergence and consistency of least-squares estimators go out the window. Developing methods that allow one to rigorously study the consequences of feedback has been a central accomplishment of the macroeconomic learning literature, at least from a technical standpoint. (See Evans and Honkapohja 2001 for a summary of this literature.)

When one turns to *inference*, however, new issues arise. First, the presence of feedback means that we cannot directly apply recent econometric advances in testing and comparing misspecified models.[3] Although

[1] Of course, it is possible to use Bayesian methods to select among a set of simple models. Bayesian purists tend to frown upon this practice, however. Also, as discussed below, our model validation approach is based more on specification testing than on model comparison.

[2] Jovanovic (2009) discusses how one might expand a model class in response to unforseen events.

[3] A highly selected sample includes White (1982), Vuong (1989), and Sin and White (1996). White (1994) and Burnham and Anderson (2002) contain textbook treatments.

we assume the agent is aware of these advances, and tries to implement them, we cannot appeal to known results to study their consequences. Second, traditionally it has been assumed that agents are unaware of feedback.[4] Although beliefs are revised in an adaptive and purposeful manner, this adaptation is strictly passive. This is a reasonable assumption in the context of learning the parameters of a single model, mainly because one is already confined to a local analysis. With multiple models, however, the distinction between local and global analysis becomes far more important, and therefore, assumptions about the agent's awareness of feedback become more important. We depart from tradition here by assuming that the agent is aware of feedback. In particular, he realizes that with model uncertainty he confronts a difficult counterfactual—How would things have been different if instead a different model had been used in the past? Fitting a model to data that were generated while a *different* model was in use could produce misleading inferences about the prospects of a given model. For the questions that we address, it is not important how exactly the agent responds to this counterfactual. What's important is that he is aware of its dangers, and takes steps to avoid becoming trapped in suboptimal self-confirming equilibria.

5.2.4 *Model comparison vs specification testing*

We assume the agent sticks with a model until sufficient evidence mounts against it. An alternative strategy would be to run a (recursive) horserace between models, by continuously comparing their relative performance. In this case, one might switch models even if the currently used model appears to be well specified. Our choice of specification testing reflects three main factors: (1) We think it is an accurate description of policy-making in most cases. (2) Specification testing can be easily embedded within a standard stochastic recursive algorithm. In particular, the orthogonality condition that drives parameter updating

[4] There have been a few notable exceptions. The early work of Bray and Savin (1986) touched on this issue, asking whether agents could use standard diagnostics, like Chow tests and Durbin–Watson statistics, to detect the parameter variation that their own learning behaviour generates. Bray and Savin (1986) found that when convergence is slow, agents are generally able to detect the misspecification of their models. Bullard (1992) and McGough (2003) studied convergence and stability when the agent's perceived law of motion allows for time-varying parameters. McGough (2003) showed that convergence to rational expectations can still occur as long as this time variation is expected to damp out at a sufficiently rapid rate. Finally, and perhaps most closely related to our own work, Sargent and Williams (2005) showed that priors about parameter drift have a strong influence on the large deviation properties of constant gain learning algorithms. However, all this prior work takes place within the confines of a single model.

can be interpreted as a score statistic, or equivalently, a localized likelihood ratio statistic, which can be used as the basis of a sequential Lagrange Multiplier test. (See, e.g., Chapter 5 of Benveniste et al. 1990.) (3) The resulting analysis is easier. In Cho and Kasa (2009) we consider the case of recursive model comparison.

5.2.5 *Model switching vs parameter revision*

Adding model uncertainty does not eliminate parameter uncertainty. We continue to assume that each model's parameters are adaptively updated using a constant gain stochastic approximation algorithm. A constant gain recognizes the potential existence of slow parameter drift. What is new here is the agent's recognition that more drastic and sudden changes to the underlying environment may also occur. These are signalled by an excessively large score statistic. When the score statistic exceeds a given threshold, it indicates that required parameter changes are faster and larger than specified by the underlying null hypothesis of gradual parameter drift.[5]

5.2.6 *Escape dynamics, type I errors, and the robustness of self-confirming equilibria*

We assume for simplicity that each model, when used, has a unique, stable, self-confirming equilibrium (SCE). This means that each model, if given the chance, is capable of passing the specification test. Of course, this does not imply that it is the 'true' data-generating process. In fact, the entire model class may be misspecified. However, with endogenous data, each model can adapt to fit the data that it itself generates. It is this possibility that wreaks havoc with the application of traditional statistical results.

Although all models are capable of passing the test, they are not all equally likely to do so on a repeated basis. Some models are more attached to their self-confirming equilibrium, while others are more apt to drift away. Model drift is driven by the fact that coefficient estimates drift in response to constant gain updating. We calibrate the testing threshold so that this kind of normal, gradual, parameter drift does not trigger model rejection. However, as first noted by Sargent (1999), constant gain algorithms also feature rare, but recurrent, 'large deviations' in their sample paths. These large deviations can be characterized

[5] Another possible response to an excessively large score statistic would be to allow the update gain to increase. See Kostyshyna (2012) for an analysis of this possibility.

analytically by the solution of a *deterministic* control problem. It is these rare 'escapes' from the self-confirming equilibrium that trigger model rejections. In a sense then, model rejections here are type I errors.[6]

The value function of the large deviations control problem is called the 'rate function', and as you would expect, it depends sensitively on the tails of the score statistic. In Cho and Kasa (2010) we show that as the update gain decreases the model with the largest rate function becomes dominant, in the sense that it is used 'almost always'. This bears some resemblence to results in the evolutionary game theory literature (Kandori et al. 1993). It also provides a selection criterion for models with multiple stable self-confirming equilbria.

5.2.7 *Experimentation*

When a model is rejected we assume the agent randomly selects a new model (which may turn out to be the existing model). This randomness is *deliberate*. It does not reflect capriciousness or computational errors, but instead reflects a strategic response to model uncertainty (Foster and Young 2003). It can also be interpreted as a form of experimentation. Of course, macroeconomic policy-makers rarely conduct explicit experiments, but they do occasionally try new things. Although the real-time dynamics of model selection naturally depend on the details of the experimentation process, our main conclusions about the stability and robustness of self-confirming equilibria do not.

5.3 Model Validation in a Cobweb Model

The cobweb model has long been a useful laboratory for analysing various issues in dynamic economics, first with constant coefficients adaptive expectations, then with rational expectations, then with adaptive least-squares learning, and most recently, with misspecified adaptive least squares. We continue this tradition by using it to study model validation dynamics. In particular, we pursue an example studied by Evans and Honkapohja (2001: 318–20). They analyse so-called restricted perceptions equilibria (RPE), in which agents (exogenously) omit relevant variables from their fitted models. In their analysis, *any* model can be a RPE, as long as its estimated coefficients adjust to account for the

[6] Note, however, that with endogenous data the concept of type I error becomes somewhat ambiguous, since the 'true model' depends on the agent's beliefs.

omitted variable bias. Here we allow the agent to *test* his model, and ask whether some RPE are more robust than others.[7]

5.3.1 *Actual and perceived laws of motion*

Suppose the true data-generating process is given by

$$p_n = \alpha E_{n-1} p_n + \beta_1 w_{1,n-1} + \beta_2 w_{2,n-1} + \varepsilon_n, \tag{5.1}$$

where $(w_{1,n}, w_{2,n})$ are Gaussian, mean zero, exogenous variables, and ε_n is an *i.i.d.*, Gaussian, mean zero shock. This model has the rational expectations equilibrium

$$p_n = \frac{1}{1-\alpha}\left(\beta_1 w_{1,n-1} + \beta_2 w_{2,n-1}\right) + \varepsilon_n.$$

Following Evans and Honkapohja (2001), suppose the agent entertains two different models, each obtained by including only one element of $\{w_1, w_2\}$ on the right-hand side of the equation.[8] We thus endow the agent with a model class $\mathcal{M} = \{\mathcal{M}_1, \mathcal{M}_2\}$, where

$$\mathcal{M}_1: \quad p_n = \gamma_1 w_{1,n-1} + v_{1,t} \tag{5.2}$$

$$\mathcal{M}_2: \quad p_n = \gamma_2 w_{2,n-1} + v_{2,t}. \tag{5.3}$$

The agent believes the disturbance process in each model is i.i.d, and orthogonal to the included regressor. Hence, each model is estimated using recursive least squares,

$$\hat{\gamma}_{1,n} = \hat{\gamma}_{1,n-1} + \eta R^{-1}_{1,n-1} w_{1,n-1}(p_n - \hat{\gamma}_{1,n-1} w_{1,n-1}) \tag{5.4}$$

$$\hat{\gamma}_{2,n} = \hat{\gamma}_{2,n-1} + \eta R^{-1}_{2,n-1} w_{2,n-1}(p_n - \hat{\gamma}_{2,n-1} w_{2,n-1}) \tag{5.5}$$

$$\hat{R}_{1,n} = \hat{R}_{1,n-1} + \eta(w^2_{1,n} - \hat{R}_{1,n-1})$$

$$\hat{R}_{2,n} = \hat{R}_{2,n-1} + \eta(w^2_{2,n} - \hat{R}_{2,n-1}),$$

where the constant gain parameter, $0 < \eta < 1$, serves to discount old data. This reflects doubts about the stationarity of the environment.

Note that in this model the agent only takes two actions: (1) He selects a model at the beginning of each period, and (2) he uses it to construct

[7] The setup here is also similar to that of Branch and Evans (2007). However, their goal is quite different. They posit a large collection of agents who randomly select between the two models, with weights determined by recent forecasting performance. In contrast, we posit a single agent who continuously challenges the existing model. Hypothesis testing generates model switches.

[8] As in Branch and Evans (2007), we suppose that all models are underparameterized.

a forecast of next period's price. These forecasts feedback to influence the actual price process as

$$p_n = \alpha(s_{1,n-1}\hat{\gamma}_{1,n-1}w_{1,n-1} + (1 - s_{1,n-1})\hat{\gamma}_{2,n-1}w_{2,n-1}) +$$
$$\beta_1 w_{1,n-1} + \beta_2 w_{2,n-1} + \varepsilon_n,$$

where $s_{1,n}$ is a model indicator, with $s_{1,n} = 1$ when $\mathcal{M}_1$ is used in period n, and zero otherwise. In Cho and Kasa (2010) we develop a more general framework, in which models are used to formulate policy actions, and these policy actions feedback to influence the true data-generating process.

5.3.2 *Mean ODEs*

A key step in our analysis is to exploit a time-scale separation between the rapidly evolving model variables, $(p_n, w_{1,n}, w_{2,n})$, and the slowly evolving coefficient estimates, $(\hat{\gamma}_{1,n}, \hat{\gamma}_{2,n})$. Following the usual procedure, we can approximate the sample paths of (5.4) and (5.5) by the following ordinary differential equations (ODEs), with continuous time units defined as $t = \eta \cdot n$:

$$\dot{\gamma}_1 = (\alpha - 1)\gamma_1 + \beta_1 + \Omega_{11}^{-1}\Omega_{12}\beta_2 = h_1(\gamma_1)$$
$$\dot{\gamma}_2 = (\alpha - 1)\gamma_2 + \beta_2 + \Omega_{22}^{-1}\Omega_{12}\beta_1 = h_2(\gamma_2).$$

As $\eta \to 0$, the coefficient estimates converge to the paths of these ODEs (see Evans and Honkapohja 2001 for a precise statement). The only subtlety here is that with potential model switching the mean ODEs could in principle become coupled, since the dynamics of a model's coefficient estimates depend on which model is used. However, it turns out that with an appropriately calibrated testing threshold, model switching effectively adds a *third* time scale, which is even slower than the rate of coefficient updating. This allows the path of each model's coefficients to be approximated with a separate ODE.[9]

5.3.3 *Self-confirming equilibria*

Suppose that $\alpha < 1$. When model $\mathcal{M}_1$ is used exclusively it has a stable self-confirming equilibrium, defined by the condition $h_1(\gamma_1^*) = 0$,[10]

[9] See Yin and Zhang (2005) for more details.
[10] Stable in the sense of E-stability, see Evans and Honkapohja (2001).

$$p_n = \frac{1}{1-\alpha}(\beta_1 + \Omega_{11}^{-1}\Omega_{12}\beta_2)w_{1,n-1} + \varepsilon_n, \tag{5.6}$$

while model $\mathcal{M}_2$ has its own stable self-confirming equilibrium

$$p_n = \frac{1}{1-\alpha}(\beta_2 + \Omega_{22}^{-1}\Omega_{12}\beta_1)w_{2,n-1} + \varepsilon_n, \tag{5.7}$$

where Ω_{ij} are the elements of the second moment matrix, $\Omega = E(ww')$. Because the self-confirming equilibria (5.6) and (5.7) are obtained by restricting the agent's beliefs to a misspecified model, Evans and Honkapohja (2001) refer to them as restricted perception equilibria. We take this idea a step further. In a sense we conduct a meta-stability analysis, and ask which of several stable RPE is likely to dominate in the long run when agents are allowed to test the specification of their models.

5.3.4 *Fluctuations/diffusion approximations*

With a constant gain, coefficient estimates do not converge to fixed numbers; they converge to a stationary distribution. A model's self-confirming equilibrium is the mean of this stationary distribution, and the above mean ODEs represent the mean path while the estimates are away from their SCE values. We can approximate the variance of the estimates around their means by constructing diffusion approximations of (5.4) and (5.5). These approximations can be interpreted as function space analogs of the central limit theorem. To do this, define the scaled processes, $\tilde{\gamma}_1(t) = (\hat{\gamma}_{1,n} - \gamma_1(t))/\sqrt{\eta}$ and $\tilde{\gamma}_2(t) = (\hat{\gamma}_{2,n} - \gamma_2(t))/\sqrt{\eta}$. A standard weak convergence argument then yields (again, see Evans and Honkapohja (2001) for details)

$$d\tilde{\gamma}_1 = (\alpha - 1)\tilde{\gamma}_1 dt + \sqrt{v_1(\gamma_1^*)}dW_1, \tag{5.8}$$

where the innovation variance, $v_1(\gamma_1^*)$ is defined at the model's SCE, and is given by

$$v_1(\gamma_1^*) = \frac{\sigma^2 + \beta_2^2\sigma_2^2(1-\rho^2)}{\sigma_1^2}, \tag{5.9}$$

where $\sigma^2 = \text{var}(\varepsilon)$, $\sigma_1^2 = \text{var}(w_1)$, $\sigma_2^2 = \text{var}(w_2)$, and $\rho = \text{corr}(w_1, w_2)$. An analagous expression applies to $\mathcal{M}_2$. Typically, $v_1(\gamma_1^*)$ will depend on third and fourth moments, as it represents the innovation variance of a least-squares orthogonality condition. However, when shocks are Gaussian, matters simplify significantly, as exhibited in (5.9).

Equation (5.8) is a standard Ornstein–Uhlenbeck process. Its variance is given by $\mathrm{var}(\tilde{\gamma}_1) = v_1(\gamma_1^*)/2(1-\alpha)$. Hence, a model's fluctuations around its mean dynamics will be larger when: (1) feedback, α, is stronger, (2) exogenous noise, σ^2, is larger, and (3) important variables are excluded from the model (e.g., in the case of $\mathcal{M}_1$, when $\beta_2^2\sigma_2^2$ is large). Conversely, fluctuations will be small when the *included* variables have high variance. High variance in a model's explanatory variables produces precise parameter estimates.

5.3.5 *Specification testing*

There is no single best way for validating a model. The right approach depends on what the model is being used for, and the nature of the relevant alternatives. In this chapter we apply a Lagrange multiplier (LM) approach. LM tests can be interpreted as likelihood ratio tests against local alternatives, or as first-order approximations of the Kullback–Leibler information criterion (KLIC). Their defining feature is that they are based solely on estimation of the null model, and do not require specification of an explicit alternative. As a result, they are often referred to as *mis*specification tests. Benveniste et al. (1990) (BMP) outline a recursive validation procedure based on LM testing principles. Their method is based on the observation that the innovation in a typical stochastic approximation algorithm is proportional to the score vector. Essentially then, what is being tested is the significance of the algorithm's update term.

Our approach is similar to that of BMP, except our null and alternative hypotheses are slightly different. BMP fix a model's coefficients and adopt the null hypothesis that the score vector is zero when evaluated at these fixed values. A rejection indicates that the coefficients (or something else) must have changed. In our setting, with multiple models and endogenous data, it is not always reasonable to interpret nonzero score vectors as model rejections. It takes time for a new model to converge to its own self-confirming equilibrium. While this convergence is underway, a model's score vector will be nonzero, as it reflects the presence of nonzero mean dynamics. We want to allow for this drift in our null hypothesis. One possible way to do this would be to incorporate a 'burn in' period after model switching, during which no testing takes place. The idea would be to give new models a chance to adapt to their own data. Another possibility would be to only update models while they are in use. Neither of these approaches seem to be widely applied in practice. Instead, we incorporate drift into the null by simply using a larger threshold than otherwise. This implicitly assumes the mean dynamics are not 'too fast' (relative to the model's escape dynamics). Given this, our alternative hypothesis is that the current model, even when making allowance for modest coefficient adjustments, has in some way become invalidated by the data, and therefore, the response is to find a new model.

To be more explicit, let $\Lambda_{i,n}$ denote the sequence of model i's (scaled) scores, given by

$$\Lambda_{i,n} = R_{i,n-1}^{-1} w_{i,n-1}(p_n - \hat{\gamma}_{i,n-1} w_{i,n-1}).$$

The null hypothesis is then, $H_0 : \Lambda_{i,n} \leq \tau$, where the threshold, τ, is sufficiently large to allow for mean dynamics-driven parameter drift. Keep in mind this is a *sequential* test, much like the well-known CUSUM test of Brown et al. (1975), or the 'monitoring stuctural change' approach of Chu et al. (1996). Hence, another reason to allow for a positive threshold is to control for the obvious size distortions induced by repeated testing.[11]

5.3.6 *Model selection*

When the LM test is rejected a new model is randomly selected. Our main conclusions are robust to the details of this selection process. (See Cho and Kasa 2010.) The only essential feature is that the support of the distribution remain full, i.e., all models must remain on the table. This ensures a form of ergodicity that is crucial for our results. For our example here, we follow tradition by assuming that selection probabilities are given by a logit function, with weights determined by each model's estimated mean-squared error (using the same constant gain estimation procedure as is used to estimate coefficients). Letting $\omega_{i,n}$ denote the period n estimate of model i's mean-squared error, we then have

$$\pi_{1,n} = \frac{e^{\phi\omega_{2,n}}}{e^{\phi\omega_{1,n}} + e^{\phi\omega_{2,n}}},$$

where ϕ is a 'choice intensity' parameter which captures the degree of experimentation. As ϕ increases, the agent is less prone to experiment.

[11] As stressed by both Brown et al. (1975) and Chu et al. (1996), an *optimal* threshold would distribute type I error probabilities evenly over time, and would result in an increasing threshold. In fact, with an infinite sample, the size is always one for any fixed threshold. The fact that our agent discounts old data effectively delivers a constant sample size, and diminishes the gains from an increasing threshold.

5.3.7 *Large deviations*

In the neighbourhood of a model's self-confirming equilibrium, the diffusion approximation in (5.8) suggests that typical fluctuations in a model's LM test statistic are determined by (5.9), i.e., the innovation variance of the coefficient update process. We calibrate the test threshold so that model rejections triggered by isolated shock realizations are extremely unlikely, both in the neighbourhood of a self-confirming equilibrium, and while a model is converging towards its self-confirming equilibrium. In this model, it is easy to place an upper bound on the influence of the mean dynamics.[12] For the parameterizations we consider, the maximum contribution of the mean dynamics to the test statistic is less than half the influence coming from the innovations. To be more specific, we suppose the test threshold for model i is $\tau_i = z \cdot \sqrt{v_i(\gamma_i^*)}$, and set $z = 4.5$. Thus, in the neighbourhood of a SCE the probability of a single large shock triggering a model rejection is extremely small, on the order of 10^{-6}.

One should keep in mind, however, that the diffusion approximations that lie behind these calculations are based on a weak convergence argument, which only captures the *average* behaviour of the process.[13] With a constant gain, coefficient estimates occasionally experience 'large deviations' from the mean dynamics. The deviations are large in the sense that their order of magnitude exceeds the $\sqrt{\eta}$ central limit scaling. A diffusion approximation predicts such large excursions are zero probability events. Although they are not zero probability events, they *are* rare. In fact, they are so rare we can actually calculate precisely how they will occur. We can also calculate their frequency, at least up to a logarithmic time scale. In what follows we shall briefly outline how to do this for our cobweb example. The model has been rigged so that calculations can be done with pencil and paper, which itself is a rare event in applications of large deviations. For a more rigorous exposition one should consult Dupuis and Kushner (1989) or Cho et al. (2002). Without loss of generality, we just focus on escapes from $\mathcal{M}_1$.

Large deviations calculations have three components: (1) An H-functional, (2) the Legendre transformation of the H-functional, and

[12] The contribution of the mean dynamics is proportional to the deviation from the SCE, with proportionality constant $1 - \alpha$. Also, we know that when a model is used its SCE coefficient value is given by (5.6)–(5.7), whereas when a model is *not* being used its SCE value becomes (in the case of $\mathcal{M}_1$) $\gamma_1 = \beta_1 + \beta_2(1 + \alpha)\Omega_{11}^{-1}\Omega_{12}$. Differencing the two implies that the maximum effect is of order $\alpha[\beta_1 - \alpha\beta_2\rho(\sigma_2/\sigma_1)]$ (with analogous expressions for $\mathcal{M}_2$).

[13] Although we ask the reader to keep this is mind, remember that we assume the agent within the model does not. He interprets large deviations as indicative of model failure.

(3) an action functional used to determine the large deviations rate function. The H-functional is the log moment generating function of the martingale difference component of the least-squares orthogonality condition. Let $\omega_{1,n}$ be the period n martingale difference component of the model 1's orthogonality condition, scaled by the slow process $R_{1,n}^{-1}$. From (5.4) and (5.1) we have

$$\omega_{1,n} = (R_{1,n}^{-1} w_{1,n}^2 - 1)[(\alpha - 1)\gamma_1 + \beta_1] + \beta_2 (R^{-1} w_{1,n} w_{2,n} - \Omega_{11}^{-1}\Omega_{12})^2 + R_{1,n}^{-1} w_{1,n}\varepsilon_n.$$

Note that $E_n(\omega_{1,n}) = 0$. Employing the usual 'complete-the-squares' trick, a brute force calculation yields the following expression for the H-functional,[14]

$$H(\gamma_1, a) \equiv \log E\left(e^{a\omega_1}\right) = -\frac{1}{2}\log(1 - 2\sigma_1^2\Phi), \tag{5.10}$$

where

$$\Phi = a\sigma_1^{-2}[(\alpha - 1)\gamma_1 + \beta_1] + .5a^2(\sigma/\sigma_1)^2 + \frac{1}{2(1-\rho^2)\sigma_2^2}\left[A^2 - \rho^2(\sigma_2^2/\sigma_1^2)\right]$$

$$A = \rho(\sigma_2/\sigma_1) + a\beta_2(1 - \rho^2)\sigma_2^2\sigma_1^2.$$

The Legendre transform of $H(\gamma_1, a)$ is defined as

$$L(\gamma_1, \lambda) = \sup_a[\lambda a - H(\gamma_1, a)]. \tag{5.11}$$

In static, *i.i.d.*, environments this is the end of the story. The probability of witnessing a large deviation of λ from the mean would be of order $\exp[-nL(\lambda)]$. However, in dynamic settings things are more complicated. The relevant sample space is now a function space, and large deviations consist of sample *paths*. Calculating the probability of a large deviation involves solving a dynamic optimization problem. The Legendre transformation $L(\gamma_1, \lambda)$ now plays the role of a flow cost function, summarizing the instantaneous probabilistic cost of any given path away from the self-confirming equilibrium. For a given boundary, the value function of this control problem captures the probability of escaping from the self-confirming equilibrium to any given point on the boundary. If only the radius of the boundary is specified, as in our specification testing problem, then one must also minimize over the

[14] Since you can't take the log of a negative number, this implies an existence condition that we shall return to once we've completed our calculations.

boundary. Fortunately, in univariate models, this dynamic optimization problem almost becomes degenerate. After all, in one dimension you only have two choices of direction! The control problem can be written as

$$S(\gamma_{1,0}) = \inf_{T>0} \inf_{\dot{\gamma}_1} \int_0^T L(\gamma_1, \dot{\gamma}_1) dt,$$

subject to the boundary conditions $\gamma_1(0) = \gamma_{1,0}$ and $\gamma_1(T) \in \partial G$, where ∂G denotes the escape boundary. For us, ∂G is just $|\tau|$. Since the action functional is stationary and T is free, the solution is characterized by the Hamilton–Jacobi–Bellman (HJB) equation

$$\inf_{\dot{\gamma}_1} \{L(\gamma_1, \dot{\gamma}_1) + S_{\gamma_1} \dot{\gamma}_1\} = 0,$$

where S_{γ_1} denotes the derivative of S with respect to γ_1. This can equivalently be written

$$\sup_{\dot{\gamma}_1} \{-S_{\gamma_1} \dot{\gamma}_1 - L(\gamma_1, \dot{\gamma}_1)\} = 0. \tag{5.12}$$

We now make an important observation. The Legendre transform in (5.11) defines a convex duality relationship between $H(\gamma_1, a)$ and $L(\gamma_1, \lambda)$. This means the HJB equation in (5.12) can be written compactly as

$$H(\gamma_1, -S_{\gamma_1}) = 0. \tag{5.13}$$

Finally, using the definition of the H-functional in (5.10) delivers the following condition characterizing the large deviations rate function,

$$\frac{1}{\sigma_1^2} \left[\sigma^2 + \beta_2^2 \sigma_2^2 (1 - \rho^2)\right] S_{\gamma_1}^2 = 2(1 - \alpha)(\gamma_1 - \gamma_1^*) S_{\gamma_1},$$

where we have used the fact that $\gamma_1^* = \beta_1 + \beta_2 \rho (\sigma_2 / \sigma_1)$. Since $S(\gamma_1^*) = 0$, a simple integration produces the solution for the rate function,[15]

$$S(\gamma_1) = \left[\frac{(1 - \alpha)\sigma_1^2}{\sigma^2 + \beta_2^2 \sigma_2^2 (1 - \rho^2)}\right] (\gamma_1 - \gamma_1^*)^2. \tag{5.14}$$

This is the key result of the analysis. If the test threshold is calibrated so that escapes trigger rejections, we have $\tau = |\gamma_1 - \gamma_1^*|$, and we obtain

[15] We can now address the existence condition noted in fn 14. Using the fact that $a = S_\gamma$, the existence condition $2\sigma_1^2 \Phi < 1$ implies the parameter restriction, $\tilde{\tau}^2 + (1 - \alpha)\tilde{\tau} < [\sigma^2 + \beta_2^2 \sigma_2^2 (1 - \rho^2)]/(4(1 - \alpha)\sigma_1^2)$, where $\tilde{\tau} = \tau / \eta$.

the following expression for model 1's mean survival time, $E(\Delta_\tau^1)$, as a function of the test threshold, τ,

$$\lim_{\eta \to 0} \{\eta \log E(\Delta_\tau^1)\} = \left[\frac{(1-\alpha)\sigma_1^2}{\sigma^2 + \beta_2^2 \sigma_2^2 (1-\rho^2)} \right] \tau^2 = S_\tau^1 .$$

Hence, the mean survival time of each model i is *exponential*,[16] i.e., $E(\Delta_\tau^i) \approx \exp[S_\tau^i/\eta]$. This implies that as $\eta \to 0$ the support of the model distribution collapses to a *single* model. We call this the 'dominant' model. In Cho and Kasa (2010) we extend this result to more general environments. We prove that dominant models have the largest large deviations rate function within the model class. We also exploit the connections between rate functions, relative entropy, and the Kullback–Leibler information criterion to relate our results to the classic results of White (1982) on the consequences of estimating misspecified models. At this point, however, it is useful to illustrate our results at work using a simple simulation.

5.3.8 *Simulation*

Figure 5.1 shows what happens when our model validation procedure is applied to the cobweb model. The parameters have been rigged to favour model 1, in the sense that the variance of w_1 is greater than the variance of w_2, so that model 2 omits the more important variable.[17] The top panel plots model use, the second panel plots the probability of selecting model 1 following a test rejection, and the bottom two panels plot the paths of the coefficient estimates.

There are several things to notice here. First, and most obviously, model 1 is used most of the time. Although we could make model 1 appear to be more dominant by increasing σ_1^2 or β_1 relative to σ_2^2 or β_2, it should be noted that in the limit, as $\eta \to 0$, even small differences imply that the proportion of time that model 1 is used converges to unity. Although the determinants of model dominance are rather obvious in this simple example, our results make predictions about model dominance when these determinants are not so obvious, e.g., when they depend on higher order moments of shock distributions. Second, the plot of the model selection probability reveals the self-

[16] The distribution of survival times is not symmetric, however. It has a long right tail, so that the median survival time is less than this.

[17] Some more details: (1) w_1 and w_2 are assumed independent ($\rho = 0$) with $\sigma_{w1}^2 = 0.45$ and $\sigma_{w2}^2 = 0.35$; (2) $\sigma_\varepsilon^2 = 0.25$; (3) $\beta_1 = \beta_2 = 1.0$; (4) $\alpha = 0.5$; (5) the update gain is set to $\eta = 0.01$; (6) the test threshold is set to $z = 4.5$; and (7) the 'choice intensity' parameter of the logit function is set to 2.0.

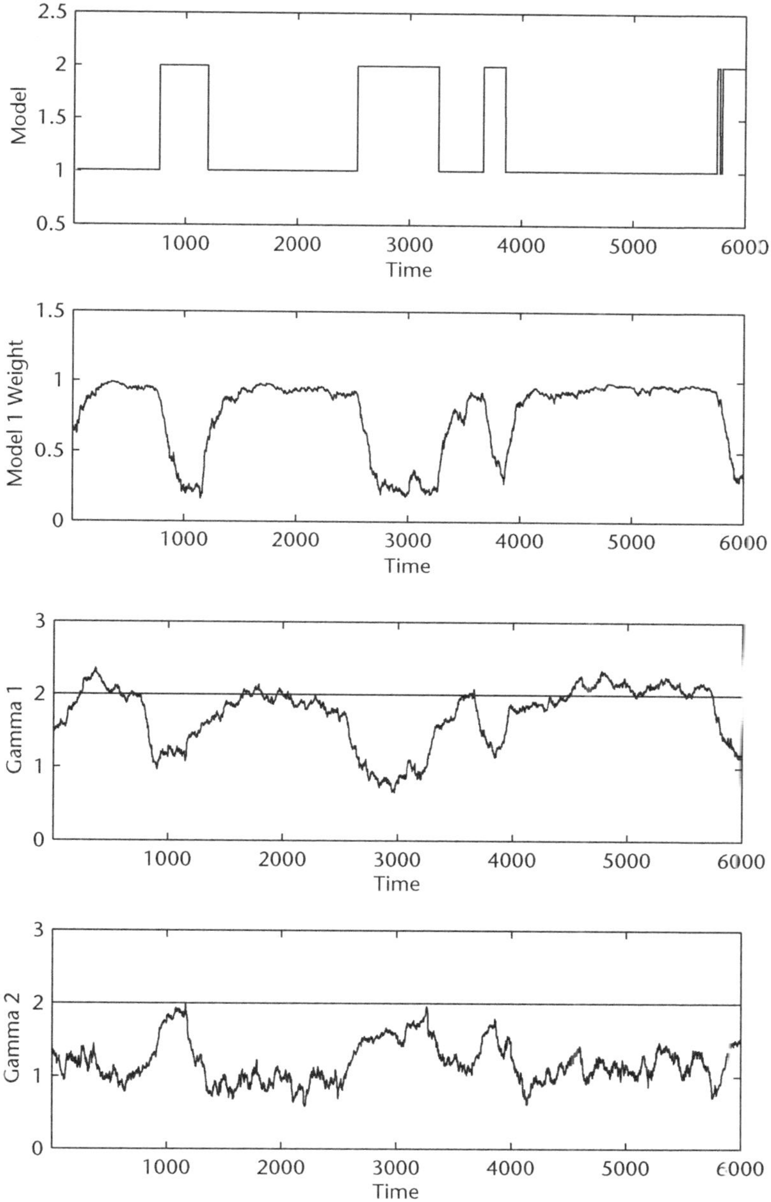

Figure 5.1 Model validation in a misspecified cobweb model.

referential aspect of the environment. Note that when a model is used, its relative performance improves. With our logit selection rule, this makes it more likely that a recently rejected model will be selected, which increases model persistence. However, as noted earlier, none of our results about model dominance depend on this particular selection protocol. Third, the bottom two plots clearly reveal that each model's coefficient estimate fluctuates between two values, the self-confirming value when it is used and the self-confirming value when the *other* model is used. Given our parameterization, the first value turns out to be 2 for both models, and the second turns out to be 1 for both models. Although it is not obvious from the plot, it is also important to note that the escape from a model's own self-confirming equilibrium occurs faster than its convergence back to it following a period of disuse. The relatively rapid pace of the escape reflects the fact that it must work against the stablizing force of the mean dynamics. Its relatively rapid rate is also what leads the agent to conclude that the model has been invalidated.

5.4 Concluding Remarks

This chapter has argued that economists should begin to incorporate model uncertainty into the adaptive learning literature. We have outlined a strategy for doing this, and have applied it to the well-known cobweb model. A virtue of our approach is that it requires only modest extensions of existing methods. We refer to our approach as *model validation*. It rests on two key ideas: (1) the interpretation of a model's parameter update term as a Lagrange multiplier specification test statistic, and (2) the deliberate injection of randomness into the model selection process following test rejections. This is designed to prevent agents from getting trapped in 'undesirable' self-confirming equilibria. Another advantage of our approach is that it is amenable to the application of large deviations methods, which enables us to provide explicit predictions about which models will survive repeated specification tests. We have purposely avoided technicalites here. Our intention has been to merely provide a taste of our results. For more details the reader should consult Cho and Kasa (2010).

References

Benveniste, A., M. Metivier, and P. Priouret (1990). *Adaptive Algorithms and Stochastic Approximations*. Berlin: Springer-Verlag.

Branch, W. A., and G. W. Evans (2007). 'Model Uncertainty and Endogenous Volatility', *Review of Economic Dynamics*, 10, 207–37.

Bray, M. M. (1982). 'Learning, Estimation and the Stability of Rational Expectations', *Journal of Economic Theory*, 26, 318–39.

—— and N. Savin (1986). 'Rational Expectatons Equilibria, Learning, and Model Specification', *Econometrica*, 54, 1129–60.

Brown, R., J. Durbin, and J. Evans (1975). 'Techniques for Testing the Constancy of Regression Relationships over Time', *Journal of the Royal Statistical Society, Series B*, 37, 149–72.

Bullard, J. (1992). 'Time-Varying Parameters and Nonconvergence to Rational Expectations under Least-Squares Learning', *Economics Letters*, 40, 159–66.

—— and K. Mitra (2002). 'Learning about Monetary Policy Rules', *Journal of Monetary Economics*, 49, 1105–29.

Burnham, K., and D. Anderson (2002). *Model Selection and Multimodel Inference: A Practical Information-Theoretic Approach*, 2nd edn. Berlin: Springer.

Cho, I.-K., and K. Kasa (2009). 'Recursive Model Selection with Endogenous Data', University of Illinois, working paper, <http://www.economics.illinois.edu/people/inkocho>.

—— and —— (2010). 'Learning and Model Validation', University of Illinois, working paper, <http://www.economics.illinois.edu/people/inkocho>.

——, N. Williams, and T. J. Sargent (2002). 'Escaping Nash Inflation', *Review of Economic Studies*, 69, 1–40.

Chu, J., M. Stinchcombe, and H. White (1996). 'Monitoring Structural Change', *Econometrica*, 64, 1045–65.

Dupuis, P., and H. J. Kushner (1989). 'Stochastic Approximation and Large Deviations: Upper Bounds and w.p.1 Convergence', *SIAM Journal of Control and Optimization*, 27, 1108–35.

Evans, G. W., and S. Honkapohja (2001). *Learning and Expectations in Macroeconomics*. Princeton, NJ: Princeton University Press.

—— and —— (2003). 'Expectations and the Stability Problem for Optimal Monetary Policy', *Review of Economic Studies*, 70, 807–24.

Foster, D. P., and H. P. Young (2003). 'Learning, Hypothesis Testing and Nash Equilibrium', *Games and Economic Behavior*, 45, 73–96.

Jovanovic, B. (2009). 'Learning and Discovery', New York University, unpublished paper, 11 May 2011, <http://www.boyanjovanovic.com/research.html>.

Kandori, M., G. Mailath, and R. Rob (1993). 'Learning, Mutation and Long Run Equilibria in Games', *Econometrica*, 61, 27–56.

Kostyshyna, O. (2012). 'Application of an Adaptive Step-Size Algorithm in Models of Hyperinflation', *Macroeconomic Dynamics*, available on CJO2012, doi:10.1017/S136510051000088X.

McGough, B. (2003). 'Statistical Learning with Time-Varying Parameters', *Macroeconomic Dynamics*, 7, 119–39.

Sargent, T. J. (1993). *Bounded Rationality in Macroeconomics*. Oxford: Clarendon Press.

—— (1999). *The Conquest of American Inflation*. Princeton, NJ: Princeton University Press.

Sargent, T. J., and N. Williams (2005). 'Impacts of Priors on Convergence and Escapes from Nash Inflation', *Review of Economic Dynamics*, 8, 360–91.

Sin, C.-Y., and H. White (1996). 'Information Criteria for Selecting Possibly Misspecified Parametric Models', *Journal of Econometrics*, 71, 207–25.

Vuong, Q. H. (1989). 'Likelihood Ratio Tests for Model Selection and Non-Nested Hypotheses', *Econometica*, 57(2), 307–33.

White, H. (1982). 'Maximum Likelihood Estimation of Misspecified Models', *Econometrica*, 50, 1–25.

——(1994). *Estimation, Inference and Specification Analysis*. Cambridge: Cambridge University Press.

Yin, G. G., and Q. Zhang (2005). *Discrete-Time Markov Chains: Two-Time-Scale Methods and Applications*. Berlin: Springer.

6

Bayesian Model Averaging, Learning, and Model Selection*

George W. Evans, Seppo Honkapohja, Thomas J. Sargent, and Noah Williams

6.1 Introduction

During the past two decades there has been a significant amount of macroeconomic research studying the implications of adaptive learning in the formation of expectations. This approach replaces rational expectations with the assumption that economic agents employ a statistical forecasting model to form expectations and update the parameters of their forecasting model as new information becomes available over time. One goal of this literature is to find the conditions under which the economy with this kind of learning converges to a rational expectations equilibrium (REE).

The basic learning setting presumes that the agents' perceptions take the form of a forecasting model with fixed unknown parameters, estimates of which they update over time.[1] Such a setting does not explicitly allow for parameter uncertainty or the use of averaging across multiple forecasting models.[2] In this chapter, we postulate that economic agents use Bayesian estimation and Bayesian model averaging to form their expectations about relevant variables.

* Any views expressed are those of the authors and do not necessarily reflect the views of the Bank of Finland.

[1] See Evans and Honkapohja (2001) for the earlier literature; for recent critical overviews see Sargent (2008) and Evans and Honkapohja (2009).

[2] A few papers have incorporated model averaging in a macroeconomic learning setting. For examples, see Cogley and Sargent (2005) and Slobodyan and Wouters (2008).

We investigate this issue both to study the robustness of some existing convergence results in the learning literature and to provide some further justification for recursive updating scheme models. It is widely understood that if agents learn by updating what they believe to be a fixed parameter, in environments with feedback their beliefs are only correct asymptotically. That is, as agents change the coefficients in their perceived laws of motion, their actions influence economic outcomes in ways that make the law of motion actually generating the data change over time. After beliefs have ultimately converged to an REE, agents' beliefs are correctly specified, but along the transition path to the REE the data-generating process has drifting coefficients. It seems natural to suppose that agents would allow the coefficients of their forecasting models to drift over time. Heuristically, that reasoning motivated the body of papers on 'constant gain' learning in which agents attempt to track drifting coefficients and learning is perpetual.[3] In this chapter, we suppose that agents subjectively entertain *two* possibilities—one that says that the data-generating process is constant, and another that says that it drifts over time. Our agents update the probabilities that they place on these two possibilities. We study the long-run behaviour of this process of jointly updating models and probabilities over models.

More precisely, we study a setting in which the pair of models used by agents includes a 'grain of truth' in the sense that the functional form of one of the models is consistent with the REE of the economy while the other model is misspecified relative to the REE.[4] In particular, as above we assume that agents also employ a time-varying parameter (TVP) model as a second available forecasting model. The analysis is carried out using a standard general setup, discussed, e.g., in Chapter 2 of Evans and Honkapohja (2001). It is known that for this model there is convergence of usual least-squares (LS) learning to a unique REE unless the expectations feedback is positive and more than one-to-one.

We thus consider a setup with Bayesian model averaging over a constant parameter model that nests the REE and a TVP model. The parameters of the models and the probability weight over models are updated in Bayesian fashion as new data become available. Does learning converge to REE?

[3] See Cho et al. (2002), Sargent and Williams (2005), and Evans et al. (2010), for examples.

[4] We note that there is also a game-theory literature on convergence of Bayesian learning and the issue of the 'grain of truth'; see Young (2004) for an overview. Here we have a setup in which the prior of agents includes a grain of truth on the REE.

- Convergence occurs for a range of structural parameters in which the influence of expectations on the current outcome is not too strong and positive.
- The set of structural parameters for which convergence occurs is less than the one-to-one feedback that is crucial for LS learning *without* model averaging.
- A striking result is that there can be convergence to the (non-REE) TVP forecasting model even though the prior puts an atom on the RE forecasting model. This happens when the expectations feedback parameter is positive and sufficiently strong but less than one-to-one.
- Learning via Bayesian model averaging usually leads to model selection. The proportion of cases of no selection in the long run is small.

One version of our general setup applies to the Muth market (or 'cobweb') model in which expectations feedback is negative. For the Muth model, learning by Bayesian model averaging converges to the REE. Our setup also covers a version of the Lucas 'island' model in which the feedback of expectations on current outcomes is positive. For that setting, the strength of the response of output to expected inflation determines the convergence outcome. If the feedback is sufficiently strong, learning by Bayesian model averaging may converge to a situation in which agents perpetually use the TVP forecasting model.

6.2 Muth model with Bayesian learning

We consider the Muth market model

$$p_t = \mu + \alpha E^*_{t-1} p_t + \delta z_{t-1} + \eta_t, \tag{6.1}$$

where p_t is the market price, $E^*_{t-1} p_t$ denotes expectations of p_t conditioned on information at date $t-1$, z_{t-1} is an exogenous observable variable following a stationary AR(1) process $z_t = \rho z_{t-1} + w_t$ with $w_t \sim \text{iid}(0, \sigma_w^2)$ and η_t is an unobserved white noise shock with $E\eta_t^2 = \bar{\sigma}_\eta^2$. We normalize $\mu = 0$. We denote the subjective expectations E^*_t to highlight that they are not necessarily the rational (mathematical) expectation.

We remark that the Muth model (6.1) can be obtained from aggregating firm supply curves that depend on $E^*_{t-1} p_t$ and a market demand curve depending on p_t, with each also depending on aggregate shocks.

The firm supply curves in turn are derived from maximization of expected profits and quadratic costs. If the demand and supply curves are, respectively, downward- and upward-sloping, the Muth market model has the parameter restriction $\alpha < 0$, so that there is a negative feedback from expectations to outcomes. More generally, as noted by Bray and Savin (1986), $\alpha < 1$, provided the demand curve crosses the supply curve from above.

The setting (6.1) also arises for a version of the Lucas aggregate supply model, in which supply depends on price surprises and aggregate demand is given by a quantity-theory type of equation. For the Lucas-type macro model the parameter restriction is $0 < \alpha < 1$, so that there is positive feedback from expectations to outcomes. See Evans and Honkapohja (2001), Chapter 2, Sections 2.2 and 2.3 for more details on the Muth and Lucas models.

The REE for model (6.1) is

$$p_t = \bar{\beta} z_{t-1} + \eta_t, \text{ where } \bar{\beta} = (1-\alpha)^{-1}\delta.$$

We begin with the case in which agents have a constant parameter forecasting model, which they estimate using Bayesian techniques. The beliefs of the agents are

$$p_t = \beta z_{t-1} + \eta_t,$$

where $\eta_t \perp z_{t-1}$ and $\eta_t \sim N(0, \sigma_\eta^2)$. The forecasting model of the agents at the end of period $t-1$, also called the perceived law of motion (PLM), is

$$p_t = b_{t-1} z_{t-1} + \eta_t,$$

where b_{t-1} is the time $t-1$ estimate of β. Note that in general we allow $\sigma_\eta^2 \neq \bar{\sigma}_\eta^2$. There is a prior distribution $\beta \sim N(b_0, V_0)$, which implies a posterior distribution of $f(\beta \mid y^{t-1})$, where $y^t = (y_t, y_{t-1}, y_{t-2}, \ldots)$ and $y_t' = (p_t, z_t)$, of the form $N(b_t, V_t)$. Here the updating of parameters b_t, V_t is given by

$$b_t = b_{t-1} + \frac{V_{t-1} z_{t-1}}{\sigma_\eta^2 + V_{t-1} z_{t-1}^2}(p_t - b_{t-1} z_{t-1})$$

$$V_t = V_{t-1} - \frac{z_{t-1}^2 V_{t-1}^2}{\sigma_\eta^2 + V_{t-1} z_{t-1}^2},$$

using the Kalman filter.

The dynamics of the system can be formulated as a stochastic recursive algorithm (SRA) as indicated in the Appendix, where it is shown that we have the following result:

Proposition 6.1 *There is convergence to the REE with probability* 1 *if* $\alpha < 1$. *Moreover, we get*

$$V_t = \frac{\sigma_\eta^2}{(t+1)S_t - z_t^2} \to 0$$

with probability 1 *for all* σ_η^2, *irrespective of whether* σ_η^2 *is correct.*[5]

Bayesian learning was already considered in a somewhat different formulation by Bray and Savin (1986), who assumed that agents have heterogeneous expectations and there is a continuum of initial priors $b_0(i), i \in [0, 1]$ with the same initial precision. Our setting could handle a finite number of classes of agents with different priors.

6.3 Bayesian learning with subjective model averaging

6.3.1 *Priors on parameter variation*

In the preceding section it was assumed that agents' beliefs treat the parameter β as an unknown constant that does not vary over time. An alternative setup would be to allow time variation in β. Papers by Bullard (1992), McGough (2003), Sargent and Williams (2005), and Evans et al. (2010) look at this issue in models with learning. Cogley and Sargent (2005) look at empirical time-varying parameter models without learning. In our self-referential setup with learning, we adopt a formulation where agents entertain multiple forecasting models and form the final forecast as a weighted average of the forecasts from the different models.

Although other extensions may be useful, we consider a simple example of multiple forecasting models below. We assume that agents have a prior that puts a weight $\pi_0 > 0$ on β constant over time and $1 - \pi_0 > 0$ on the TVP model $\beta_t = \beta_{t-1} + v_t$, where $v_t \overset{\text{iid}}{\sim} N(0, \sigma_v^2)$. In general, σ_v^2 could be unknown, but we assume that it is known. The next steps are (i) the computation of the model-weighted forecast and (ii) the updating of the parameters in the forecasting models and of the models weights as new information becomes available.

[5] In particular, we get convergence to the REE whether or not the actual η_t is normal.

We now develop these ideas in a simple setting using model (6.1) and the assumption that agents employ two different forecasting models.

6.3.2 *Model averaging*

Thus there are just two forecasting models in use: a constant coefficient model, and a TVP model with $\beta_t = \beta_{t-1} + v_t$, where $v_t \overset{\text{iid}}{\sim} N(0, \sigma_v^2)$ and $\sigma_v^2 > 0$ is known.[6] More specifically, and changing notation somewhat, the PLMs of the agents are

$$p_t = \beta_t(i) z_{t-1} + \sigma_p(i)\varepsilon_{pt}, \text{ for } i = 0, 1$$
$$\beta_t(i) = \beta_{t-1}(i) + \sigma_\beta(i)\varepsilon_{\beta t}, \text{ for } i = 0, 1,$$

where z_t is an exogenous observable. Here the first equation is the PLM for p_t of subjective model i. Various assumptions about $\sigma_p(i)$ are possible. They can be assumed known or unknown and equal or allowed to be different for $i = 0, 1$. The second equation specifies the perceived parameter drift in each subjective model. We will assume $0 \leq \sigma_{\beta(0)} < \sigma_{\beta(1)}$ are known. A third equation, specified below, gives the subjective probability weight for subjective model 1, with a prior placing (say) an equal weight on the two models. The ε_{jt}, $j = p, \beta$ are *i.i.d.* standard normal and mutually independent. Agents have normal priors on the $\beta_0(i)$ and a given prior probability π_0 that model 0 is correct. We will usually take $\pi_0 = 0.5$.

Expectations of agents are given by subjective model averaging, i.e.,

$$E_{t-1}^* p_t = \left(\pi_{t-1}(0)\hat{\beta}_{t|t-1}(0) + \pi_{t-1}(1)\hat{\beta}_{t|t-1}(1)\right) z_{t-1},$$

where $\hat{\beta}_{t|t-1}(0)$ and $\hat{\beta}_{t|t-1}(1)$ are the means of the posterior distribution for $\beta_t(0)$ and $\beta_t(1)$ and where $\pi_{t-1}(i)$ is the posterior probability that model i is correct, i.e.,

$$\pi_{t-1}(i) = \Pr(i|p^{t-1}, z^{t-1}]),$$

for $i = 0, 1$. The actual evolution of price p_t is given by

$$p_t = \alpha E_{t-1}^* p_t + \delta z_{t-1} + \sigma_a \varepsilon_{at},$$

[6] We adopt this formulation for simplicity. Clearly a useful extension will be to have finitely many subjective models.

where the exogenous observables z_{t-1} are a stationary AR(1) process, i.e.,

$$z_t = \rho z_{t-1} + \sigma_z \varepsilon_{zt}.$$

For simplicity, we have set all the intercepts to be zero. Otherwise, subjective intercepts for each model would also need to be estimated and agents would plausibly also allow for parameter drift for intercepts. As noted above, in the Muth market model we usually have $\alpha < 0$, but in 'Lucas-type' models $0 < \alpha < 1$.

We are especially interested in how the weight $\pi_t(1)$ of the TVP model evolves. Suppose that $\sigma_\beta(0) = 0$ and $\sigma_\beta(1) > 0$. Will we have $\pi_t(1) \to 0$ and $\hat{\beta}_t \to \bar{\beta} = \delta(1-\alpha)^{-1}$ as $t \to \infty$, with probability 1, so that there is convergence to REE? We suspect that this will depend on the magnitudes of both α and $\sigma_\beta(1)$. We venture an initial guess that the most 'stable' cases are possibly in the range $-1 < \alpha < 0.5$. The basis for this guess is that in the standard LS learning setting parameter values in the range $0.5 < a < 1$ may yield slow convergence to REE and in the case $\alpha < -1$ a possible problem of overshooting can emerge when agents overparameterize the PLM under LS learning. For $\alpha = 0$ the p_t process is exogenous and here we certainly expect $\pi_t(1) \to 0$ and $\hat{\beta}_t \to \delta$ with probability 1. We would therefore expect $\pi_t(1) \to 0$ and convergence to REE also for α near 0. However, there does seem to be the possibility with $\alpha \neq 0$ that $\pi_t(1)$ remains near 1 for long periods or even that $\pi_t(1) \to 1$. In what follows we examine these issues by means of numerical simulations.

We now give the recursive updating equations for $i = 0, 1$. The Kalman filter, see, e.g., Hamilton (1994), pp. 399 and 380, gives the updating equations for the mean $\hat{\beta}_{t+1|t}(i)$ of the (Gaussian) posterior distribution of $\beta_{t+1}(i)$ as

$$\hat{\beta}_{t+1|t}(i) = \hat{\beta}_{t|t-1}(i) + \frac{V_{t|t-1}(i)z_{t-1}}{\sigma_p^2(i) + V_{t|t-1}(i)z_{t-1}^2}(p_t - \hat{\beta}_{t|t-1}(i)z_{t-1})$$

$$V_{t+1|t}(i) = V_{t|t-1}(i) - \frac{z_{t-1}^2 V_{t|t-1}(i)^2}{\sigma_p^2(i) + V_{t|t-1}(i)z_{t-1}^2} + \sigma_\beta^2(i).$$

Here $\text{var}(\hat{\beta}_{t|t-1}(i) - \beta_t(i)) = V_{t|t-1}(i)$. We will also need the mean and variance of the conditional distribution for β_t conditional on information through t, which are given by $\hat{\beta}_{t|t}(i) = \hat{\beta}_{t+1|t}(i)$ and $V_{t|t}(i) = V_{t+1|t}(i) - \sigma_\beta^2(i)$.

6.3.3 *Updating formulae for model probabilities*

Finally, we need the updating formula for $\pi_t(i) = \Pr(i|p^t, z^t)$. We will make use of Cogley and Sargent (2005), Appendix A to get the recursion. Writing $\pi_t(i) = \Pr(i|p^t, z^t)$, we have

$$\pi_t(i) = \frac{f(p^t, z^t|i)\pi_0(i)}{f(p^t, z^t)} \propto m_{it}\pi_0(i),$$

where

$$\begin{aligned} m_{it} &= f(p^t, z^t|i) \\ &= \int L(p^t, z^t|\beta_0(i); i) f(\beta_0(i)) d\beta_0(i). \end{aligned}$$

Here $f(\beta_0(i))$ denotes the prior distribution for $\beta_0(i)$, $f(p^t, z^t|i)$ denotes the probability density for (p^t, z^t) conditional on the model, $L(p^t; z^t; \beta_0(i)|i)$ is the likelihood function for model i, and $\pi_0(i)$ is the prior probability for model $i = 0, 1$ (with $\pi_0(1) = \pi_0$ and $\pi_0(0) = 1 - \pi_0(1)$). Moreover, $f(p^t, z^t)$ is the marginal distribution of the sample across models. Thus, m_{it} is the marginalized likelihood for model i. Since $\sigma_{\beta(0)}$ and $\sigma_{\beta(1)}$ are assumed known, we have not made the dependence of the distributions on them explicit.

First note that

$$\begin{aligned} f(\beta_t(i)|p^t, z^t; i) \times m_{it} = L(p_t, z_t|p^{t-1}, z^{t-1}, \beta_t(i); i) \times f(\beta_t(i)|p^{t-1}, z^{t-1}; i) \\ \times f(p^{t-1}, z^{t-1}|i), \text{ or} \end{aligned}$$

$$\frac{m_{it}}{m_{i,t-1}} = \frac{L(p_t, z_t|p^{t-1}, z^{t-1}, \beta_t(i); i) \times f(\beta_t(i)|p^{t-1}, z^{t-1}; i)}{f(\beta_t(i)|p^t, z^t; i)} \equiv \tilde{A}_t(i).$$

Here $f(\beta_t(i)|p^{t-1}, z^{t-1}; i)$ denotes the normal density with mean $\hat{\beta}_{t|t-1}(i)$ and variance $V_{t|t-1}(i)$, i.e.,

$$f(\beta|p^{t-1}, z^{t-1}; i) = (2\pi V_{t|t-1}(i))^{-1/2} \exp\left\{-\frac{1}{2}\frac{(\beta - \hat{\beta}_{t|t-1}(i))^2}{V_{t|t-1}(i)}\right\}.$$

Similarly,

$$f(\beta|p^t, z^t; i) = (2\pi V_{t|t}(i))^{-1/2} \exp\left\{-\frac{1}{2}\frac{(\beta - \hat{\beta}_{t|t}(i))^2}{V_{t|t}(i)}\right\},$$

and

$$L(p_t, z_t|p^{t-1}, z^{t-1}, \beta; i) = f(p_t|z_{t-1}, \beta; i) \times f(z_t|z_{t-1}),$$

where

$$f(p_t|z_{t-1}, \beta; i) = (2\pi\sigma_p^2(i))^{-1/2} \exp\left\{-\frac{1}{2}\frac{(p_t - z_{t-1}\beta)^2}{\sigma_p^2(i)}\right\}, \text{ and}$$

$$f(z_t|z_{t-1}) = (2\pi\sigma_z^2)^{-1/2} \exp\left\{-\frac{1}{2}\frac{(z_t - z_{t-1}\rho)^2}{\sigma_z^2}\right\}.$$

It can be verified that $m_{it}/m_{i,t-1}$ does not depend on $\beta_t(i)$ even though each of the three terms in the expression does.[7] In fact,

$$\tilde{A}_t(i) = f(z_t|z_{t-1})A_t(i),$$

where

$$A_t(i) = \exp\left\{-\frac{(p_t - \hat{\beta}_{t|t-1}(i)z_{t-1})^2}{2(\sigma_p^2(i) + V_{t|t-1}(i)z_{t-1}^2)}\right\}\left(2\pi(\sigma_p^2(i) + V_{t|t-1}(i)z_{t-1}^2)\right)^{-1/2}.$$

Since

$$\pi_t(i) = \Pr(i|p^t, z^t) = \frac{f(p^t, z^t|i)\pi_0(i)}{f(p^t, z^t)},$$

the posterior odds ratio for the two models is given by

$$r_t = \frac{\pi_t(1)}{\pi_t(0)} = \frac{f(p^t, z^t|i = 1)\pi_0(1)}{f(p^t, z^t|i = 0)\pi_0(0)} = \frac{m_{1t}}{m_{0t}}$$

assuming $\pi_0(1) = \pi_0(0)$ for the prior of the two models. (More generally, the prior odds ratio would come in.) We thus have

$$\frac{m_{1,t+1}}{m_{0,t+1}} = \frac{m_{1,t}}{m_{0,t}}\frac{A_{t+1}(1)}{A_{t+1}(0)}.$$

We then use the fact that $m_{1,t}/m_{0,t} = \pi_t(1)/(1 - \pi_t(1))$ in the last equation. Solving for $\pi_{t+1}(1)$ then gives

$$\pi_{t+1}(1) = \frac{\pi_t(1)A_{t+1}(1)}{A_{t+1}(0) - \pi_t(1)A_{t+1}(0) + \pi_t(1)A_{t+1}(1)}.$$

This equation describes the updating of the model weights over time and completes our specification of the formulae for the posteriors of the parameters of both forecasting models and for the posterior probabilities of the two models.

[7] A Mathematica routine for this is available on request.

6.4 Simulation results

We now present simulation results for our setup. Key parameters are the model parameters α and ρ and the belief parameter $\sigma_\beta(1)$. We set $\sigma_\beta(0) = 0$. Other model parameters are set at values $\delta = 0.5, \sigma_Z = 1$, and $\sigma_a = 1$ in the simulations. We assume that agents set $\sigma_P(1) = \sigma_P(0) = 1$. Their priors at $t = 1$ are assumed to be

$$V_{1|0}(i) = 0.2 \text{ for } i = 0, 1$$

$$\hat{\beta}_{1|0}(i) = \bar{b} + \varepsilon_b\sqrt{V_{1|0}(i)} \text{ for } i = 0, 1,$$

where ε_b is a standard normal random variable. In addition we set the model priors as

$$\pi_0(i) = 0.5 \text{ for } i = 0, 1.$$

Except where otherwise stated, we simulate for $T = 40,000$ periods and do $N = 10,000$ simulations. In our tables we report the proportion of the simulations in which each model is selected. To assess this we say that model 1 is selected if $\pi_T(1) > 0.99999999$ and model 0 is selected if $\pi_T(1) < 0.00000001$. In our benchmark table the role of α is studied, and the other key parameters are set at $\sigma_\beta(1) = 0.005$ and $\rho = 0$. The results are in Table 6.1.

The results in Table 6.1 are intriguing, and are further illustrated in Figure 6.1. For $\alpha \ll 0.5$ learning with Bayesian model averaging converges to the REE with high (empirical) probability. As the value of α

Table 6.1 The role of expectations feedback in model selection

α	% Model 1	% Model 0	% Unselect
−0.5	0	100.0	0
0.1	0	100.0	0
0.4	0.2	95.8	4.0
0.5	5.7	82.7	11.6
0.6	32.7	60.5	6.8
0.7	56.0	43.3	0.7
0.85	70.0	30.0	0
0.95	61.6	38.2	0.2
0.99	49.3	50.7	0

Percentage of 10,000 simulation runs selecting either model 1 or model 2, or neither after 40,000 periods.

gets closer to 0.5 the probability starts to fall below 1 and for values near $\alpha = 0.5$ both cases of selection of the TVP model and of non-selection have small positive probabilities. As the value of α is raised above 0.5 the frequency of selection of the TVP model increases but in a non-monotonic way as $\alpha \to 1$.

It can be seen from Figure 6.1 that a fairly strong positive expectational feedback creates the possibility that agents come to believe that the economy is generated by the time-varying parameter model 1. When there is negative expectations feedback, as in the Muth cobweb model with normal supply and demand slopes, then agents learn the REE asymptotically. Convergence to the REE also occurs when there is positive expectational feedback that is not too strong, i.e., for $\alpha \ll 0.5$. However, for $\alpha > 0.5$ there is a clear possibility of convergence to a non-RE equilibrium in which agents believe that the endogenous variable p_t is generated by a time-varying model of the form $p_t = b_t z_{t-1} + \varepsilon_{pt}$, where b_t follows a random walk.

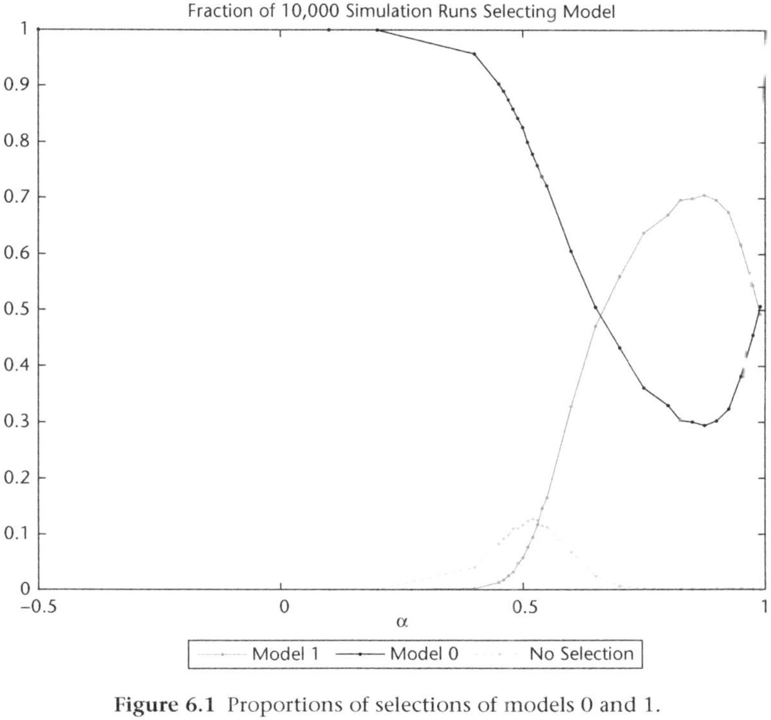

Figure 6.1 Proportions of selections of models 0 and 1.

Interestingly, the dependence of the selection result on α is non-monotonic. As α increases from 0.1, the proportion of simulations selecting model 1 increases until around $\alpha = 0.85$. At that point, further increases in α lead to reductions in selection of model 1, and as α gets very close to 1 the proportions are nearly 50–50. Thus, sufficiently strong expectations feedback makes agents more likely to believe in the drifting parameter model, but with very strong feedback they are just as likely to believe in the constant parameter model.

We remark that for cases in which model 1 is selected at $T = 40,000$ we have found that in longer simulations of $T = 100,000$ the convergence is to $\pi_T(1) = 1$ up to computer accuracy. This implies that such a numerical simulation would deliver $\pi_t(1) = 1$ for all $t > T$.

Next we consider the sensitivity of the outcomes to the parameters ρ and $\sigma_\beta(1)$. We fix $\alpha = 0.65$ and $\sigma_\beta(1) = 0.005$, and first consider different values of ρ. The results are reported in Table 6.2. It can be seen that the impact of ρ, the correlation in z_t, is fairly small. Larger values of ρ, either positive or negative, increase the likelihood of model 1 being selected. However, this impact is not very substantial.

Finally, for $\alpha = 0.65$ and $\rho = 0$ we consider variations in $\sigma_\beta(1)$. The results are shown in Table 6.3. As the perceived parameter variation in the forecasting model 1 falls, the proportion of simulations converging to model 0 decreases and, apparently falls to 0 for $\sigma_\beta(1)$ sufficiently small. However, for small values of $\sigma_\beta(1)$ Table 6.3 suggests the possibility of non-selection between the two models. To study this further we considered longer simulations of $T = 1,000,000$ for the cases when $\sigma_\beta(1) < 0.005$. These results are shown in the second section of the table. There we see that the instances of non-selection eventually resolve, and the proportion of simulations converging to model 1 continues to increase as the variability in its random walk

Table 6.2 Robustness of results with respect to autocorrelation of observable shocks

ρ	% Model 1	% Model 0	% Unselect
0.99	60.8	39.2	0
0.90	54.5	45.4	0.1
0.75	50.5	48.8	0.6
0.25	46.7	51.0	2.3
0	46.8	50.6	2.6
−0.25	47.2	50.2	2.6
−0.75	50.3	49.2	0.5
−0.90	54.0	45.9	0.1
−0.99	60.6	39.5	0

Table 6.3 Role of standard deviation of random walk in model selection

$\sigma_\beta(1)$	% Model 1	% Model 0	% Unselect
$T = 40,000$			
1.0000	3.2	96.8	0
0.5000	7.0	93.0	0
0.2500	14.1	85.9	0
0.1000	21.3	78.7	0
0.0500	29.6	70.4	0
0.0100	41.4	58.5	0.1
0.0050	47.3	50.7	2.0
0.0025	42.2	30.1	27.7
0.0010	31.1	0	68.9
0.0005	22.8	0	77.2
$T = 1,000,000$			
0.0050	48.4	51.7	0
0.0025	52.8	47.2	0
0.0010	59.1	40.9	0
0.0005	62.9	36.9	0.2

innovation decreases. Intuitively, for $\sigma_\beta(1)$ small it is more difficult for agents to distinguish between the two models, which is why the selection results require longer samples. Nevertheless, for large enough samples, model 1 is increasingly selected. For this case of $\alpha = 0.65$ there is sufficient dependence on expectations to make the time-varying parameter model a possible outcome, but the likelihood of this outcome increases as the drift in coefficients becomes smaller. That is, a slowly varying random walk seems to be a better fit for the actual law of motion than a model with substantial parameter drift.[8]

We normally do not see switching between $\pi_t(1)$ near 0 and near 1 within a simulation. There may possibly be such cases for α near 0.5, since we have observed a few cases when $\alpha = 0.4$ and $\sigma_\beta(1) = 0.001$ in which $\pi_t(1)$ is near 1 at t =40,000, which might resolve to $\pi_t(1) = 0$ eventually.

6.5 Additional interpretation and analysis

The preceding results are not straightforward to interpret, because a number of forces are at play. In this section we provide two auxiliary

[8] For $\alpha = 0.4$ it is also the case that for $\sigma_\beta(1)$ sufficiently small the possibility of non-selection increases with relatively shorter T. But as T is increased the proportion of non-selecting simulations falls and agents increasingly select model 0.

results that will help in obtaining a partial interpretation of the surprising result that non-RE forecasting model 1 has a fair chance to get selected when the expectational feedback is sufficiently strong.

The first result is about comparison of rational and non-rational mean forecast errors. At any moment of time, for each model $i = 0, 1$ agents have estimates $\hat{\beta}_{t|t-1}(i)$ of β_t, which are used to form forecasts of p_t. For convenience, we use the temporary notation

$$b = \pi_{t-1}(0)\hat{\beta}_{t|t-1}(0) + \pi_{t-1}(1)\hat{\beta}_{t|t-1}(1).$$

Then the following result will be useful in interpreting our results.

Lemma 6.2 *Suppose at time t agents believe in the PLM*

$$p_t = bz_{t-1} + \varepsilon_{pt}$$

with probability 1, where $b \neq \bar{b} = \delta/(1-\alpha)$. (Here $\bar{b}$ is the REE coefficient value.) Then under the resulting actual law of motion (ALM), the forecast $E^*_{t-1}p_t = bz_{t-1}$ has lower conditional MSE (mean square forecast error, conditional on z_{t-1}) than the 'REE forecast' $E^*_{t-1}p_t = \bar{b}z_{t-1}$, provided $1/2 < \alpha < 1$.

Suppose that model 0 converges to $\bar{b}$, i.e., $\hat{\beta}_{t|t-1}(0) \to \bar{b}$ as $t \to \infty$. We know this is the case if only model 0 is used by agents, but it plausibly holds more generally when both models are in play. In that case, the forecasts from model 1 will be more accurate, in the conditional MSE sense, if and only if $\alpha > 0.5$. On average the more accurate forecasting model will lead to an upward revision in its probability. Thus, for $\alpha > 0.5$ one would expect $\pi_t(1)$ to tend to increase over time. This suggests that one may have $\pi_t(1) \to 1$ when $\alpha > 0.5$.[9]

Special case. *Agents set $\pi_t(1) = 1$ for all t. Here the 'small constant gain' approximation (i.e. small $\sigma_\beta(1)$) is employed, making the framework similar to that used in Evans et al. (2010). Formally, the setting is now*

$$p_t = \beta_t z_{t-1} + \sigma_p \varepsilon_{pt},$$

and

$$\beta_t = \beta_{t-1} + \sigma_\beta \varepsilon_{\beta t}$$

[9] The Lemma also holds for $\alpha \geq 1$, but $\alpha < 1$ is a maintained assumption (the standard condition for stability under LS learning).

for the PLM, where for brevity the index to model 1 has been omitted in β_t, σ_p *and* σ_β. *The rest of the system is*

$$p_t = \alpha E^*_{t-1} p_t + \delta z_{t-1} + \sigma_a \varepsilon_{at},$$

$$E^*_{t-1} p_t = \hat{\beta}_{t|t-1} z_{t-1},$$

$$\hat{\beta}_{t+1|t} = \hat{\beta}_{t|t-1} + \frac{V_{t|t-1} z_{t-1}}{\sigma_p^2 + V_{t|t-1} z_{t-1}^2} (p_t - \hat{\beta}_{t|t-1} z_{t-1})$$

$$V_{t+1|t} = V_{t|t-1} - \frac{z_{t-1}^2 V_{t|t-1}^2}{\sigma_p^2 + V_{t|t-1} z_{t-1}^2} + \sigma_\beta^2.$$

The ALM is $p_t = (\hat{\beta}_{t|t-1} + \delta) z_{t-1} + \sigma_a \varepsilon_{at}$. *We analyse this system in the Appendix to this chapter. The analysis implies that asymptotically* $\hat{\beta}_{t+1|t}$ *is approximately an AR(1) process, with mean equal to the RE value, and with (i) a variance proportional to* $\sigma_\beta^2(1)$ *and (ii) a first-order autocorrelation parameter that tends to 1 as* $\sigma_\beta^2(1)$ *tends to 0.*

The result for the special case and the above Lemma suggest the reason for convergence of Bayesian updating to the TVP model 1, provided $\sigma_\beta^2(1) > 0$ is small enough. A sketch of the argument is as follows (we are assuming $\sigma_\beta^2(1) > 0$, $\sigma_\beta^2(0) = 0$). Suppose that $\pi_t(1) = 1$, all t, i.e., agents believe in the TVP model 1 w.p.1 for all t. Under model 0, we expect $\beta_{t+1|t}(0) \to \bar{b}$ as $t \to \infty$, based on the approximation results. Under model 1 we will have $\beta_{t+1|t}(1)$ converging to a distribution centred on $\bar{b}$, with deviations that are strongly and positively serially correlated. Hence by the Lemma the average forecast error under model 1 will be less than under model 0 if $0.5 < \alpha < 1$. Since actual squared errors strongly impact the evolution of $\pi_t(1)$ this strongly suggests that $\pi_t(1) = 1$ can be a stable outcome. (However, other factors influence the $\pi_t(1)$ updating.) This argument also suggests that for $\alpha < 0$ and for $0 \leq \alpha < 0.5$ model 1 will not be a fixed point asymptotically.

6.6 Conclusions

It is natural to assume that in situations with imperfect knowledge economic agents try to use multiple models and weighted averages of forecasts when they form expectations about the future. We consider the consequences of such practices in a simple self-referential model in which expectations affect outcomes and agents learn using appropriate Bayesian techniques. At the outset we impose the assumption that one of the forecasting models employed by agents contains a 'grain of truth', i.e., for particular parameter values that model corresponds to the correct forecasting model in an REE.

The central result in this chapter shows that convergence of learning with Bayesian model averaging to an REE occurs only when the feedback of agents' expectations on actual outcomes is relatively weak, less than 0.5. See Table 6.1 and Figure 6.1. This observation should be contrasted with Proposition 6.1, where it is showed that when agents only use the correctly specified forecasting model Bayesian learning converges to the REE provided that expectations feedback has coefficient less than 1.

More generally, it is seen from Table 6.1 and Figure 6.1 that learning by Bayesian model averaging leads to selection of a unique forecasting model with very high probability. However, the selection can be a misspecified forecasting model when the expectations feedback parameter has sufficiently high value. We allow agents to consider a drifting coefficients model and use it to form expectations. If the feedback from expectations to outcomes is sufficiently high, then the resulting drift in the actual data-generating process may justify selecting the drifting coefficients model. Thus, even though a constant parameter model is correctly specified asymptotically, the process of learning may make agents doubt that model.

Appendix

Proof of Proposition 6.1 (outline). Define

$$S_{t-1}^{-1} = \frac{tV_{t-1}}{\sigma_\eta^2 + V_{t-1}z_{t-1}^2}.$$

Then we have

$$S_{t-1} = \frac{1}{t}(\sigma_\eta^2 + V_{t-1}z_{t-1}^2)/V_{t-1}, \tag{6.2}$$

or

$$\sigma_\eta^2/V_{t-1} = tS_{t-1} - z_{t-1}^2 \tag{6.3}$$

and

$$V_t = V_{t-1}\left(1 - \frac{z_{t-1}^2 V_{t-1}}{\sigma_\eta^2 + V_{t-1}z_{t-1}^2}\right) = V_{t-1}\frac{\sigma_\eta^2}{\sigma_\eta^2 + V_{t-1}z_{t-1}^2}$$

$$= V_{t-1}\frac{\sigma_\eta^2/V_{t-1}}{\sigma_\eta^2/V_{t-1} + z_{t-1}^2} = V_{t-1}\frac{tS_{t-1} - z_{t-1}^2}{tS_{t-1}}.$$

Using the last expression and (6.3), we also have

$$V_t = \frac{\sigma_\eta^2}{(t+1)S_t - z_t^2} = \frac{\sigma_\eta^2}{tS_{t-1} - z_{t-1}^2}\,\frac{tS_{t-1} - z_{t-1}^2}{tS_{t-1}}$$

and so

$$\frac{1}{(t+1)S_t - z_t^2} = \frac{1}{tS_{t-1}}$$

or

$$(t+1)S_t - z_t^2 = tS_{t-1},$$

from which we get

$$S_t = \frac{t}{t+1}S_{t-1} + \frac{1}{t+1}z_t^2$$

$$= S_{t-1} + \frac{1}{t+1}(z_t^2 - S_{t-1}).$$

Since $E_{t-1}^* p_t = b_{t-1}z_{t-1}$ note that $p_t = (\alpha b_{t-1} + \delta)z_{t-1} + \eta_t$.

Collecting the results together, the system under Bayesian learning is

$$b_t = b_{t-1} + t^{-1}S_{t-1}^{-1}z_{t-1}(p_t - b_{t-1}z_{t-1})$$

$$S_t = S_{t-1} + t^{-1}\left(\frac{t}{t+1}\right)(z_t^2 - S_{t-1})$$

$$p_t = (\alpha b_{t-1} + \delta)z_{t-1} + \eta_t,$$

$$z_t = \rho z_{t-1} + w_t.$$

Since

$$b_t = b_{t-1} + t^{-1}S_{t-1}^{-1}z_{t-1}(z_{t-1}(\alpha - 1)b_{t-1} + \delta z_{t-1} + \eta_t),$$

we can apply standard results on stochastic recursive algorithms to show convergence. Note that the starting point is $S_0 = \frac{V_0}{\sigma_\eta^2+V_0 z_0^2}$. As usual,

$$\lim_{t\to\infty}(b_t, S_t) = ((1-\alpha)^{-1}\delta, \bar{S}).$$

Q.E.D.

Proof of Lemma 6.2. The actual model is $p_t = \alpha E^*_{t-1}p_t + \delta z_{t-1} + \varepsilon_{at}$. For this PLM the ALM is

$$p_t = (\alpha b + \delta)z_{t-1} + \varepsilon_{at}.$$

Thus, the forecast $E^*_{t-1}p_t = bz_{t-1}$ has lower conditional MSE than $E^*_{t-1}p_t = \bar{b}z_{t-1}$ when

$$\left|(\alpha b+\delta) - b\right| < \left|(\alpha b + \delta) - \bar{b}\right|, \text{ i.e.}$$

$$\left|(\alpha - 1)(b - \bar{b})\right| < \left|\alpha(b-\bar{b})\right|, \text{ or}$$

$$|\alpha - 1| < |\alpha|,$$

which holds for $\alpha > 0.5$ and fails to hold for $\alpha < 0$ and for $0 \le \alpha < 0.5$. Q.E.D.

Analysis of the case. $\pi_t(1) = 1$: Letting $\hat{P}_t = P_t/\sigma_\beta^2$, we get

$$\hat{\beta}_{t+1|t} = \hat{\beta}_{t|t-1} + \sigma_\beta^2 \frac{\hat{P}_t z_{t-1}}{1+\sigma_\beta^2 \hat{P}_t z_{t-1}^2}[(p_t - \hat{\beta}_{t|t-1}z_{t-1}) + \sigma_a \varepsilon_{at}]$$

$$\hat{P}_{t+1} = \hat{P}_t + \sigma_\beta^2\left[\frac{1}{\sigma_p^2} - \frac{z_{t-1}^2 \hat{P}_t^2}{1+\sigma_\beta^2 \hat{P}_t z_{t-1}^2}\right],$$

which is a constant-gain stochastic recursive algorithm (SRA) when σ_β^2 is treated as the gain. The associated differential equation is

$$\frac{d\beta}{d\tau} = \hat{P}\sigma_z^2[(\alpha-1)\beta + \delta] \tag{6.4}$$

$$\frac{d\hat{P}}{d\tau} = \frac{1}{\sigma_p^2} - \hat{P}^2\sigma_z^2 \tag{6.5}$$

with fixed point

$$\bar{\beta} = \delta(1-\alpha)^{-1}$$
$$\bar{P} = \frac{1}{\sigma_Z \sigma_p}.$$

We consider the stochastic differential equation approximation to the algorithm. Introduce the notation

$$\theta = \begin{pmatrix} \beta \\ \hat{P} \end{pmatrix}.$$

The mean dynamics $\tilde{\theta}(\tau, a)$ are given by (6.4)–(6.5) and we write the system in vector form as

$$\frac{d\theta}{d\tau} = h(\theta). \tag{6.6}$$

We also define

$$U^{\sigma_\beta^2}(\tau) = \sigma_\beta^{-1}[\theta^{\sigma_\beta^2}(\tau) - \tilde{\theta}(\tau, a)],$$

where a is the initial condition for (6.6). As $\sigma_\beta^2 \to 0$, the normalized deviation $U^{\sigma_\beta^2}(\tau)$ for $0 \leq \tau \leq \bar{\tau}$ converges weakly to the solution $\bar{U}(\tau)$ of

$$dU(\tau) = D_\theta h(\tilde{\theta}(\tau, a))U(\tau)d\tau + R^{1/2}(\tilde{\theta}(\tau, a))dW(\tau) \tag{6.7}$$

with initial condition $U(0) = 0$.[10] Here

$$A = Dh(\bar{\theta}) = \begin{pmatrix} \hat{P}\sigma_Z^2(\alpha - 1) & 0 \\ 0 & -2\frac{\sigma_Z}{\sigma_p} \end{pmatrix},$$

where $\bar{\theta}' = (\bar{\beta}, \bar{P})'$. Writing the SRA in vector form as

$$\theta_t = \theta_{t-1} + \gamma H(\theta_{t-1}, X_t),$$

where $X_t' = (z_{t-1}, \varepsilon_{at})$ we consider (6.7) from the starting point $\bar{\theta}$, i.e.,

$$dU(\tau) = D_\theta h(\bar{\theta})U(\tau)d\tau + \bar{R}^{1/2}dW(\tau), \text{ where } \bar{R} = R(\bar{\theta}).$$

The elements of $\bar{R}$ are given by

$$\bar{R}^{ij} = \sum_{k=-\infty}^{\infty} cov[H_i(\bar{\theta}, X_k), H_j(\bar{\theta}, X_0)].$$

[10] We use the results in Section 7.4 of Evans and Honkapohja (2001).

In particular, for

$$\bar{R}^{11} = \sum_{k=-\infty}^{\infty} cov[H_1(\bar{\theta}, X_k), H_1(\bar{\theta}, X_0)]$$

we get

$$H_1(\bar{\theta}, X_t) = \frac{\bar{P}z_{t-1}}{1 + 1 + \sigma_\beta^2 \bar{P} z_{t-1}^2}[((\alpha - 1)\bar{\beta} + \delta)z_{t-1} + \sigma_a \varepsilon_{at}]$$

$$= \frac{\bar{P}\sigma_a z_{t-1}}{1 + \sigma_\beta^2 \bar{P} z_{t-1}^2} z_{t-1}\varepsilon_{at}.$$

It follows that

$$\text{cov}[H_1(\bar{\theta}, X_k), H_1(\bar{\theta}, X_0)] = 0 \text{ for } k \neq 0$$

since $\{\varepsilon_{ak}\}$ is independent of $\{z_t\}$ and $E\varepsilon_{ak}\varepsilon_{a0} = 0$. Thus,

$$\bar{R}^{11} = \text{var}(H_1(\bar{\theta}, X_t)) = \bar{P}\sigma_a^4 \text{var}\left(\frac{z_{t-1}}{1 + \sigma_\beta^2 \bar{P} z_{t-1}^2}\right).$$

In particular,

$$\bar{R}^{11} \to \bar{P}\sigma_a^4 \text{var}(z_t) \text{ as } \sigma_\beta^2 \to 0,$$

where $\bar{P} = \sigma_z^{-1}\sigma_p^{-1}$. If $\sigma_a = \sigma_p$ then $\bar{R}^{11} \to \sigma_p^3 \sigma_z$.

Next, we compute

$$\text{cov}[U(\tau), U(\tau - \hat{\tau})] \equiv \rho(\tau, \tau - \hat{\tau}) = \exp(\hat{\tau}A).C,$$

where

$$C = \int_0^\infty \exp(vA)\bar{R}\exp(vA)dv.$$

Note also that $\bar{R}^{12} = 0$ as $H_2(\bar{\theta}, X_0)$ does not depend on ε_{at}. It follows that $\exp(vA)\bar{R}\exp(vA)$ is diagonal and

$$C^{11} = \bar{R}^{11} \int_0^\infty \exp(v\sigma_z\sigma_p^{-1}(\alpha - 1)2)dv$$

$$= \bar{R}^{11}\frac{\sigma_p}{2(1-\alpha)\sigma_z} = \frac{\sigma_p^4}{2(1-\alpha)}$$

since $\bar{R}^{11} \to \sigma_p^3 \sigma_Z$ as noted above. This implies that the autocorrelation function of $U(\tau)$ is $\tilde{r}(\hat{\tau}) = \exp(-\hat{\tau} \frac{\sigma_Z}{\sigma_p}(1-\alpha))$. As $\bar{\theta} + \sigma_\beta^2 U^{\sigma_\beta^2}(\tau) = \theta^{\sigma_\beta^2}(\tau)$ we have the approximation $\theta^{\sigma_\beta^2}(\tau) \approx \theta_t$, where $\tau = \sigma_\beta^2 t$. Using the notation $\hat{\beta}_t = \hat{\beta}_{t+1|t}$ we have

$$\begin{aligned} \text{cor}(\hat{\beta}_t, \hat{\beta}_{t-k}) &= \text{cor}[U_\beta^{\sigma_\beta^2}(\tau)(\sigma_\beta^{-2}\tau), U_\beta^{\sigma_\beta^2}(\tau)(\sigma_\beta^{-2}\tau - k)] \\ &= \tilde{r}_\beta(\sigma_\beta^2 k) = \exp[-\sigma_\beta^2 \frac{\sigma_Z}{\sigma_p}(1-\alpha)k]. \end{aligned}$$

Thus, for any $k > 1$, $\text{cor}(\hat{\beta}_t, \hat{\beta}_{t-k}) \to 1$ as $\sigma_\beta^2 - 0$.

References

Bray, M., and N. Savin (1986). 'Rational Expectations Equilibria, Learning, and Model Specification', *Econometrica*, 54, 1129–60.

Bullard, J. (1992). 'Time-Varying Parameters and Nonconvergence to Rational Expectations under Least Squares Learning', *Economics Letters*, 40, 159–66.

Cho, I.-K., N. Williams, and T. J. Sargent (2002). 'Escaping Nash Inflation', *Review of Economic Studies*, 69, 1–40.

Cogley, T., and T. J. Sargent (2005). 'The Conquest of US Inflation: Learning and Robustness to Model Uncertainty', *Review of Economic Dynamics*, 8, 528–63.

Evans, G. W., and S. Honkapohja (2001). *Learning and Expectations in Macroeconomics*. Princeton, NJ: Princeton University Press.

—— and —— (2009). 'Learning and Macroeconomics', *Annual Review of Economics*, 1, 421–51.

——, ——, and N. Williams (2010). 'Generalized Stochastic Gradient Learning', *International Economic Review*, 51, 237–62.

Hamilton, J. D. (1994). *Time Series Analysis*. Princeton, NJ: Princeton University Press.

McGough, B. (2003). 'Statistical Learning and Time Varying Parameters', *Macroeconomic Dynamics*, 7, 119–39.

Sargent, T. J. (2008). 'Evolution and Intelligent Design', *American Economic Review*, 98, 5–37.

—— and N. Williams (2005). 'Impacts of Priors on Convergence and Escapes from Nash Inflation', *Review of Economic Dynamics*, 8, 360–91.

Slobodyan, S., and R. Wouters (2008). 'Estimating a Medium-Scale DSGE Model with Expectations Based on Small Forecasting Models', mimeo.

Young, H. P. (2004). *Strategic Learning and Its Limits*. Oxford: Oxford University Press.

7

History-Dependent Public Policies

*David Evans and Thomas J. Sargent**

7.1 Introduction

For the purpose of making some general points about history-dependent public policies and their representations, we study a model in which a benevolent tax authority is forced to raise a prescribed present value of revenues by imposing a distorting flat rate tax on the output of a competitive representative firm that faces costs of adjusting its output. That the firm lives within a rational expectations equilibrium imposes restrictions on the tax authority.[1]

We compare two timing protocols. In the first, an infinitely lived benevolent tax authority solves a Ramsey problem. This means that the authority chooses a sequence of tax rates once-and-for-all at time 0. In the second timing protocol, there is a sequence of tax authorities, each choosing only a time t tax rate. Under both timing protocols, optimal tax policies are history-dependent. But the history dependence reflects different economic forces across the two timing protocols. In the first, history dependence expresses the time-inconsistency of the Ramsey plan. In the second, it reflects the unfolding of constraints that assure that at a time t government wants to confirm the representative firm's expectations about government actions. We discuss recursive representations of history-dependent tax policies under both timing protocols.

The first timing protocol models a policy-maker who can be said to 'commit'. To obtain a recursive representation of a Ramsey policy, we compare two methods. We first apply a method proposed by Kydland and Prescott (1980) that uses a promised marginal utility to augment

* We thank Marco Bassetto for very helpful comments.

[1] We could also call a competitive equilibrium a rational expectations equilibrium.

authentic state variables. We then apply a closely related method of Miller and Salmon (1985), Pearlman et al. (1986), and Backus and Driffill (1986). This method uses a 'co-state on a co-state' variable to augment the authentic state variables. After applying both methods, we describe links between them and confirm that they recover the same Ramsey plan.

Turning to the second timing protocol in which the tax rate is chosen sequentially, we use the notion of a sustainable plan proposed by Chari and Kehoe (1990), also referred to as a credible public policy by Stokey (1989). A key idea here is that history-dependent policies can be arranged so that, when regarded as a representative firm's forecasting functions, they confront policy-makers with incentives to confirm them. We follow Chang (1998) in expressing such history-dependent plans recursively. Credibility considerations contribute an additional auxiliary state variable (above and beyond the auxiliary state variable appearing in the first timing protocol). This new state variable is a promised value to the planner. It expresses how things must unfold to give the government the incentive to confirm private sector expectations when the government chooses sequentially.

We write this chapter partly because we observe occasional confusions about the consequences of our two timing protocols and about recursive representations of government policies under them. It is erroneous to regard a recursive representation of the Ramsey plan as in any way 'solving' a time-inconsistency problem. In contrast, the evolution of the auxiliary state variable that augments the authentic ones under our first timing protocol ought to be viewed as *expressing* the time inconsistency of a Ramsey plan. Despite that, in literatures about practical monetary policy one frequently sees efforts to 'sell' Ramsey plans in settings where our second, sequential timing protocol more accurately characterizes decision-making. One of our purposes is to issue a warning to beware of discussions of credibility if you don't see recursive representations of policies with the complete list of state variables appearing in the Chang (1998)-like analysis of Section 7.9 below.

7.2 Rational expectations equilibrium

A representative competitive firm sells output q_t for price p_t, where market-wide output is Q_t. The market as a whole faces a downward sloping inverse demand function

$$p_t = A_0 - A_1 Q_t, \quad A_0 > 0, A_1 > 0. \tag{7.1}$$

The representative firm has given initial condition q_0, endures quadratic adjustment costs $\frac{d}{2}(q_{t+1} - q_t)^2$, and pays a flat rate tax τ_t per unit of output. The firm faces what it regards as exogenous sequences $\{p_t, \tau_t\}_{t=0}^{\infty}$ and chooses $\{q_{t+1}\}_{t=0}^{\infty}$ to maximize

$$\sum_{t=0}^{\infty} \beta^t \{p_t q_t - \frac{d}{2}(q_{t+1} - q_t)^2 - \tau_t q_t\}. \tag{7.2}$$

Let $u_t = q_{t+1} - q_t$ be the firm's 'control' variable at time t. First-order conditions for the firm's problem are

$$u_t = \frac{\beta}{d} p_{t+1} + \beta u_{t+1} - \frac{\beta}{d} \tau_{t+1} \tag{7.3}$$

for $t \geq 0$.

Notation. For any scalar x_t, let $\vec{x} = \{x_t\}_{t=0}^{\infty}$.

To compute a rational expectations equilibrium, it is appropriate to take (7.3), eliminate p_t in favour of Q_t by using (7.1), and then set $q_t = Q_t$, thereby making the representative firm representative.[2] We arrive at

$$u_t = \frac{\beta}{d} \left[A_0 - A_1 Q_{t+1}\right] + \beta u_{t+1} - \frac{\beta}{d} \tau_{t+1}. \tag{7.4}$$

We also have

$$Q_{t+1} = Q_t + u_t. \tag{7.5}$$

Equations (7.1), (7.4), and (7.5) summarize competitive equilibrium sequences for $(\vec{p}, \vec{Q}, \vec{u})$ as functions of the path $\{\tau_{t+1}\}_{t=0}^{\infty}$ for the flat rate distorting tax τ.

Definition 7.2.1 *Given a tax sequence $\{\tau_{t+1}\}_{t=0}^{\infty}$, a competitive equilibrium is a price sequence $\{p_t\}_{t=0}^{\infty}$ and an output sequence $\{Q_t\}_{t=0}^{\infty}$ that satisfy (7.1), (7.4), and (7.5).*

Definition 7.2.2 *For any sequence $\vec{x} = \{x_t\}_{t=0}^{\infty}$, $\vec{x}_1 \equiv \{x_t\}_{t=1}^{\infty}$ is called a* continuation *sequence or simply a* continuation.

Remark 7.2.3 *A competitive equilibrium consists of a first period value $u_0 = Q_1 - Q_0$ and a continuation competitive equilibrium with initial condition Q_1. A continuation of a competitive equilibrium is a competitive equilibrium.*

Following the lead of Chang (1998), we shall make extensive use of the following property:

[2] It is important not to set $q_t = Q_t$ prematurely. To make the firm a price taker, this equality should be imposed *after* and not *before* solving the firm's optimization problem.

Remark 7.2.4 *A continuation $\vec{\tau}_1 = \{\tau_{t+1}\}_{t=1}^{\infty}$ of a tax policy $\vec{\tau}$ influences u_0 via (7.4) entirely through its impact on u_1. A continuation competitive equilibrium can be indexed by a u_1 that satisfies (7.4).*

Definition 7.2.5 *With some abuse of language, in the spirit of Kydland and Prescott (1980) and Chang (1998) we shall use u_{t+1} to describe what we shall dub a 'promised marginal value' that a competitive equilibrium offers to a representative firm.*

Remark 7.2.6 *We should instead, perhaps with more accuracy, define a promised marginal value as $\beta(A_0 - A_1 Q_{t+1}) - \beta\tau_{t+1} + \beta d u_{t+1}$, since this is the object to which the firm's first-order condition instructs it to equate to the marginal cost du_t of $u_t = q_{t+1} - q_t$.*[3] *But given (u_t, Q_t), the representative firm knows (Q_{t+1}, τ_{t+1}), so it is adequate to take u_{t+1} as the intermediate variable that summarizes how $\vec{\tau}_{t+1}$ affects the firm's choice of u_t.*

Definition 7.2.7 *Define a history $Q^t = [Q_0, \ldots, Q_t]$. A history-dependent tax policy is a sequence of functions $\{\sigma_t\}_{t=0}^{\infty}$ with time t component σ_t mapping Q^t into a choice of τ_{t+1}.*

Below we shall study history-dependent tax policies that either (a) solve a Ramsey plan or (b) are credible. We shall describe recursive representations of both types of history-dependent policies.

7.3 Ramsey problem

The planner's objective is cast in terms of consumer surplus net of the firm's adjustment costs. Consumer surplus is

$$\int_0^Q [A_0 - A_1 x] dx = A_0 Q - \frac{A_1}{2} Q^2,$$

so the planner's one-period return function is

$$A_0 Q_t - \frac{A_1}{2} Q_t^2 - \frac{d}{2} u_t^2. \tag{7.6}$$

At time 0, a Ramsey planner faces the intertemporal budget constraint

$$\sum_{t=1}^{\infty} \beta^t \tau_t Q_t = G_0. \tag{7.7}$$

Note that (7.7) precludes taxation of initial output Q_0.

[3] This choice would align better with how Chang (1998) chose to express his competitive equilibrium recursively.

Definition 7.3.1 *The Ramsey problem is to choose a tax sequence $\vec{\tau}$ and a competitive equilibrium outcome $(\vec{Q}, \vec{u})$ that maximize*

$$\sum_{t=0}^{\infty} \beta^t \left[A_0 Q_t - \frac{A_1}{2} Q_t^2 - \frac{d}{2} u_t^2 \right] \tag{7.8}$$

subject to (7.7).

Definition 7.3.2 *Ramsey timing protocol.*

1. *At time 0, knowing (Q_0, G_0), the Ramsey planner chooses $\{\tau_{t+1}\}_{t=0}^{\infty}$.*
2. *Given $(Q_0, \{\tau_{t+1}\}_{t=0}^{\infty})$, a competitive equilibrium outcome $\{u_t, Q_{t+1}\}_{t=0}^{\infty}$ emerges (see Definition 7.2.1).*

Remark 7.3.3 *In bringing out the timing protocol associated with a Ramsey plan, we run head on to a set of issues analysed by Bassetto (2005). This is because in Definition 7.3.2 of the Ramsey timing protocol, we have not completely described conceivable actions by the government and firms as time unfolds. For example, we are silent about how the government would respond if firms, for some unspecified reason, were to choose to deviate from the competitive equilibrium associated with the Ramsey plan, thereby possibly violating budget balance (7.7). Our definition of a Ramsey plan says nothing about how the government would respond. This is an example of the issues raised by Bassetto (2005), who identifies a class of government policy problems whose proper formulation requires supplying a complete and coherent description of all actors' behaviour across all possible histories. Implicitly, we are assuming that a more complete description of a government strategy than we have included could be specified that (a) agrees with ours along the Ramsey outcome, and (b) suffices uniquely to implement the Ramsey plan by deterring firms taking actions that deviate from the Ramsey outcome path.*

7.3.1 *Computing a Ramsey plan*

The planner chooses $\{u_t\}_{t=0}^{\infty}, \{\tau_t\}_{t=1}^{\infty}$ to maximize (7.8) subject to (7.4), (7.5), and (7.7). To formulate this problem as a Lagrangian, attach a Lagrange multiplier μ to the budget constraint (7.7). Then the planner chooses $\{u_t\}_{t=0}^{\infty}, \{\tau_t\}_{t=1}^{\infty}$ to maximize and the Lagrange multiplier μ to minimize

$$\sum_{t=0}^{\infty} \beta^t \left[A_0 Q_t - \frac{A_1}{2} Q_t^2 - \frac{d}{2} u_t^2 \right] + \mu \left[\sum_{t=0}^{\infty} \beta^t \tau_t Q_t - G_0 - \tau_0 Q_0 \right] \tag{7.9}$$

subject to (7.4) and (7.5).

7.4 Implementability multiplier approach

The Ramsey problem is a special case of the linear quadratic dynamic Stackelberg problem analysed in Ljungqvist and Sargent (2004, Ch. 18). The idea is to construct a recursive representation of a Ramsey plan by taking as state variables Lagrange multipliers on implementability constraints that require the Ramsey planner to choose among competitive equilibrium allocations. The motion through time of these Lagrange multipliers become components of a recursive representation of a history-dependent plan for taxes. For us, the key implementability conditions are (7.4) for $t \geq 0$.

Holding fixed μ and G_0, the Lagrangian (7.9) for the planning problem can be abbreviated as

$$\max_{\{u_t\},\{\tau_{t+1}\}} \sum_{t=0}^{\infty} \beta^t \left[A_0 Q_t - \frac{A_1}{2} Q_t^2 - \frac{d}{2} u_t^2 + \mu \tau_t Q_t \right]$$

Define

$$y_t = \begin{pmatrix} z_t \\ u_t \end{pmatrix} = \begin{pmatrix} 1 \\ Q_t \\ \tau_t \\ u_t \end{pmatrix},$$

where $z_t = \begin{pmatrix} 1 \\ Q_t \\ \tau_t \end{pmatrix}$ are genuine state variables and u_t is a jump variable. We include τ_t as a state variable for bookkeeping purposes: it helps to map the problem into a linear regulator problem with no cross products between states and controls. However, it will be a redundant state variable in the sense that the optimal tax τ_{t+1} will not depend on τ_t. The government chooses τ_{t+1} at time t as a function of the time t state. Thus, we can rewrite the Ramsey problem as

$$\max_{\{y_t\},\{\tau_{t+1}\}} - \sum_{t=0}^{\infty} \beta^t y_t' R y_t \tag{7.10}$$

subject to z_0 given and the law of motion

$$\begin{pmatrix} z_{t+1} \\ u_{t+1} \end{pmatrix} = A \begin{pmatrix} z_t \\ u_t \end{pmatrix} + B \tau_{t+1}, \tag{7.11}$$

where

$$R = \begin{pmatrix} 0 & -\frac{A_0}{2} & 0 & 0 \\ -\frac{A_0}{2} & \frac{A_1}{2} & \frac{-\mu}{2} & 0 \\ 0 & \frac{-\mu}{2} & 0 & 0 \\ 0 & 0 & 0 & \frac{d}{2} \end{pmatrix},\ A = \begin{pmatrix} 1 & 0 & 0 & 0 \\ 0 & 1 & 0 & 1 \\ 0 & 0 & 0 & 0 \\ -\frac{A_0}{d} & \frac{A_1}{d} & 0 & \frac{A_1}{d} + \frac{1}{\beta} \end{pmatrix},\ \text{and } B = \begin{pmatrix} 0 \\ 0 \\ 1 \\ \frac{1}{d} \end{pmatrix}.$$

Because this problem falls within the Ljungqvist and Sargent (2004, Ch. 18) framework, we can proceed as follows. Letting λ_t be a vector of Lagrangian multipliers on the transition laws summarized in Eq. (7.11), it follows that $\lambda_t = Py_t$, where P solves the Riccati equation

$$P = R + \beta A'PA - \beta^2 A'PB(\beta B'PB)^{-1}B'PA$$

and $\tau_{t+1} = -Fy_t$, where

$$F = \beta(\beta B'PB)^{-1}B'PA.$$

This we can rewrite as

$$\begin{pmatrix} \lambda_{zt} \\ \lambda_{ut} \end{pmatrix} = \begin{pmatrix} P_{11} & P_{12} \\ P_{21} & P_{22} \end{pmatrix} \begin{pmatrix} z_t \\ u_t \end{pmatrix}.$$

Solve for u_t to get

$$u_t = -P_{22}^{-1}P_{21}z_t + P_{22}^{-1}\lambda_{ut},$$

where now the multiplier λ_{ut} becomes our authentic state variable, one that measures the costs of confirming the public's prior expectations about time t government actions. Then the complete state at time t becomes $\begin{pmatrix} z_t \\ \lambda_{ut} \end{pmatrix}$. Thus,

$$y_t = \begin{pmatrix} z_t \\ u_t \end{pmatrix} = \begin{pmatrix} I & 0 \\ -P_{22}^{-1}P_{21} & P_{22}^{-1} \end{pmatrix} \begin{pmatrix} z_t \\ \lambda_{ut} \end{pmatrix}$$

so

$$\tau_{t+1} = -F\begin{pmatrix} I & 0 \\ -P_{22}^{-1}P_{21} & P_{22}^{-1} \end{pmatrix} \begin{pmatrix} z_t \\ \lambda_{ut} \end{pmatrix}.$$

The evolution of the state is

$$\begin{pmatrix} z_{t+1} \\ \lambda_{ut+1} \end{pmatrix} = \underbrace{\begin{pmatrix} I & 0 \\ P_{21} & P_{22} \end{pmatrix} (A - BF) \begin{pmatrix} I & 0 \\ -P_{22}^{-1}P_{21} & P_{22}^{-1} \end{pmatrix}}_{G} \begin{pmatrix} z_t \\ \lambda_{ut} \end{pmatrix}$$

with initial state

$$\begin{pmatrix} z_0 \\ \lambda_{u0} \end{pmatrix} = \begin{pmatrix} 1 \\ Q_0 \\ \tau_0 \\ 0 \end{pmatrix}. \tag{7.12}$$

Equation (7.12) incorporates the Ljungqvist and Sargent (2004, Ch. 18) finding that the Ramsey planner finds it optimal to set λ_{u0} to 0.

7.5 Kydland–Prescott (1980) approach

Kydland and Prescott (1980) or Chang (1998) would formulate our Ramsey problem in terms of the Bellman equation

$$v(Q_t, \tau_t, u_t) = \max_{\tau_{t+1}} \left\{ A_0 Q_t - \frac{A_1}{2} Q_t^2 - \frac{d}{2} u_t^2 + \mu \tau_t Q_t + \beta v(Q_{t+1}, \tau_{t+1}, u_{t+1}) \right\},$$

where the maximization is subject to the constraints

$$Q_{t+1} = Q_t + u_t$$

and

$$u_{t+1} = -\frac{A_0}{d} + \frac{A_1}{d} Q_t + \left(\frac{A_1}{d} + \frac{1}{\beta} \right) u_t + \frac{1}{d} \tau_{t+1}.$$

We now regard u_t as a state. It plays the role of a promised marginal utility in the Kydland and Prescott (1980) framework. Define the state vector to be

$$y_t = \begin{pmatrix} 1 \\ Q_t \\ \tau_t \\ u_t \end{pmatrix} = \begin{pmatrix} z_t \\ u_t \end{pmatrix},$$

where $z_t = \begin{pmatrix} 1 \\ Q_t \\ \tau_t \end{pmatrix}$ are authentic state variables and u_t is a variable whose time 0 value is a 'jump' variable but whose values for dates $t \geq 1$ will become state variables that encode history dependence in the Ramsey plan. Write a dynamic programming problem in the style of Kydland and Prescott (1980) as

$$v(y_t) = \max_{\tau_{t+1}} \left\{ -y_t' R y_t + \beta v(y_{t+1}) \right\}, \tag{7.13}$$

where the maximization is subject to the constraint

$$y_{t+1} = Ay_t + B\tau_{t+1},$$

where

$$R = \begin{pmatrix} 0 & -\frac{A_0}{2} & 0 & 0 \\ -\frac{A_0}{2} & \frac{A_1}{2} & \frac{-\mu}{2} & 0 \\ 0 & \frac{-\mu}{2} & 0 & 0 \\ 0 & 0 & 0 & \frac{d}{2} \end{pmatrix},\ A = \begin{pmatrix} 1 & 0 & 0 & 0 \\ 0 & 1 & 0 & 1 \\ 0 & 0 & 0 & 0 \\ -\frac{A_0}{d} & \frac{A_1}{d} & 0 & \frac{A_1}{d} + \frac{1}{\beta} \end{pmatrix},\ \text{and } B = \begin{pmatrix} 0 \\ 0 \\ 1 \\ \frac{1}{d} \end{pmatrix}.$$

Functional equation (7.13) is an optimal linear regulator problem. It has solution

$$v(y_t) = -y_t' P y_t,$$

where P solves

$$P = R + A'PA - A'PB(B'PB)^{-1}B'PA$$

and the optimal policy function is given by

$$\tau_{t+1} = -Fy_t, \tag{7.14}$$

where

$$F = \beta(\beta B'PB)^{-1}B'PA = (B'PB)^{-1}B'PA. \tag{7.15}$$

Note that since the formulas for A, B, and R are identical it follows that F and P are the same as in the Lagrangian multiplier approach of Section 7.4. The optimal choice of u_0 satisfies

$$\frac{\partial v}{\partial u_0} = 0.$$

If we partition P as

$$P = \begin{pmatrix} P_{11} & P_{12} \\ P_{21} & P_{22} \end{pmatrix},$$

then we have

$$\begin{aligned} 0 &= \frac{\partial}{\partial u_0}\left(z_0'P_{11}z_0 + z_0'P_{12}u_0 + u_0'P_{21}z_0 + u_0'P_{22}u_0\right) \\ &= P_{12}'z_0 + P_{21}u_0 + 2P_{22}u_0, \end{aligned}$$

which implies that

$$u_0 = -P_{22}^{-1} P_{21} z_0. \tag{7.16}$$

Thus, the Ramsey plan is

$$\tau_{t+1} = -F \begin{pmatrix} z_t \\ u_t \end{pmatrix} \text{ and } \begin{pmatrix} z_{t+1} \\ u_{t+1} \end{pmatrix} = (A - BF) \begin{pmatrix} z_t \\ u_t \end{pmatrix},$$

with initial state $\begin{pmatrix} z_0 \\ -P_{22}^{-1} P_{21} z_0 \end{pmatrix}$.

7.5.1 *Comparison of the two approaches*

We can compare the outcome from the Kydland–Prescott approach to the outcome of the Lagrangian multiplier on the implementability constraint approach of Section 7.4. Using the formula

$$\begin{pmatrix} z_t \\ u_t \end{pmatrix} = \begin{pmatrix} I & 0 \\ -P_{22}^{-1} P_{21} & P_{22}^{-1} \end{pmatrix} \begin{pmatrix} z_t \\ \lambda_{ut} \end{pmatrix}$$

and applying it to the evolution of the state

$$\begin{pmatrix} z_{t+1} \\ \lambda_{ut+1} \end{pmatrix} = \underbrace{\begin{pmatrix} I & 0 \\ P_{21} & P_{22} \end{pmatrix} (A - BF) \begin{pmatrix} I & 0 \\ -P_{22}^{-1} P_{21} & P_{22}^{-1} \end{pmatrix}}_{G} \begin{pmatrix} z_t \\ \lambda_{ut} \end{pmatrix},$$

we get

$$\begin{pmatrix} z_{t+1} \\ u_{t+1} \end{pmatrix} = (A - BF) \begin{pmatrix} z_t \\ u_t \end{pmatrix} \tag{7.17}$$

or

$$y_{t+1} = A_F y_t, \tag{7.18}$$

where $A_F \equiv A - BF$. Then using the initial state value $\lambda_{u,0} = 0$, we obtain

$$\begin{pmatrix} z_0 \\ u_0 \end{pmatrix} = \begin{pmatrix} z_0 \\ -P_{22}^{-1} P_{21} z_0 \end{pmatrix}. \tag{7.19}$$

This is identical to the initial state delivered by the Kydland–Prescott approach. Therefore, as expected, the two approaches provide identical Ramsey plans.

7.6 Recursive representation

An outcome of the preceding results is that the Ramsey plan can be represented recursively as the choice of an initial marginal utility (or rate of growth of output) according to a function

$$u_0 = \upsilon(Q_0|\mu) \tag{7.20}$$

that obeys (7.19) and the following updating equations for $t \geq 0$:

$$\tau_{t+1} = \tau(Q_t, u_t|\mu) \tag{7.21}$$

$$Q_{t+1} = Q_t + u_t \tag{7.22}$$

$$u_{t+1} = u(Q_t, u_t|\mu). \tag{7.23}$$

We have conditioned the functions υ, τ, and u by μ to emphasize how the dependence of F on G appears indirectly through the Lagrange multiplier μ. We'll discuss how to compute μ in Section 7.7, but first want to consider the following numerical example.

7.6.1 *Example*

We computed the Ramsey plan for the following parameter values: $[A_0, A_1, d, \beta, Q_0] = [100, 0.05, 0.2, 0.95, 100]$. Figure 7.1[4] reports the Ramsey plan for τ and the Ramsey outcome for Q, u for $t = 0, \ldots, 20$. The optimal decision rule is[5]

$$\tau_{t+1} = -248.0624 - 0.1242Q_t - 0.3347u_t. \tag{7.24}$$

Note how the Ramsey plan calls for a high tax at $t = 1$ followed by a perpetual stream of lower taxes. Taxing heavily at first, less later sets up a time-inconsistency problem that we'll characterize formally after first discussing how to compute μ.

[4] The computations are executed in Matlab programs Evans_Sargent_Main.m and ComputeG.m. ComputeG.m solves the Ramsey problem for a given μ and returns the associated tax revenues (see Section 7.7) and the matrices F and P. Evans_Sargent_Main.m is the main driving file and with ComputeG.m computes the time series plotted in Figure 7.1.

[5] As promised, τ_t does not appear in the Ramsey planner's decision rule for τ_{t+1}.

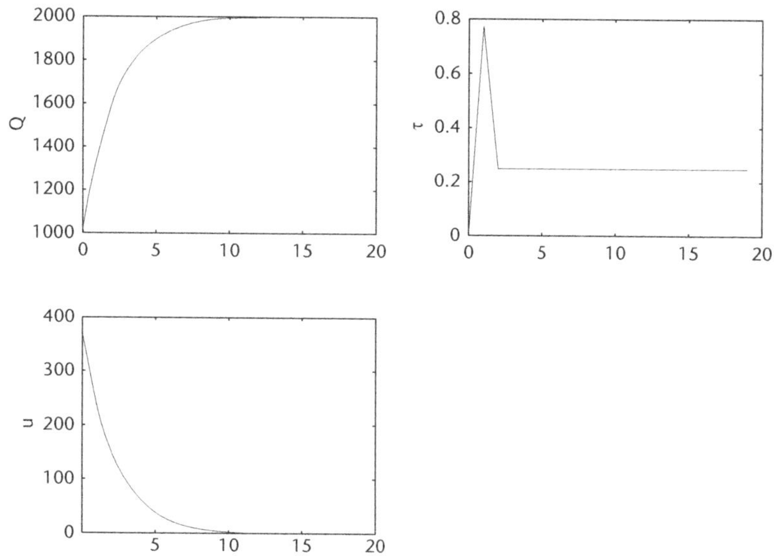

Figure 7.1 Ramsey plan and Ramsey outcome. From upper left to right: first panel, Q_t; second panel, τ_t; third panel, $u_t = Q_{t+1} - Q_t$.

7.7 Computing μ

Define the selector vectors $e_\tau = \begin{bmatrix} 0 & 0 & 1 & 0 \end{bmatrix}'$ and $e_Q = \begin{bmatrix} 0 & 1 & 0 & 0 \end{bmatrix}'$. Then express $\tau_t = e_\tau' y_t$ and $Q_t = e_Q' y_t$. Evidently, tax revenues $Q_t \tau_t = y_t' e_Q e_\tau' y_t = y_t' S y_t$ where $S \equiv e_Q e_\tau'$. We want to compute

$$T_0 = \sum_{t=1}^{\infty} \beta^t \tau_t Q_t = \beta \tau_1 Q_1 + \beta T_1,$$

where $T_1 = \sum_{t=2}^{\infty} \beta^{t-1} Q_t \tau_t$. The present values T_0 and T_1 are connected by

$$T_0 = \beta y_0' A_F' S A_F y_0 + \beta T_1.$$

Guess a solution that takes the form $T_t = y_t' \Omega y_t$ then find an Ω that satisfies

$$\Omega = \beta A_F' S A_F + \beta A_F' \Omega A_F. \tag{7.25}$$

Equation (7.25) is a discrete Lyapunov equation that can be solved for Ω using the Matlab program `dlyap` or `doublej2`.

The matrix F and therefore the matrix $A_F = A - BF$ depend on μ. To find a μ that guarantees that

$$T_0 = G, \tag{7.26}$$

we proceed as follows:

1. Guess an initial μ, compute a tentative Ramsey plan and the implied $T_0 = y_0' \Omega(\mu) y_0$.
2. If $T_0 > G$, lower μ; if $T_0 < \mu$, raise μ.
3. Continue iterating on step 3 until $T_0 = G$.

7.8 Time inconsistency

Recall that the Ramsey planner chooses $\{u_t\}_{t=0}^{\infty}, \{\tau_t\}_{t=1}^{\infty}$ to maximize

$$\sum_{t=0}^{\infty} \beta^t \left[A_0 Q_t - \frac{A_1}{2} Q_t^2 - \frac{d}{2} u_t^2 \right]$$

subject to (7.4), (7.5), and (7.7). In this section, we note that a Ramsey plan is time-inconsistent, which we express as follows:

Proposition 7.8.1 *A continuation of a Ramsey plan is not a Ramsey plan.*

Let

$$w(Q_0, u_0 | \mu_0) = \sum_{t=0}^{\infty} \beta^t \left[A_0 Q_t - \frac{A_1}{2} Q_t^2 - \frac{d}{2} u_t^2 \right], \tag{7.27}$$

where $\{Q_t, u_t\}_{t=0}^{\infty}$ are evaluated under the Ramsey plan whose recursive representation is given by (7.21), (7.22), (7.23) and where μ_0 is the value of the Lagrange multiplier that assures budget balance, computed as described in Section 7.7. Evidently, these continuation values satisfy the recursion

$$w(Q_t, u_t | \mu_0) = A_0 Q_t - \frac{A_1}{2} Q_t^2 - \frac{d}{2} u_t^2 + \beta w(Q_{t+1}, u_{t+1} | \mu_0) \tag{7.28}$$

for all $t \geq 0$, where $Q_{t+1} = Q_t + u_t$. Under the timing protocol affiliated with the Ramsey plan, the planner is committed to the outcome of iterations on (7.21), (7.22), (7.23). In particular, when time t comes, he is committed to the value of u_t implied by the Ramsey plan and receives continuation value $w(Q_t, u_t|\mu_0)$.

That the Ramsey plan is time-inconsistent can be seen by subjecting it to the following 'revolutionary' test. First, define continuation revenues G_t that the government raises along the original Ramsey outcome by

$$G_t = \beta^{-1}(G_0 - \sum_{s=1}^{t} \beta^s \tau_s Q_s), \tag{7.29}$$

where $\{\tau_t, Q_t\}_{t=0}^{\infty}$ is the original Ramsey outcome.[6] Then at time $t \geq 1$, take (Q_t, G_t) inherited from the original Ramsey plan as initial conditions, and invite a brand new Ramsey planner to compute a new Ramsey plan, solving for a new u_t, to be called $\check{u}_t$, and for a new μ, to be called $\check{\mu}_t$. The revised Lagrange multiplier $\check{\mu}_t$ is chosen so that, under the new Ramsey Plan, the government is able to raise enough continuation revenues G_t given by (7.29). Would this new Ramsey plan be a continuation of the original plan? The answer is no because along a Ramsey plan, for $t \geq 1$, in general it is true that

$$w\big(Q_t, v(Q_t|\check{\mu}_t)|\check{\mu}_t\big) > w\big(Q_t, u_t|\mu_0\big), \tag{7.30}$$

which expresses a continuation Ramsey planner's incentive to deviate from a time 0 Ramsey plan by resetting u_t according to (7.20) and adjusting the Lagrange multiplier on the continuation appropriately to account for tax revenues already collected.[7] Inequality (7.30) expresses the time-inconsistency of a Ramsey plan.

To bring out the time inconsistency of the Ramsey plan, in Figure 7.2 we compare the time t values of τ_{t+1} under the original Ramsey plan with the value $\check{\tau}_{t+1}$ associated with a new Ramsey plan begun at time t with initial conditions (Q_t, G_t) generated by following the *original* Ramsey plan, where $G_t = \beta^{-t}(G_0 - \sum_{s=1}^{t} \beta^s \tau_s Q_s)$. Associated with the new Ramsey plan at t is a value μ_t of the Lagrange multiplier on the continuation government budget constraint. In Figure 7.3, we compare the time t outcome for u_t under the original Ramsey plan with the time t value of this new Ramsey problem starting from (Q_t, G_t). To

[6] The continuation revenues G_t are the time t present value of revenues that must be raised to satisfy the original time 0 government intertemporal budget constraint, taking into account the revenues already raised from $s = 1, \ldots, t$ under the original Ramsey plan.

[7] For example, let the Ramsey plan yield time 1 revenues $Q_1\tau_1$. Then at time 1, a continuation Ramsey planner would want to raise continuation revenues, expressed in units of time 1 goods, of $\tilde{G}_1 \equiv \frac{G-\beta Q_1 \tau_1}{\beta}$. To finance the remainder revenues, the continuation Ramsey planner would find a continuation Lagrange multiplier μ by applying the three-step procedure from the previous section to revenue requirements $\tilde{G}_1$.

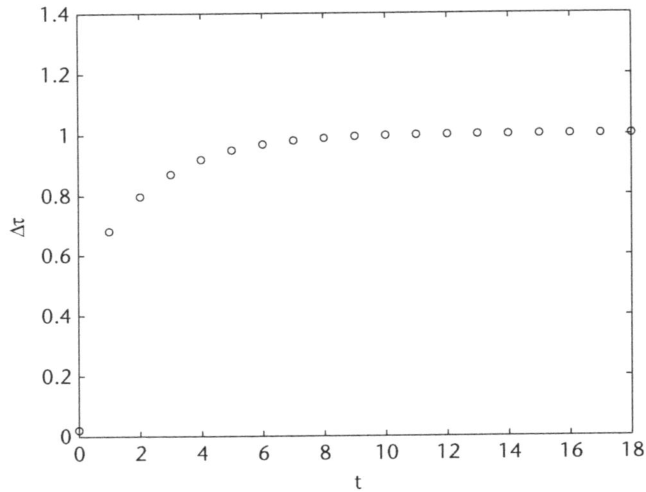

Figure 7.2 Difference $\check{\tau}_{t+1} - \tau_{t+1}$ where τ_{t+1} is along Ramsey plan and $\check{\tau}_{t+1}$ is for Ramsey plan restarted at t when Lagrange multiplier is frozen at μ_0.

compute u_t under the new Ramsey plan, we use the following version of formula (7.16):

$$\check{u}_t = -P_{22}^{-1}(\mu_t)P_{21}(\mu_t)z_t, \tag{7.31}$$

for z_t evaluated along the Ramsey outcome path, where we have included μ_t to emphasize the dependence of P on the Lagrange multiplier μ_0.[8] To compute u_t along the Ramsey path, we just iterate the recursion (7.17) starting from the initial Q_0 with u_0 being given by formula (7.16). Figure 7.2 plots the associated $\check{\tau}_{t+1} - \tau_{t+1}$. Figure 7.3, which plots $\check{u}_t - u_t$, indicates how far the reinitiated $\check{u}_t$ value departs from the time t outcome along the Ramsey plan. Note that the restarted plan raises the time $t+1$ tax and consequently lowers the time t value of u_t. Figure 7.4 plots the value of μ_t associated with the Ramsey plan that restarts at t with the required continued revenues G_t implied by the original Ramsey plan.

These figures help us understand the time inconsistency of the Ramsey plan. One feature to note is the large difference between $\check{\tau}_{t+1}$ and τ_{t+1} in Figure 7.2. If the government is able to reset to a new Ramsey plan at time t, it chooses a significantly higher tax rate than if it were

[8] It can be verified that this formula puts non-zero weight only on the components 1 and Q_t of z_t.

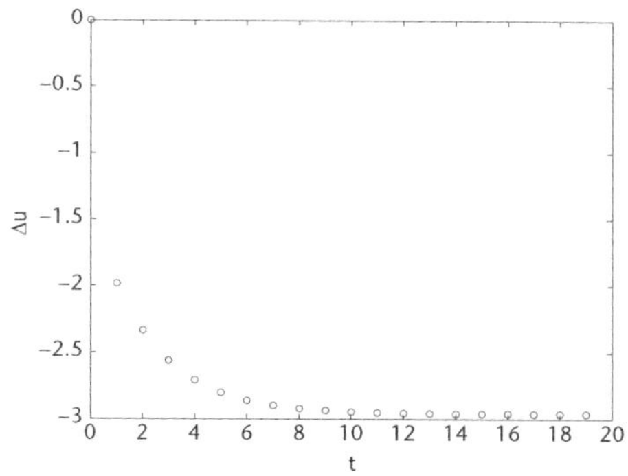

Figure 7.3 Difference $\check{u}_t - u_t$ where u_t is outcome along Ramsey plan and $\check{u}_t$ is for Ramsey plan restarted at t when Lagrange multiplier is frozen at μ_0.

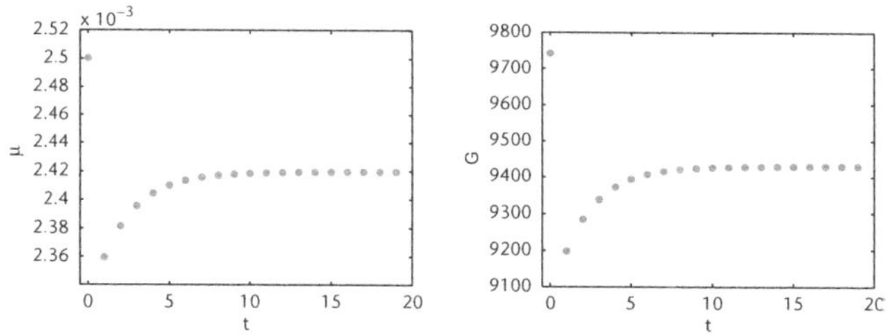

Figure 7.4 Value of Lagrange multiplier $\check{\mu}_t$ associated with Ramsey plan restarted at t (left), and the continuation G_t inherited from the original time 0 Ramsey plan G_t (right).

required to maintain the original Ramsey plan. The intuition here is that the government is required to finance a given present value of expenditures with distorting taxes τ. The quadratic adjustment costs prevent firms from reacting strongly to variations in the tax rate for next period, which tilts a time t Ramsey planner towards using time $t+1$ taxes. As was noted before, this is evident in Figure 7.1, where the government taxes the next period heavily and then falls back to a constant tax from then on. This can also been seen in Figure 7.4, where the government pays off a significant portion of the debt using the first period tax rate. The similarities between two graphs in Figure 7.4 reveals that there is a one-to-one mapping between G and μ. The Ramsey plan can then only be time consistent if G_t remains constant over time, which will not be true in general.

7.9 Credible policy

The theme of this section is conveyed in the following:

Remark 7.9.1 *We have seen that in general, a continuation of a Ramsey plan is not a Ramsey plan. This is sometimes summarized by saying that a Ramsey plan is not* credible. *A continuation of a credible plan is a credible plan.*

The literature on a credible public policy or credible plan introduced by Chari and Kehoe (1990) and Stokey (1989) describes history-dependent policies that arrange incentives so that public policies can be implemented by a *sequence* of government decision-makers. In this section, we sketch how recursive methods that Chang (1998) used to characterize credible policies would apply to our model.

A credibility problem arises because we assume that the timing of decisions differs from the Definition 7.3.1 Ramsey timing. Throughout this section, we now assume the following:

Definition 7.9.2 *Sequential timing protocol:*

1. *At each $t \geq 0$, given Q_t and expectations about a continuation tax policy $\{\tau_{s+1}\}_{s=t}^{\infty}$ and a continuation price sequence $\{p_{s+1}\}_{s=t}^{\infty}$, the representative firm chooses u_t.*
2. *At each t, given (Q_t, u_t), a government chooses τ_{t+1}.*

Item (2) captures that taxes are now set sequentially, the time $t+1$ tax being set after *the government has observed u_t.*

Of course, the representative firm sets u_t in light of its expectations of how the government will ultimately choose to set future taxes. A credible tax plan $\{\tau_{s+1}\}_{s=t}^{\infty}$ is one that is anticipated by the representative firm and also one that the government chooses to confirm.

We use the following recursion, closely related to but different from (7.28), to define the continuation value function for Ramsey planner:

$$J_t = A_0 Q_t - \frac{A_1}{2} Q_t^2 - \frac{d}{2} u_t^2 + \beta J_{t+1}(\tau_{t+1}, G_{t+1}). \tag{7.32}$$

This differs from (7.28) because continuation values are now allowed to depend explicitly on values of the choice τ_{t+1} and continuation government revenue to be raised G_{t+1} that need not be ones called for by the prevailing government policy. Thus, deviations from that policy are allowed, an alteration that recognizes that τ_t is chosen sequentially.

Express the government budget constraint as requiring that the $G = G_0$, where G_0 solves the difference equation

$$G_t = \beta \tau_{t+1} Q_{t+1} + \beta G_{t+1}, \tag{7.33}$$

subject to the terminal condition $\lim_{t \to +\infty} \beta^t G_t = 0$. Because the government is choosing sequentially, it is convenient to take G_t as a state variable at t and to regard the time t government as choosing τ_{t+1}, G_{t+1} subject to constraint (7.33).

To express the notion of a credible government plan concisely, we expand the strategy space by also adding J_t itself as a state variable and allow policies to take the following recursive forms.[9] Regard J_0 as a discounted present value promised to the Ramsey planner and take it as an initial condition. Then after choosing u_0 according to

$$u_0 = \upsilon(Q_0, G_0, J_0), \tag{7.34}$$

choose subsequent taxes, outputs, *and* continuation values according to recursions that can be represented as

$$\hat{\tau}_{t+1} = \tau(Q_t, u_t, G_t, J_t) \tag{7.35}$$

$$u_{t+1} = \xi(Q_t, u_t, G_t, J_t, \tau_{t+1}) \tag{7.36}$$

$$G_{t+1} = \beta^{-1} G_t - \tau_{t+1} Q_{t+1} \tag{7.37}$$

$$J_{t+1}(\tau_{t+1}, G_{t+1}) = \nu(Q_t, u_t, G_{t+1}, J_t, \tau_{t+1}). \tag{7.38}$$

Here $\hat{\tau}_{t+1}$ is the time $t+1$ government action called for by the plan, while τ_{t+1} is possibly some one-time deviation that the time $t+1$ government contemplates and G_{t+1} is the associated continuation tax collections. The plan is said to be *credible* if, for each t and each state (Q_t, u_t, G_t, J_t), the plan satisfies the incentive constraint

$$\begin{aligned} J_t &= A_0 Q_t - \frac{A_1}{2} Q_t^2 - \frac{d}{2} u_t^2 + \beta J_{t+1}(\hat{\tau}_{t+1}, \hat{G}_{t+1}) \\ &\geq A_0 Q_t - \frac{A_1}{2} Q_t^2 - \frac{d}{2} u_t^2 + \beta J_{t+1}(\tau_{t+1}, G_{t+1}) \end{aligned} \tag{7.39}$$

for all tax rates $\tau_{t+1} \in \mathbf{R}$ available to the government. Here $\hat{G}_{t+1} = \beta^{-1} G_t - \hat{\tau}_{t+1} Q_{t+1}$. Inequality (7.39) expresses that continuation values adjust to deviations in ways that discourage the government from deviating from the prescribed $\hat{\tau}_{t+1}$.

[9] This choice is the key to what Ljungqvist and Sargent (2004) call 'dynamic programming squared'.

Inequality (7.39) indicates that *two* continuation values J_{t+1} contribute to sustaining time t promised value J_t; $J_{t+1}(\hat{\tau}_{t+1}, \hat{G}_{t+1})$ is the continuation value when the government chooses to confirm e private sector's expectations, formed according to the decision rule (7.35);[10] $J_{t+1}(\tau_{t+1}, G_{t+1})$ tells the continuation consequences should the government disappoint the private sector's expectations. The internal structure of the plan deters deviations from it. That (7.39) maps *two* continuation values $J_{t+1}(\tau_{t+1}, G_{t+1})$ and $J_{t+1}(\hat{\tau}_{t+1}, \hat{G}_{t+1})$ into one promised value J_t reflects how a credible plan arranges a system of private sector expectations that induces the government to choose to confirm them. Chang (1998) builds on how inequality (7.39) maps two continuation values into one.

Remark 7.9.3 *Let* J *be the set of values associated with credible plans. Every value* $J \in$ J *can be attained by a credible plan that has a recursive representation of form* (7.35), (7.36), (7.37). *The set of values can be computed as the largest fixed point of an operator that maps sets of candidate values into sets of values. Given a value within this set, it is possible to construct a government strategy of the recursive form* (7.35), (7.36), (7.37) *that attains that value. In many cases, there is a* set *of values and associated credible plans. In those cases where the Ramsey outcome is credible, a multiplicity of credible plans* must *be a key part of the story because, as we have seen earlier, a continuation of a Ramsey plan is not a Ramsey plan. For it to be credible, a Ramsey outcome must be supported by a worse outcome associated with another plan, the prospect of reversion to which sustains the Ramsey outcome.*

7.10 Concluding remarks

The term 'optimal policy', which pervades an important applied monetary economics literature, means different things under different timing protocols. Under the 'static' Ramsey timing protocol (i.e., choose a sequence once-and-for-all), we obtain a unique plan. Here the phrase 'optimal policy' seems to fit well, since the Ramsey planner optimally reaps early benefits from influencing the private sector's beliefs about the government's later actions. But if we adopt the sequential timing protocol associated with credible public policies, 'optimal policy' is a more ambiguous description. There is a multiplicity of credible plans. True, the theory explains how it is optimal for the government to confirm the private sector's expectations about its actions along a

[10] Note the double role played by (7.35): as the decision rule for the government and as the private sector's rule for forecasting government actions.

credible plan but some credible plans have very bad outcomes. And these bad outcomes are central to the theory because it is the presence of bad credible plans that makes possible better ones by sustaining the low continuation values that appear in the second line of incentive constraint (7.39).

Recently, many have taken for granted that 'optimal policy' means 'follow the Ramsey plan'.[11] In pursuit of more attractive ways of describing a Ramsey plan when policy-making is in practice done sequentially, some writers have repackaged a Ramsey plan in the following way. Take a Ramsey *outcome*—a sequence of endogenous variables under a Ramsey plan—and reinterpret it (or perhaps only a subset of its variables) as a *target path* of relationships among outcome variables to be assigned to a sequence of policy-makers.[12] If appropriate (infinite dimensional) invertibility conditions are satisfied, it can happen that following the Ramsey plan is the *only* way to hit the target path.[13] The spirit of this work is to say, 'in a democracy we are obliged to live with the sequential timing protocol, so let's constrain policy makers' objectives in way that will force them to follow a Ramsey plan in spite of their benevolence'.[14] By this slight of hand, we acquire a theory of an optimal outcome target path.

This 'invertibility' argument leaves open two important loose ends: (1) implementation, and (2) time consistency. As for (1), repackaging a Ramsey plan (or the tail of a Ramsey plan) as a target outcome sequence does not confront the delicate issue of *how* that target path is to be implemented.[15] As for (2), it is an interesting question whether the 'invertibility' logic can repackage and conceal a Ramsey plan well enough to make policy-makers forget or ignore the benevolent intentions that give rise to the time inconsistency of a Ramsey plan in the first place. To attain such an optimal output path, policy-makers must forget their benevolent intentions because there will inevitably occur temptations to deviate from that target path, and the implied relationship among variables like inflation, output, and interest rates along it. The continuation of such an optimal target path is not an optimal target path.

[11] It is possible to read Woodford (2003) and Giannoni and Woodford (2010) as making some carefully qualified statements of this type. Some of the qualifications can be interpreted as advice 'eventually' to follow a tail of Ramsey plan.

[12] In our model, the Ramsey outcome would be a path $(\vec{p}, \vec{Q})$.

[13] See Giannoni and Woodford (2010).

[14] Sometimes the analysis is framed in terms of following the Ramsey plan only from some future date T onwards.

[15] See Bassetto (2005) and Atkeson et al. (2010).

References

Atkeson, A., V. V. Chari, and P. J. Kehoe (2010). 'Sophisticated Monetary Policies'. *Quarterly Journal of Economics*, 47–89.

Backus, D. and J. Driffill (1986). 'The Consistency of Optimal Policy in Stochastic Rational Expectations Models'. CEPR Discussion Papers 124.

Bassetto, M. (2005). 'Equilibrium and Government Commitment'. *Journal of Economic Theory*, 124(1), 79–105.

Chang, R. (1998). 'Credible Monetary Policy in an Infinite Horizon Model: Recursive Approaches'. *Journal of Economic Theory*, 81(2), 431–61.

Chari, V. V., and P. J. Kehoe (1990). 'Sustainable Plans'. *Journal of Political Economy*, 98(4), 783–802.

Giannoni, M. P., and M. Woodford (2010). 'Optimal Target Criteria for Stabilization Policy'. NBER Working Papers 15757, National Bureau of Economic Research.

Kydland, F. E., and E. C. Prescott (1980). 'Dynamic Optimal Taxation, Rational Expectations and Optimal Control'. *Journal of Economic Dynamics and Control*, 2(1), 79–91.

Ljungqvist, L., and T. J. Sargent (2004). *Recursive Macroeconomic Theory, Second Edition*. Cambridge, MA: MIT Press.

Miller, M., and M. Salmon (1985). 'Dynamic Games and the Time Inconsistency of Optimal Policy in Open Economies'. *Economic Journal*, 95(380a), 124–37.

Pearlman, J., D. Currie, and P. Levine (1986). Rational expectations models with partial information. *Economic Modelling*, 3(2), 90–105.

Stokey, N. L. (1989). 'Reputation and Time Consistency'. *American Economic Review*, 79(2), 134–9.

Woodford, M. (2003). *Interest and Prices: Foundations of a Theory of Monetary Policy*. Princeton, NJ: Princeton University Press.

8

Finite-Horizon Learning*

William Branch, George W. Evans, and Bruce McGough

8.1 Introduction

The rational expectations (RE) hypothesis of the 1970s places individual optimization and expectation formation at the forefront of macroeconomic research. Although RE is the natural benchmark for expectation formation, it is at the same time a very strong assumption, subject both to theoretical criticisms[1] and to plausible modifications that allow for a broader notion of bounded rationality.[2]

Today, dynamic stochastic general equilibrium (DSGE) models are the mainstay of macroeconomic modelling. To the extent that DSGE models embracing RE are unable to account adequately for the co-movements and time-series properties observed in the macroeconomic data, alternative mechanisms for expectation formation provide a plausible avenue for reconciliation; and, in the 30 years since the birth of the literature, adaptive learning has become rationality's benchmark replacement.[3] While this literature originally focused on the conditions under which an equilibrium would be stable when rational expectations are replaced with an adaptive learning rule, increasingly there has been an emphasis on transitional or persistent learning dynamics that have the potential for generating new phenomena.

In the early literature, adaptive learning was applied either to ad hoc models or to models with repeated, finite horizons such as the Muth model (Bray 1982, Bray and Savin 1986) and the overlapping gen-

* Financial support from National Science Foundation Grant SES-1025011 is gratefully acknowledged.

[1] See, for example, Guesnerie (2005).
[2] See Sargent (1993) for a survey of possible approaches.
[3] For a recent discussion see Evans and Honkapohja (2010).

erations model of money (Woodford 1990). However, micro-founded infinite-horizon DSGE models provide a distinct challenge. The first attempts at modelling adaptive learning in infinite-horizon DSGE models employed what we call 'reduced-form learning', in which RE are replaced in the equilibrium conditions with a boundedly rational expectations operator and the stability of the equilibrium is then studied (see, e.g., Evans and Honkapohja 2001 and Bullard and Mitra 2002).

While this was a natural first step in the study of equilibrium stability in a DSGE model, the ad hoc nature of reduced-form learning is disconnected from the underlying micro-foundations of modern macroeconomic models. To address this concern, and to better understand the link between agents' choices and their forecasts in the context of an infinite-horizon model, Honkapohja et al. (2002) and Evans and Honkapohja (2006) provide a model of bounded rationality, which they called 'Euler-equation learning', in which individual agents are assumed to make forecasts both of the relevant prices and of their own behaviour, and then make decisions based on these forecasts to satisfy their perceived Euler equation. The Euler equation itself is taken as a behavioural primitive, capturing individual decision-making. Evans and Honkapohja (2006) show, in a New Keynesian model, that Euler-equation learning is equivalent to reduced-form learning.

The literature has proposed other learning mechanisms as alternatives to Euler-equation learning. Infinite-horizon learning, developed in Marcet and Sargent (1989), and emphasized by Preston (2005), posits that agents make decisions to meet their Euler equations at all forward iterates and, where appropriate, also imposes their expected lifetime budget constraint.[4] Shadow price learning, developed in Evans and McGough (2010), assumes that agents make choices conditional on the perceived value of additional future state variables. These alternative learning mechanisms are discussed in more detail in Section 8.3.2.

Euler-equation learning identifies agents as two-period planners: they make decisions today based on their forecasts of tomorrow. Under rationality, this type of behaviour is optimal: forecasts of tomorrow contain all the information needed to make the best possible decision today. If agents are boundedly rational, however, it is less clear that a two-period planning horizon is optimal, or even adequate: perhaps a longer planning horizon is appropriate. The infinite-horizon approach takes this position to the extreme by positing an infinite planning horizon. By incorporating the lifetime budget constraint into the choice process, the agent is making decisions to satisfy his (perceived) Euler equation at

[4] See also Sargent (1993), 122–5.

all iterations and his transversality condition; in fact, infinite-horizon learning can be interpreted as assuming that private agents each period fully solve their dynamic programming problem, given their beliefs. While this has appeal in that it is consistent with the micro-foundations of the associated model, it has a number of drawbacks:

1. Agents are required to make forecasts at all horizons, even though most forecasters in fact have a finite horizon;
2. Agents are assumed to have sufficient sophistication to solve their infinite-horizon dynamic programming problem; and
3. Agents' behaviour is predicated upon the assumption that their beliefs are *correct*.

This last point, in particular, is a strong assumption.[5] In an adaptive learning model, agents' beliefs are updated by an estimation procedure—for example, recursive least squares—and therefore in any given period they will not correctly capture the joint distribution of the model's endogenous variables. If an agent knows his beliefs are wrong and likely to change in the future, that is, if an agent recognizes that his parameter estimates will evolve over time, it is no longer obvious that the agent's optimal decision is determined by the fully optimal solution to his dynamic programming problem *given his current beliefs*. While this point holds both for short- and long-horizon learning, it is most telling in the case of infinite-horizon learning, in which considerable weight is placed on distant forecasts, using a forecasting model that may become greatly revised. This reasoning suggests that agents may do best with finite-horizon models that look further ahead than one period but do not attempt to forecast beyond some suitable finite horizon.

This chapter generalizes the existing approaches to decision-making to environments in which agents form expectations adaptively. We bridge the gap between Euler-equation learning and infinite-horizon learning, by developing a theory of finite-horizon learning. We ground our analysis in a simple dynamic general equilibrium model, the Ramsey model, and our approach is to allow agents to make decisions based on a planning horizon of a given finite length N. Euler-equation learning is particularly easy to generalize: we iterate the Euler equation forward N periods and assume agents make consumption decisions today based on forecasts of consumption N periods in the future, and on forecasts of the evolution of interest rates during those N periods. We call this implementation of learning 'N-step Euler-equation learning'.

[5] The approach is typically justified by appealing to an anticipated utility framework. See Kreps (1998) and Cogley and Sargent (2008).

For reasons discussed below, N-step Euler-equation learning does not reduce to infinite-horizon learning in the limit as the horizon approaches infinity. In fact, a distinct learning mechanism is required to provide a finite-horizon analog to infinite-horizon learning. We accomplish this by incorporating the Euler equation, iterated forward n periods for $1 < n \leq N$, into the budget constraint, which itself is discounted and summed N times. Through this construction, decisions are conditional on savings yesterday, the future evolution of interest rates and wages, and on expected future savings. We call the resulting learning mechanism 'N-step optimal learning' because it leads to decisions which would be optimal given an N-period problem *conditional on expected future savings.*

We show that for both learning mechanisms and all horizon lengths, the Ramsey model's unique rational expectations equilibrium is stable under learning. There are, however, important differences along a transition path. By examining the expected paths of agents' beliefs, we find that both learning mechanisms impart oscillatory dynamics. However, for longer planning horizons, these oscillations become negligible.

8.2 The Ramsey model and reduced-form learning

The Ramsey model provides a simple, tractable laboratory for our exploration of finite-horizon learning (FHL). In this section, we review the model and analyse the stability of its unique rational expectations equilibrium under reduced-form learning.

8.2.1 *The Ramsey model*

We consider a standard version of the Ramsey model. There are many identical households with CRRA preferences who supply their unit endowment of labour inelastically and face a consumption/savings decision. The representative household's problem is given by

$$\max_{\{c_t,k_t\}_{t\geq 0}} \quad E\sum_{t\geq 0} \beta^t u(c_t)$$

$$\text{s.t.} \quad s_t = w_t + (1+r_t)s_{t-1} - c_t + \pi_t,$$

where s_{t-1} is the savings (in the form of capital) held by the household at the beginning of time t, c_t is the time t consumption level, r_t is the real return on savings, w_t is the real wage, and π_t is profit from the household's portfolio of firm shares. Here s_{-1} is given, and $s_t \geq 0$ and $0 \leq c_t \leq w_t + (1+r_t)s_{t-1}$ are additional constraints.

The associated Euler equation is given by

$$u'(c_t) = \beta E_t(1+r_{t+1})u'(c_{t+1}),$$

which we may linearize as

$$c_t = E_t c_{t+1} + aE_t r_{t+1} \tag{8.1}$$

where $a = -r\beta/\sigma$, and σ is the relative risk aversion. Also, all variables are now written in proportional deviation from steady-state form.

There are many identical firms, each having access to a Cobb–Douglas production function $F = k^{\alpha}n^{1-\alpha}$ in capital and labour.[6] Firms rent capital and hire labour in competitive factor markets, sell in a competitive goods market, and face no adjustment costs. This simple modelling of firm behaviour, together with the assumptions on the production function, implies that factor prices are equal to the associated marginal products and firms' profits are zero. Incorporating these implications into the flow budget constraint and using market clearing to identify s_t with k_{t+1} provides the capital accumulation equation. Imposing equilibrium interest rates into the household's Euler equation results in the following reduced-form system of expectational difference equations:

$$k_{t+1} = \delta_1 c_t + \delta_2 k_t \tag{8.2}$$

$$c_t = E_t c_{t+1} + bk_{t+1}. \tag{8.3}$$

The coefficients are $\delta_1 = -c/k$, $\delta_2 = (1 + F_k - \delta)$, and $b = akF_{kk}/r$, where variables without time subscripts are steady-state levels and all derivatives are evaluated at the steady state. Note that because capital is predetermined there is no expectations operator in front of k_{t+1}. The system (8.2), (8.3) is generically determinate (under the usual assumptions on utility and technology), and the unique REE may be written $c_t = \hat{A}k_t$ and $k_t = (\delta_1\hat{A} + \delta_2)k_{t-1}$.

8.2.2 *Reduced-form learning*

In order to form rational expectations, agents in the economy must know the actual distributions of all variables, which depend in part on their own behaviour and beliefs. Instead of adopting this framework,

[6] Typically there would be a stochastic productivity component in the production function. Without a loss of generality, the analysis in this chapter assumes a non-stochastic economy.

Evans and Honkapohja (2001) assume that agents behave as econometricians: given a forecasting model whose specification is consistent with the equilibrium of interest, agents form conditional expectations and update their perceived coefficients as new data become available. Specifically, throughout the remainder of the chapter, we attribute to agents a *perceived law of motion* for consumption:

$$c_t = H + Ak_t. \tag{8.4}$$

Since only the Euler equation depends explicitly on expectations, it seems reasonable to assume that agents know the coefficients for the capital accumulation equation (8.2) and the manner in which real interest rates are related to the capital stock. We could have agents estimate these coefficients, but since there is no feedback involved in this estimation, stability results would not be affected.

In the present case of reduced-form learning we will not be precise about the 'actions' taken given the forecasts and whether these are consistent with economic equilibrium. Therein lies the fundamental difference between RF learning and agent-based learning mechanisms.

We take as given the reduced-form equation

$$c_t = E_t^* c_{t+1} + bE_t^* k_{t+1}, \tag{8.5}$$

which has been modified to incorporate bounded rationality: E_t^* is taken to be a boundedly rational expectations operator based on the agents' forecast model. Conditional on the perceived law of motion (8.4), expectations are

$$E_t^* c_{t+1} = H + AE_t^* k_{t+1}.$$

It remains to identify agents' forecasts of the future capital stock, and we do so by assuming agents know the coefficients in the capital accumulation equation (8.2), δ_i, so that

$$E_t^* k_{t+1} = \delta_1 c_t + \delta_2 k_t.$$

Plugging in expectations into the reduced-form equation (8.5) leads to the following actual law of motion (ALM) for consumption:

$$c_t = \frac{H}{1-(A+b)\delta_1} + \frac{(A+b)\delta_2}{1-(A+b)\delta_1} k_t. \tag{8.6}$$

Much like when employing the method of undetermined coefficients, there is a mapping from the perceived coefficients in (8.4) to the actual coefficients in (8.6) that are implied by the PLM. Note, in particular, that the PLM for consumption consists of a constant and a coefficient on the current capital stock. In the actual law of motion, which depends on these beliefs, actual consumption depends on a constant and the current capital stock. Referring to the mapping from the PLM to the ALM as the 'T-map', it is immediate that the ALM identifies the T-map as

$$A \to \frac{(A+b)\delta_2}{1-(A+b)\delta_1}$$

$$H \to \frac{H}{1-(A+b)\delta_1}.$$

Note that the unique REE $(0, \hat{A})$ is a fixed point to the T-map. The T-map plays a prominent role in expectational stability analysis as we see next.

Expectational stability analysis asks whether reasonable learning rules based on PLMs like (8.4) will converge to a rational expectations equilibrium. It turns out that a straightforward and intuitive condition governs whether an equilibrium is E-stable. Let $\Theta = (H, A)'$ summarize the household's beliefs. Since the REE is a fixed point of the T-map it is also a resting point of the ordinary differential equation (ODE)

$$\dot{\Theta} = T(\Theta) - \Theta. \tag{8.7}$$

The right-hand side of the ODE is the difference between the actual coefficients and the perceived coefficients. According to the ODE, a reasonable learning rule should adjust perceived coefficients towards actual coefficients, with the resting point being an REE. The E-stability principle states that if an REE corresponds to a Lyapunov stable rest point of the E-stability differential equation then it is locally stable under least-squares learning. An REE will be E-stable when the T-map contracts to the unique REE. Thus stability under learning may be assessed by analysing the stability properties of (8.7). Below, we compute the T-map for each learning environment and assess the E-stability properties.

While the reduced-form learning mechanism is simple and appealing, it is vague on the interaction between forecasts and the implied agent behaviour. The argument for this mechanism is that agents form forecasts and then 'act accordingly', and that the implications of their actions are well captured by the reduced-form equation (8.5). This may be greeted with some suspicion because, while (8.5) is developed from the agent's Euler equation, it already has equilibrium prices imposed. More sophisticated DSGE models, such as RBC or New Keynesian models, have reduced-form equations that are considerably more complicated, thus making interpretation of reduced-form learning that much more difficult.

8.3 Euler-equation learning and alternatives

To place learning in DSGE models on a more firm footing, Evans and Honkapohja (2006) introduce Euler-equation learning. Evans and Honkapohja take the Euler equation (8.1) as the behavioural primitive, and take care to distinguish between individual quantities and aggregate variables. As it will serve as a platform to launch our investigations of finite-horizon learning, we review Euler-equation learning in detail; then we provide some discussion of other learning mechanisms.

8.3.1 *Euler-equation learning*

Under Euler-equation learning, the Euler equation is taken as the primitive equation capturing agent behaviour. Intuitively, agents make consumption decisions today to equate marginal loss with expected marginal benefit. For each agent i, there is an Euler equation,

$$c_t^i = E_t^i c_{t+1}^i + aE_t^i r_{t+1}, \tag{8.8}$$

where E^i is agent i's (possibly) boundedly rational expectations operator. We emphasize the behavioural assumption identifying Euler-equation learning as follows:

Euler-equation learning behavioural assumption. *The Euler-equation learning assumption identifying consumption behaviour in terms of future forecasts is given by (8.8).*

Agent i forms forecasts of r_{t+1} and c_{t+1}^i, and then uses these forecasts to determine demand for the current period's consumption goods. Since

$$r_t = \left(F_{kk}k/r\right) k_t \equiv Bk_t,$$

that is, since there is no feedback in the determination of the dependence of r on k, we assume agents know $r_t = Bk_t$, and thus forecast future interest rates by forecasting future aggregate capital. To forecast future consumption, we assume that agents adopt a perceived law of motion which conditions on current interest rates and current wealth. For simplicity, and to promote comparison to real time learning, we exploit the homogeneity of the model and assume agents recognize that past wealth has been equal to aggregate capital, and that they forecast future wealth accordingly. Together, these assumptions provide the forecasting model

$$c_t^i = H^i + A^i k_t.$$

As for reduced-form learning, we assume that agents know the values of δ_i. Therefore,

$$\begin{aligned} E_t^i r_{t+1} &= B\delta_1 c_t + B\delta_2 k_t \\ E_t^i c_{t+1}^i &= H^i + A^i(\delta_1 c_t + \delta_2 k_t). \end{aligned}$$

Given these forecasts, we may use (8.8) to identify agent i's consumption decision:

$$c_t^i = H^i + (A^i + aB)\delta_1 c_t + (A^i + aB)\delta_2 k_t.$$

Imposing homogeneity, so that $c^i = c$, $H^i = H$, and $A^i = A$, allows us to compute the equilibrium dynamics given beliefs:

$$c_t = \frac{H}{1-(A+aB)\delta_1} + \frac{(A+aB)\delta_2}{1-(A+aB)\delta_1} k_t.$$

These dynamics comprise the ALM for the economy and thus identify the Euler-equation learning model's T-map,

$$A \to \frac{(A+b)\delta_2}{1-(A+aB)\delta_1} \tag{8.9}$$

$$H \to \frac{H}{1-(A+aB)\delta_1}, \tag{8.10}$$

which may then be used to analyse stability under learning. Since $aB = b$, we note that Euler-equation learning provides the same T-map as reduced-form learning. In this way, Evans and Honkapohja are able to justify and provide a foundation for reduced-form learning.

8.3.2 *Other implementations of learning*

The coupling of agent level decision-making and boundedly rational forecasting has been considered by a variety of other authors, and in this section we discuss two alternate implementations of learning in infinite-horizon models: shadow price learning and infinite-horizon learning.

The infinite-horizon learning mechanism was first developed by Marcet and Sargent (1989) and has received renewed attention in

Preston (2005) and Eusepi and Preston (2011). Under infinite-horizon learning, agents make decisions so as to meet their Euler equations at all forward iterates and their expected lifetime budget constraint. Notably, this requires that agents account, a priori, for their transversality condition; in this way, agents are making optimal decisions given their beliefs, which are captured by their forecasting model. Preston has found that in some circumstances the stability conditions implied by infinite-horizon learning are different (and more restrictive) than the conditions implied by Euler-equation learning. A nice comparison of Euler-equation learning and infinite-horizon learning is provided by Evans et al. (2009). In the next section, we establish infinite-horizon learning as a limiting case of one of our finite-horizon learning implementations.

Evans and McGough (2010) take a different approach to coupling decision theory and learning agents: they model agents as two-period planners who choose controls today based on their perceived value of the state tomorrow. Evans and McGough call this simple behavioural procedure 'shadow price learning', and establish a general result showing that under shadow price learning, agents will eventually learn to make optimal decisions. They further show that, in certain circumstances, shadow price learning reduces to Euler-equation learning.

8.4 Stability under finite-horizon learning

By modelling the representative household as an Euler-equation learner, we impose that decisions be made based on one-period-ahead forecasts. This assumption is in sharp contrast to the benchmark behaviour of the rational agent and to the imposed behaviour in infinite-horizon learning: each is required to form forecasts at all horizons. Existing models involve only the two extreme cases—one-period horizon and infinite horizon—which are at odds with the casual observation that most forecasters have a finite forecasting horizon. This section presents our generalization of adaptive learning to environments with finite planning/forecasting horizons.

We construct two finite-horizon learning mechanisms: 'N-step Euler equation learning', which generalizes Euler-equation learning to an N-period planning horizon; and, 'N-step optimal learning', where agents solve an N-period optimization problem with boundedly rational forecasts. We note that N-step optimal learning has infinite-horizon learning as a limiting case.

8.4.1 *N-step Euler-equation learning*

We modify Euler-equation learning to allow for more far-sighted individuals by iterating (8.8) forward N periods:

$$c_t^i = E_t^i c_{t+N}^i + aE_t^i \sum_{s=1}^{N} r_{t+s}. \tag{8.11}$$

We interpret this equation as capturing individuals who are concerned about long run consumption levels and short run price fluctuations, and we call this learning mechanism 'N-step Euler-equation learning'.

N-step Euler-equation learning behavioural assumption. *The* N*-step Euler-equation learning assumption identifying consumption behaviour in terms of future forecasts is given by (8.11).*

To forecast, for example, k_{t+n+1}, agent i must forecast c_{t+n}—an issue we did not encounter when investigating Euler-equation learning. One option would be to provide agent i with a forecasting model for aggregate consumption. For simplicity and comparability, we make the alternative assumption that agent i thinks he is 'average' and so his best forecast of c_{t+n} is c_{t+n}^i.

It remains to specify how agents form forecasts of c_{t+n}^i. As above we provide agent i with a forecasting model that is linear in aggregate capital: $c_t^i = H^i + A^i k_t$. These assumptions yield the forecasts

$$\begin{aligned} E_t^i c_{t+n}^i &= H^i + A^i E_t^i k_{t+n} \\ E_t^i k_{t+n} &= \delta_1 E_t^i c_{t+n-1}^i + \delta_2 E_t^i k_{t+n-1} \\ &= H^i S_n(A^i) + (\delta_1 A^i + \delta_2)^{n-1}(\delta_1 c_t + \delta_2 k_t) \\ E_t^i r_{t+n} &= BE_t^i k_{t+n}, \end{aligned}$$

where

$$S_n(A^i) = \delta_1 \sum_{m=0}^{n-2} (\delta_1 A^i + \delta_2)^m.$$

These forecasts may be combined with the behavioural equation (8.11) to determine agent i's consumption decision: for appropriate functions $\hat{C}_j$ we have

$$c_t^i = \hat{C}_0(A^i)H^i + \hat{C}_1(A^i)c_t + \hat{C}_2(A^i)k_t. \tag{8.12}$$

Equation (8.12) determines the behaviour of agent i given our implementation of N-step learning. Note that agent i's behaviour depends on his beliefs and on aggregate realizations.

Imposing homogeneity provides the equilibrium dynamics dictated by (8.12). Let $\psi(A) = \delta_1 A + \delta_2$, and set

$$\gamma_1(A,N) = 1 + A\delta_1\left(\frac{1-\psi(A)^{N-1}}{1-\psi(A)}\right) + \frac{aB\delta_1}{1-\psi(A)}\left(N-1-\psi(A)\left(\frac{1-\psi(A)^{N-1}}{1-\psi(A)}\right)\right)$$

$$\gamma_2(A,N) = A\psi(A)^{N-1} + aB\left(\frac{1-\psi(A)^{N}}{1-\psi(A)}\right).$$

Then the T-map is given by

$$A \to \frac{\delta_2\gamma_2(A,N)}{1-\delta_1\gamma_2(A,N)} \tag{8.13}$$

$$H \to \frac{\gamma_1(A,N)H}{1-\delta_1\gamma_2(A,N)}. \tag{8.14}$$

This map may be used to assess stability under N-step Euler-equation learning.

8.4.2 N-*step optimal learning*

Under N-step Euler-equation learning, savings behaviour is passive in that it is determined by the budget constraint after the consumption decision is made; and because of this assumption, individual wealth enters into the agent's decision only if it influences the agent's forecasts of either future consumption or future interest rates. An alternative formulation of agent behaviour, which we call 'N-step optimal learning', takes wealth—both current and expected future values—as central by incorporating the budget constraint into consumption decisions.

To develop N-step optimal learning, set

$$R_t^n = \prod_{k=1}^{n}(1+r_{t+k})^{-1},$$

with $R_0^t = 1$. Iterate agent i's flow budget constraint forward N periods to get

$$\sum_{n=0}^{N} R_n^t c_{t+n}^i = \sum_{n=0}^{N} R_n^t w_{t+n} + (1 + r_t) s_{t-1}^i - R_N^t s_{t+N}^i. \tag{8.15}$$

Log-linearize (8.15) and assume agent *i* makes decisions so that it binds in expectation. Thus agent *i*'s behaviour must satisfy

$$c_t^i + c \sum_{n=1}^{N} \beta^n E_t^i c_{t+n}^i = \zeta_1 s_{t-1}^i + \zeta_2(N) E_t^i s_{t+N}^i$$
$$+ \sum_{n=0}^{N} \zeta_2(N, n) E_t^i r_{t+n} + w \sum_{n=0}^{N} \beta^n E_t^i w_{t+n},$$

for appropriate functions ζ_i.

We now use agent *i*'s Euler equation iterated forward appropriately to eliminate explicit dependence of consumption today on expected future consumption; this yields the behavioural equation[7]

$$c_t^i = \phi_1(N) s_{t-1}^i + \phi_2(N) E_t^i s_{t+N}^i$$
$$+ \sum_{n=1}^{N} \phi_3(N, n) E_t^i r_{t+n} + \phi_4(N) \sum_{n=1}^{N} \beta^n E_t^i w_{t+n}. \tag{8.16}$$

Here

$$\beta(N, n) = \frac{\beta^n}{1-\beta}\left(1 - \beta^{N-n+1}\right)$$
$$\phi_1(N) = \frac{s\beta^{-1}}{c\beta(N, 0)}$$
$$\phi_2(N) = -\frac{\beta^N s}{c\beta(N, 0)}$$
$$\phi_3(N) = \frac{1}{c\beta(N, 0)}\left(\left(cr\beta\left(1 - \frac{1}{\sigma}\right) - wr\beta\right)\beta(N, n) + rs\beta^{N+1}\right)$$
$$\phi_4(N) = \frac{w}{c\beta(N, 0)}.$$

N-step optimal learning behavioural assumption. *The N-step optimal learning assumption identifying consumption behaviour in terms of future forecasts and current savings is given by (8.16).*

[7] Because the production function has constant returns to scale, the explicit dependence of consumption on current real wage and real interest rates washes out.

To close the model, we must specify how these forecasts are formed. To remain consistent with, and comparable to N-step Euler-equation learning, we assume agent i forecasts his future savings as being equal to aggregate capital holdings: $E_t^i s_{t+N}^i = E_t^i k_{t+N+1}$; modelled this way, only a PLM for aggregate consumption is required. As above, assume agent i forecasts k_{t+n} using the known aggregate capital accumulation equation. This requires forecasts of aggregate consumption c_{t+n}. Because agent i is no longer forecasting individual consumption, we provide him with a forecasting model for aggregate consumption: $c_t = H^i + A^i k_t$. Finally, we assume agents know $w_t = \alpha k_t$.

Imposing homogeneity provides the equilibrium dynamics, which yields the T-map

$$A \to R(A,N)\left(\phi_1(N) + \delta_2\theta_N(A)\psi(A)^{N-1} + \delta_2 \sum_{n=1}^{N-1} \eta(N,n)\psi(A)^{n-1}\right) \tag{8.17}$$

$$H \to R(A,N)\left(\delta_1\phi_2(N) + \theta_N(A)S_N(A) + \sum_{n=1}^{N-1} \eta(N,n)S_n(A)\right), \tag{8.18}$$

where

$$\begin{aligned}
\eta(N,n) &= B\phi_3(N,n) + \alpha\phi_4(N)\beta^n \\
\theta_n(A) &= \phi_2(n)\psi(A) + \eta(N,N) \\
R(A,N) &= \left(1 - \delta_1\theta_N(A)\psi(A)^{N-1} - \delta_1 \sum_{n=1}^{N-1} \eta(N,n)\psi(A)^{n-1}\right)^{-1}.
\end{aligned}$$

This map may be used to assess stability under N-step optimal learning.

8.4.3 *Discussion*

Two observations concerning N-step Euler-equation learning are immediate. First, N-step Euler-equation learning is a generalization of the Euler-equation learning mechanism, as developed by Evans and Honkapohja: indeed, by setting the horizon $N = 1$, the behavioural assumption (8.11) reduces to (8.8) and the T-maps (8.13) and (8.14) reduce to (8.9) and (8.10), respectively. On the other hand, it is not possible to provide an interpretation of N-step Euler-equation learning at an infinite horizon. To see this, note that at the rational expectations equilibrium, captured by $\hat{A}$, the time path for capital is given by $k_{t+1} = \psi(\hat{A})k_t$, and must converge to the steady state; thus, $|\psi(\hat{A})| < 1$. Since $a > 0, B > 0$ and $\delta_1 < 0$, it follows that $\gamma_1(\hat{A}, N) \to -\infty$ as the planner horizon gets large. This does not overturn stability; however, it does prevent identifying an 'infinite-horizon' version of Euler-equation learning, and suggests that the planning horizon may strongly influence the path taken by beliefs—and hence the economy—along a path that converges to the rational expectations equilibrium.

N-step optimal learning is like N-step Euler-equation learning in that the behavioural primitive governing N-step optimal learning asserts that agents make decisions today based on forecasts of future prices, and on their own future behaviour—consumption in case of Euler-equation learning and savings in case of optimal learning; however, unlike N-step Euler-equation learning, N-step optimal learning conditions also on current savings. Second, as suggested by the nomenclature, under N-step optimal learning, the agent is behaving *optimally* conditional on current wealth *and conditional on expected future wealth*; that is, she is behaving as if she is solving an N-period problem with terminal wealth taken as given. Finally, it can be shown that provided beliefs imply $|\psi(A)| < 1$, the T-map given by (8.17)–(8.18) above converges to the T-map obtained under infinite-horizon learning: in this way, N-step optimal learning may be viewed as the finite-horizon version of infinite-horizon learning.

8.4.4 *Stability under finite-horizon learning*

To conduct stability analysis of the Ramsey model's unique REE under finite-horizon learning, we appeal to Evans and Honkapohja's E-stablity principle, and thus examine the Lyapunov stability of the systems of differential equations of the form (8.7), corresponding either to Eqs. (8.17) and (8.18) or to Eqs. (8.13) and (8.14). While there is nothing difficult in principle about this type of stability analysis—simply compute $DT - I$ and see whether the real parts of the eigenvalues are negative—the dependence of DT on the planning horizon and on the model's deep parameters is quite complicated, and prevents analytic results. Instead, we rely on numerical analysis, and we obtain the following result:

Result. *For all parameter constellations examined, for all planning horizons* N, *and for both learning mechanisms, the unique REE is E-stable.*

Our numerical result indicates that planning horizon and learning mechanisms are irrelevant asymptotically, but they are not pairwise equivalent. While this will be explored in more detail in the next section, we can get a taste for the potential differences here by plotting the derivatives of the T-maps evaluated at the REE. Note that both T-map systems decouple so that the derivatives with respect to A and H may be evaluated separately. For the numerical analysis presented here and throughout the chapter we use the standard calibration

$$\alpha = 1/3, \quad \beta = .99, \quad \delta = .025, \quad \sigma = 1.$$

Figure 8.1 plots DT_A and DT_H for both N-step Euler-equation learning and N-step optimal learning, for $N \in \{2, \ldots, 100\}$. The solid curves indicate the values of DT_A and the dashed curves indicate values of DT_H. E-stability requires that these eigenvalues have real parts less than 1. Note that while stability obtains for all values of N, the magnitude of the derivatives vary across both horizon length and implementation type. While the connection is not completely understood nor particularly precise, there are formal results and numerical evidence to suggest that small values of DT imply faster convergence. In this way, Figure 8.1 suggests that Euler-equation learning is faster than optimal

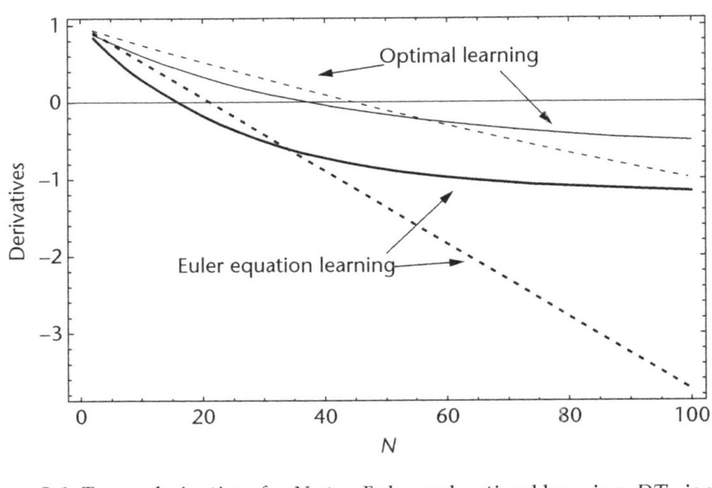

Figure 8.1 T-map derivatives for N-step Euler and optimal learning. DT_A is solid and DT_H is dashed.

learning, and longer horizons provide more rapid convergence to the REE.

8.5 Transition dynamics of finite-horizon learning

The behavioural assumption of N-step Euler-equation learning implies strong negative feedback for large N: this is evidenced by the failure of N-step Euler-equation learning to exist in the limit (as $N \to \infty$) and by the exploding behaviour of DT_H in Figure 8.1. Intuitively, an agent forecasting above average aggregate consumption for the next N periods (corresponding to the belief $H > 0$) will subsequently forecast low aggregate capital stocks and high real interest rates for these periods as well; high real interest rate forecasts raise the relative price of consumption today and the agent responds by lowering c_t^i. A long planning horizon exacerbates this effect.

The same thought experiment leads to a different intuition for N-step optimal learning. By incorporating the budget constraint into the optimal decision, our use of log utility washes the income/substitution effect of expected interest rate movements: this may be seen in the expression for $\phi_3(N)$. Interest rates still affect consumption through a wealth effect. Thus an expected decrease in future capital stock, leading to an increase in expected interest rates, reduces the present value of future wage earnings, and thus puts downward pressure on consumption. This effect is compounded by the decrease in expected future wage resulting from the expected decrease in future capital stock. However, both of these effects are mitigated by the expectation that future savings falls: a reduction in expected future savings leads to an increase in consumption today; while this may seem counter-intuitive, remember that the N-step optimal learner is, in effect, solving an N-period planning problem, taking expected future savings as given; a reduction in expected future savings relaxes the agent's constraint and so allows for increased consumption today.

While both learning implementations imply negative feedback for large N, the magnitude of the implied feedback is smaller for N-step optimal learning. Also, given a particular learning implementation—either N-step optimal learning or N-step Euler-equation learning—the feedback varies dramatically across planning horizon. These observations suggest that the transition dynamics—the time path of beliefs as convergence to the REE obtains—should vary across both planning horizon and learning implementation. To investigate these possibilities we analyse the different learning algorithms' 'mean dynamics'.

8.5.1 *Mean dynamics*

Let $\Theta = (H, A)'$ capture a representative agent's beliefs. The mean dynamics are given by

$$\dot{\Theta} = S^{-1}M(\Theta)(T(\Theta) - \Theta)$$
$$\dot{S} = M(\Theta) - S,$$

where S is the sample second moment matrix of the regressors $(1, k_t)$ and M is the corresponding population second moment matrix assuming fixed beliefs Θ. Intuitively, the mean dynamics provide an approximation to the expected time path of beliefs given that agents are using recursive least squares to estimate their forecasting model: for more details, see Evans and Honkapohja (2001).[8]

Figure 8.2 plots the time path for beliefs implied by the mean dynamics under N-step Euler-equation learning, and given the initial condition $A = 0.357$, $H = 0.99$.[9] The time paths for A are solid curves and those for H are dashed. The REE value for A is approximately 0.6. We note that the beliefs on capital, A, oscillates as it approaches its REE value; also, while convergence is indicated for all planning horizons, convergence is much faster for larger N.

In Figure 8.3, we plot the time path for beliefs implied by the mean dynamics under N-step optimal learning, and for the same initial conditions. As with N-step Euler-equation learning, a longer planning horizon results in faster convergence. Also, the oscillatory nature of the time paths under N-step optimal equation learning are quite similar to N-step Euler-equation learning; however, under N-step Euler-equation learning, these oscillations largely disappear, whereas they remain for optimal learners.

[8] Because our model is non-stochastic, the matrix M, which captures the asymptotic second moment of the regressors under fixed beliefs in the recursive least-squares updating algorithm, must be modified. We follow the ridge regression literature and perturb $M(\Theta)$ by adding εI. For the graphs in this chapter, $\varepsilon = 0.05$. The qualitative features of the analysis are not affected by small changes in ε.

[9] The matrix S must also be given an initial condition. In a stochastic model, the natural initial condition for this matrix is the regressor's covariance; however, since our model is non-stochastic, our initial condition is necessarily ad hoc. While the time paths do depend quantitatively on the initial condition chosen, we found that the qualitative results to be quite robust.

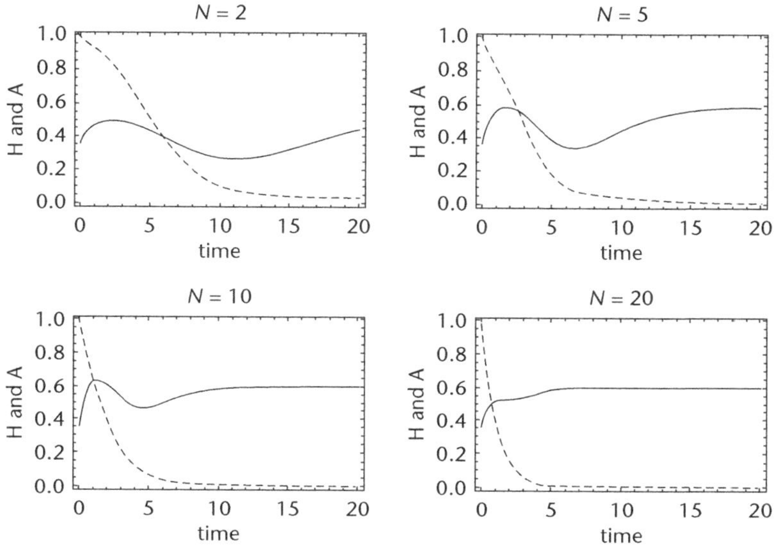

Figure 8.2 Time path for beliefs under Euler-equation learning. A is solid curve and H is dashed curve.

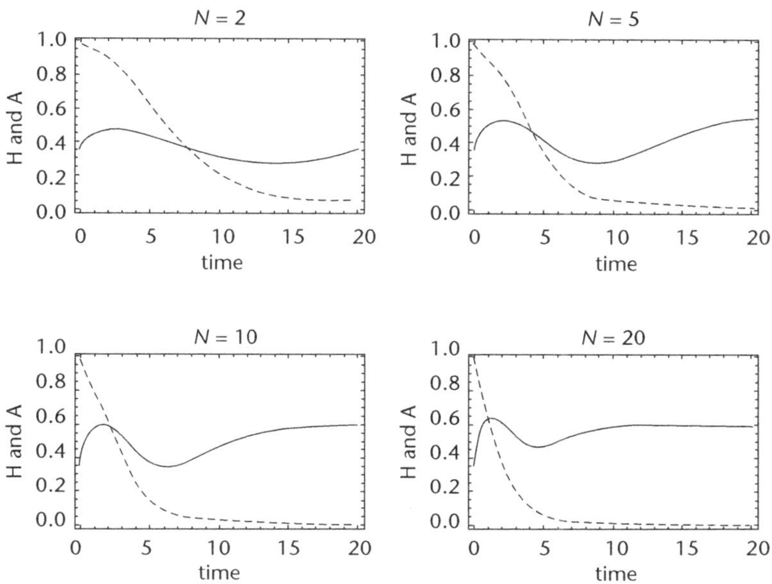

Figure 8.3 Time path for beliefs under optimal equation learning. A is solid curve and H is dashed curve.

8.5.2 *Phase plots*

The possibility of intriguing oscillatory dynamics is not evident from the T-maps or from the E-stability differential system; and, in fact, the oscillations are caused not by the T-maps themselves, but rather by the interaction of the beliefs with the covariance matrix S. To expose this dichotomy more effectively, consider Figure 8.4 where we plot, in phase space, the time path of beliefs under Euler-equation learning: see solid curves in the various panels. However, we plot this time path against the vector field capturing the E-stability differential equation (8.7). The vector field indicates that the REE is a sink; however, the mean dynamics impart a path for beliefs that, at times, moves away from the REE values, against the direction dictated by the E-stability vector field. The figure indicates the potential importance of using mean dynamics rather than the E-stability differential system to study transition paths.

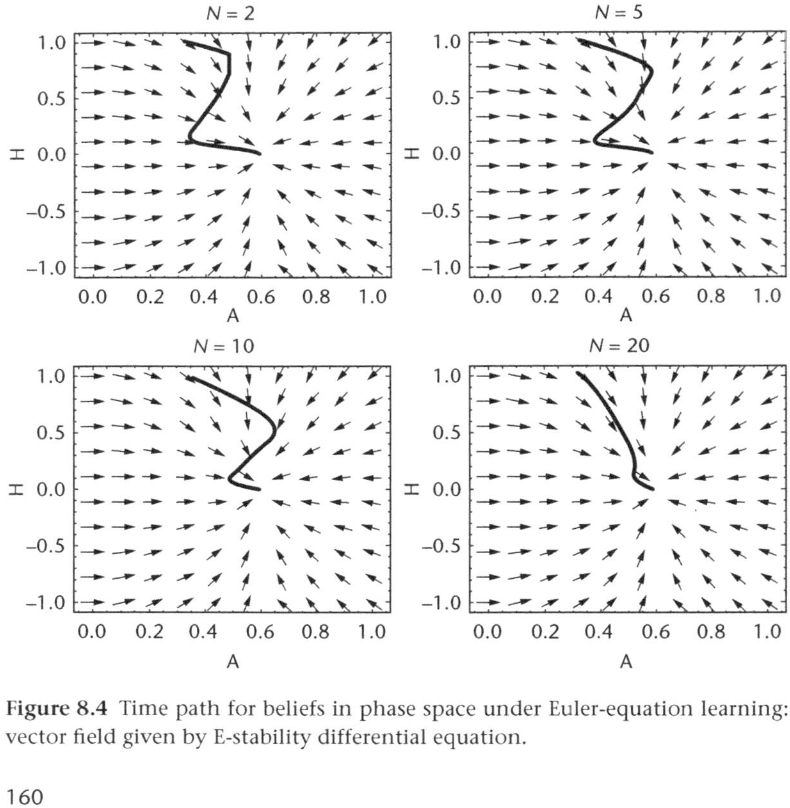

Figure 8.4 Time path for beliefs in phase space under Euler-equation learning: vector field given by E-stability differential equation.

8.5.3 *Discussion*

The mean dynamics capture the expected transition to the model's rational expectations equilibrium, and the evidence presented in Figures 8.2–8.4 above indicates that the transition depends on both planning horizon and learning mechanism: short horizon learning models indicate slower convergence and the potential for oscillations in beliefs; these oscillations persist under optimal learning as the planning horizon increases, but under Euler-equation learning, the strength of the feedback at long planning horizon dominates and washes out the oscillations.

The distinctive transitional behaviour indicated by planning horizon and learning mechanism suggests empirical implications. Coupling finite-horizon learning with constant-gain recursive updating, and then embedding these mechanisms in more realistic DSGE models—for example, real business cycle models or New-Keynesian models—may improve fit, better capture internal propagation, and allow for reduced reliance on exogenous shocks with unrealistic, or at least unmodelled, time-series properties.

8.6 Conclusion

To the extent that DSGE and finance models that embrace the rational expectations hypothesis are unable to account for co-movements in the data, alternative expectation formation mechanisms are clearly a natural focus; and, in the 30 years since birth of the literature, adaptive learning has become rationality's benchmark replacement. Originally, adaptive learning and the corresponding stability analysis was applied to either ad hoc models or models with repeated, finite horizons; however, micro-founded infinite-horizon DSGE models provided a distinct challenge. On the one hand, Euler-equation learning has been offered as a simple behavioural rule providing a boundedly rational justification for examining adaptive learning within one-step ahead reduced-form systems. On the other hand, the principal alternative proposal has been to assume that agents solve their infinite-horizon dynamic optimization problem each period, using current estimates of the forecasting model to form expectations infinitely far into the future. In contrast, introspection and common sense suggests that boundedly rational decision-making is usually based on a finite horizon, the length of which depends on many factors.

This chapter has explored a generalization of Euler-equation learning that extends the planning horizon to any finite number of periods. We have also formulated a new type of mechanism—optimal learning—designed explicitly to provide a finite-planning horizon analogue to infinite-horizon learning. The asymptotic stability implications of finite-horizon learning within the Ramsey model are simple to summarize: all roads lead to rationality. This is good news to those researchers hoping to justify the rational expectations hypothesis and to those researchers who have relied on Euler-equation learning, or reduced-form learning, to conduct their stability analysis.

Equally important to the stability analysis, though, are the results on transitional dynamics—results which, under constant-gain learning, would carry over to persistent learning dynamics. Our results indicate that agents' choices are strongly affected by planning horizon. If these results hold in more realistic models then researchers interested in embedding learning agents into fitted DSGE models should consider the planning horizon as a key parameter that needs to be estimated.

References

Bray, M. (1982). 'Learning, Estimation, and the Stability of Rational Expectations Equilibria', *Journal of Economic Theory*, 26, 318–39.

Bray, M., and N. Savin (1986). 'Rational Expectations Equilibria, Learning, and Model Specifcation', *Econometrica*, 54, 1129–60.

Bullard, J., and K. Mitra (2002). 'Learning About Monetary Policy Rules', *Journal of Monetary Economics*, 49, 1105–29.

Cogley, T., and T. J. Sargent (2008). 'Anticipated Utility and Rational Expectations as Approximations of Bayesian Decision Making', *International Economic Review*, 49, 185–221.

Eusepi, S., and B. Preston (2011). 'Expectations, Learning and Business Cycle Fluctuations', *American Economic Review*, 101, 2844–72.

Evans, G. W., and S. Honkapohja (2001). *Learning and Expectations in Macroeconomics*. Princeton, NJ: Princeton University Press.

—— and —— (2006). 'Monetary Policy, Expectations and Commitment', *Scandinavian Journal of Economics*, 108, 15–38.

—— and —— (2010). 'Learning as a Rational Foundation for Macroeconomics and Finance', mimeo.

——, ——, and K. Mitra (2009). 'Anticipated Fiscal Policy and Learning', *Journal of Monetary Economics*, 56, 930–53.

—— and B. McGough (2010). 'Learning to Optimize', mimeo.

Guesnerie, R. (2005). *Assessing Rational Expectations 2: Eductive Stability in Economics*. Cambridge, MA: MIT Press.

Honkapohja, S., K. Mitra, and G. W. Evans (2002). 'Notes on Agents. Behavioral Rules Under Adaptive Learning and Recent Studies of Monetary Policy', manuscript, www.valt.helsinki.fi/RAKA/seppo.hmtl, and http://darkwing.uoregon.edu/~gevans.

Jacobs, D., E. Kalai, and M. Kamien (eds) (1998). *Frontiers of Research in Economic Theory*. Cambridge: Cambridge University Press.

Kreps, D. M. (1998). 'Anticipated Utility and Dynamic Choice', in D. Jacobs, E. Kalai, and M. Kamien (eds), *Frontiers of Research in Economic Theory*. Cambridge: Cambridge University Press, pp. 242–74.

Marcet, A., and T. J. Sargent (1989). 'Convergence of Least-Squares Learning Mechanisms in Self-Referential Linear Stochastic Models', *Journal of Economic Theory*, 48, 337–68.

Preston, B. (2005). 'Learning about Monetary Policy Rules when Long-Horizon Expectations Matter', *International Journal of Central Banking*, 1, 81–126.

Sargent, T. J. (1993). *Bounded Rationality in Macroeconomics*. Oxford: Oxford University Press.

Woodford, M. (1990). 'Learning to Believe in Sunspots', *Econometrica*, 58, 277–307.

9

Regime Switching, Monetary Policy, and Multiple Equilibria*

Jess Benhabib

9.1 Introduction

In simple settings the conditions under which monetary policy can lead to indeterminacy are well understood: active Taylor rules generate determinacy and passive rules generate indeterminacy. When monetary policy is subject to regime switches, presumably because monetary policy must shift randomly with changes in some underlying economic conditions, like output growth or employment, the situation becomes more complex, especially if policy is active in some regimes and passive in others.[1] It is natural then to expect that some average over the regimes, possibly weighted by transition probabilities, would allow the characterization of determinacy versus indeterminacy, once indeterminacy is appropriately defined. The question has been studied by Davig and Leeper (2007) and then by Farmer et al. (2009a, b). We hope to further clarify the conditions for indeterminacy by characterizing the moments of the stationary distribution of inflation when monetary policy can switch across active and passive regimes according to a Markov process.

* I thank Florin Bilbiie, Troy Davig, Roger Farmer, and Eric Leeper for very useful comments and suggestions.

[1] We have in mind simple Taylor rules in simple settings where a policy is active if the central bank changes the nominal rate by more than the change in the inflation rate, and passive otherwise. One possibility is that output growth follows a Markov chain, and policy is active or passive depending on whether output growth is above a treshold.

9.2 A simple model

We start with the simplest possible model, and leave the extensions for later. The simplest model has flexible prices where π_t is the inflation rate, r_t is the real rate, and R_t is the nominal rate at time t. The Fisher equation is satisfied, that is

$$R_t = E(\pi_{t+1}) + r_t, \tag{9.1}$$

and the monetary authority sets the nominal rate according to the Taylor rule:

$$R_t = \tilde{R} + \phi_t (\pi_t - \tilde{\pi}). \tag{9.2}$$

We assume that $\{r_t\}_t$ is a bounded *i.i.d.* random variable with mean $\tilde{r}$, that $\{\phi_t\}_t$ is an irreducible, aperiodic, stationary Markov chain over state space $\Phi = (\bar{\phi}_1, \ldots \bar{\phi}_s)$ with transition matrix P and stationary distribution $\nu = (\nu_1, \ldots \nu_s)$, and that the target inflation rate is $\tilde{\pi} = \tilde{R} - \tilde{r}$. Then, substituting (9.2) into (9.1) and subtracting $\tilde{r}$ from both sides, we have

$$\begin{aligned}
\tilde{R} - \tilde{r} + \phi_t (\pi_t - \tilde{\pi}) &= E(\pi_{t+1}) + r_t - \tilde{r} \\
\phi_t (\pi_t - \tilde{\pi}) &= E(\pi_{t+1}) - \left(\left(\tilde{R} - \tilde{r}\right) - (r_t - \tilde{r})\right) \\
\phi_t (\pi_t - \tilde{\pi}) &= E(\pi_{t+1}) - (\tilde{\pi} - (r_t - \tilde{r})) \\
\phi_t (\pi_t - \tilde{\pi}) &= E(\pi_{t+1} - \tilde{\pi}) + (r_t - \tilde{r}).
\end{aligned}$$

If we set $q_t = \pi_t - \tilde{\pi}$, and we define $\varepsilon_t = r_t - \tilde{r}$ so that $E(\varepsilon_t) = 0$, we get

$$\phi_t q_t = E(q_{t+1}) + \varepsilon_t. \tag{9.3}$$

We can then explore additional solutions of (9.3) that satisfy

$$q_{t+1} = \phi_t q_t + \varepsilon_t. \tag{9.4}$$

By repeated substitution we obtain

$$q_{t+N} = \left(\prod_{l=0}^{N-1} \phi_{t+l}\right) q_t + \sum_{l=0}^{N-1} \varepsilon_{t+1} \prod_{m=l+1}^{N-1} \phi_{t+m}. \tag{9.5}$$

It is clear that if $\bar{\phi}_i > 1$ for $i = 1, \ldots s$, the only solution satisfying (9.3) that is bounded or that has finite moments is the minimum state variable solution (MSV) (see McCallum 1983),

$$q_t = \frac{\varepsilon_t}{\phi_t}. \tag{9.6}$$

When $\bar{\phi}_s < 1$ for one or more values of s, indeterminacy can become an issue and solutions of (9.3) other than (9.6) may emerge. For any initial q_0 and bounded *i.i.d.* sunspot process $\{\gamma_t\}_t$ with $E_t(\gamma_{t+1}) = 0$ for all t, there may be other ergodic solutions of (9.3) satisfying

$$q_{t+1} = \phi_t q_t - \varepsilon_t + \gamma_{t+1} \tag{9.7}$$

that are bounded or have finite moments. It may therefore be useful to consider what the set of admissible solutions to (9.3) are.

Typically, transversality conditions associated with underlying optimization problems are given in terms of the expected discounted value of assets in the limit as time goes to infinity. If, for example, the supply of nominal bonds or nominal balances are fixed, fast unbounded deflations may generate real asset levels that go to infinity, violating transversality conditions. Fast unbounded inflations that drive the real value of money to 0 may also be inefficient or infeasible if money is essential for the functioning of the economy, so it is indeed reasonable from the perspective of optimizing agents to impose conditions assuring that at least the mean of the stationary distribution of $\{q_t\}_t$ exists. Other more stringent criteria may only require the existence of second or even higher moments.

9.3 Indeterminacy

If ϕ_t were fixed, it is well known that a standard condition for indeterminacy, or a multiplicity of bounded solutions that would satisfy underlying transversality conditions of the agents, is $\phi < 1$. When ϕ is stochastic, or is a Markov chain, we may surmise that a condition for indeterminacy, admitting solutions to (9.3) other than (9.6), is given by $E(\phi) < 1$, where the expectation is taken with respect to the stationary distribution of ϕ. This, however, is not necessary: we will show that even when $E(\phi) < 1$, that is when the Taylor rule is passive on average, solutions of (9.3) other than the (9.6) will exist but may not have first, second, or higher moments, so that transversality conditions for the agents may fail. Therefore determinacy or uniqueness may be assured even if the Taylor rule is passive on average.

Let us first start with the existence of stationary solutions of (9.7). Since $\{\varepsilon_t\}_t$ and $\{\gamma_t\}_t$ zero mean *i.i.d.* processes, and $\{\phi\}_t$ has a stationary distribution, we can immediately apply a theorem of Brandt (1986). Recall that ν is the stationary probability induced by the transition matrix P. Brandt (1986) shows that if the condition $\nu \ln|\Phi'| < 0$ holds, that is if the expected value of $\ln\ |\phi|$ taken with respect to the stationary probabilities induced by the transition matrix P is negative, then (9.7) has a unique ergodic stationary distribution. Thus we see that the existence of stationary solutions requires not that $|\bar{\phi}_i| < 1$ for every i, but that the average over $\ln|\Phi'|$, computed using stationary probabilities for the Taylor coefficient ϕ, is negative. Clearly, the condition $\nu \ln|\Phi'| < 0$ cannot be satisfied if $|\bar{\phi}_i| > 1$ for all i. (See footnote 4.)

But this is not much help since a stationary distribution need not have finite moments, let alone be bounded. In fact it is precisely the finiteness of moments that will be the focus next. For this we invoke a recent Theorem of Saporta (2005).[2] Let Q be the diagonal matrix with diagonal entries $\bar{\phi}_i$.

Theorem 9.1 *(Saporta 2005, Thm 2) Let*

$$q_{t+1} = \phi_t q_t - \varepsilon_t + \gamma_{t+1}.$$

Assume: (i) $\nu \ln|\Phi'| < 0$,[3] *and (ii) $\ln\phi_i$ $i = 1, \ldots s$ are not integral multiples of the same number.*[4] *Then for $x = \{-1, 1\}$, the tails of the stationary distribution of q_n, $Pr(q_n > q)$, are asymptotic to a power law*

$$Pr(xq_n > q) \sim L(x)\, q^{-\mu},$$

with $L(1) + L(-1) > 0$, where $\mu > 0$ satisfies

$$\lambda\left(Q^{\mu}P'\right) = 1$$

and where $\lambda\left(Q^{\mu}P'\right)$ is the dominant root of $Q^{\mu}P'$.

Remark 9.1 *The stationary distribution of $\{q_t\}_t$ is two-tailed because realizations of ε_t and γ_t as well as $\bar{\phi}_i$ may be positive or negative.*[5]

Remark 9.2 *Note that the i'th column sum of the matrix QP' gives the expected value of the Taylor coefficient conditional on starting at state i.*

Remark 9.3 *Most importantly, it follows from power law tails that if the solution of $\mu = \hat{\mu}$, then the stationary distribution has only moments $m < \hat{\mu}$.*

[2] In a very different context Benhabib et al. (2011) use similar techniques to study wealth distribution with stochastic returns to capital as well as stochastic earnings.

[3] Condition (i) may be viewed as a passive logarithmic Taylor rule in expectation. We will also use an expected passive Taylor rule in Assumption 9.1 and Proposition 9.1 but not in logarithms.

[4] Condition (ii) is a non-degeneracy condition often used to avoid lattice distributions in renewal theory, and that will hold generically.

[5] The distribution would only have a right tail if we had $-\varepsilon_t + \gamma_{t+1} > 0$, and $\bar{\phi}_i > 0$ for all i, that is we would have $L(-1) = 0$. See Saporta (2005), Thm 1.

The above result is still not sharp enough because it does not sufficiently restrict the range of μ. Suppose, for example, on grounds of microfoundations, we wanted to make sure that $\hat{\mu} > m$ for some m. To assure that the first moment of the stationary distribution of $\{q_t\}_t$ exists, we would want $\hat{\mu} > 1$, or if we wanted the variance to exist (mean square stability) we would want $\hat{\mu} > 2$. The assumptions to guarantee this, however, are easy to obtain and trivial to check, given the transition matrix P and the state space Φ.

Define $\Phi^m = \left((\phi_1)^m, \ldots (\phi_1)^m\right)$ for some positive integer m that we choose.

Assumption 9.1 *(a) Let the column sums of $Q^m P'$ be less than unity, that is $P\left(\Phi^m\right)' < \mathbf{1}$, where $\mathbf{1}$ is a vector with elements equal to 1, (b) let $P_{ii} > 0$ for all i, and (c) assume that there exists some i for which $\bar{\phi}_i > 1$.*

Remark 9.4 *In Assumption 9.1, (a) implies, for $m = 1$, that the expected value of the Taylor coefficient ϕ_t conditional on any realization of ϕ_{t-1}, is less than 1, that is that the policy is passive in expectation, (b) implies that there is a positive probability that the Taylor coefficient does not change from one period to the next, and (c) implies that there exists a state in which the Taylor rule is active.*

We now turn to our result on the conditions for indeterminacy.

Proposition 9.1 *Let Assumption 9.1 hold. The stationary distribution of inflation exists and has moments of order m or lower.*

Proof. We have to show that there exists a solution $\hat{\mu} > m$ of $\lambda\left(Q^\mu P'\right) = \mathbf{1}$. Saporta shows that $\mu = 0$ is a solution for $\lambda\left(Q^\mu P'\right) = \mathbf{1}$, or equivalently for $\ln\left(\lambda\left(Q^\mu P'\right)\right) = 0$. This follows because $Q^0 = I$ and P is a stochastic matrix with a unit dominant root. Let $E \ln q$ denote the expected value of $\ln q$ evaluated at its stationary distribution. Saporta, under the assumption $E \ln q < 0$, shows that $\frac{d \ln \lambda(Q^\mu P')}{d\mu} < 0$ at $\mu = 0$, and that $\ln\left(\lambda\left(Q^\mu P'\right)\right)$ is a convex function of μ.[6] Therefore, if there exists another solution $\mu > 0$ for $\ln\left(\lambda\left(Q^\mu P'\right)\right) = 0$, it is positive and unique. To assure that $\hat{\mu} > m$ we replace the condition $E \ln q < 0$ with $P\left(\Phi^m\right)' < \mathbf{1}$. Since $Q^m P'$ is positive and irreducible, its dominant root is smaller than the maximum column sum. Therefore for $\mu = m$, $\lambda\left(Q^\mu P'\right) < 1$. Now note that if $P_{ii} > 0$ and $\overline{\phi}_i > 1$ for some i, the trace of $Q^\mu P'$ goes to infinity if $\mu\ \phi_t$ does (see also Saporta 2004, Proposition 2.7). But the trace is the sum of the roots so that the dominant root of

[6] This follows because $\lim_{n\to\infty} \frac{1}{n} \ln E\left(q_0 q_{-1} \ldots q_{n-1}\right)^\mu = \ln\left(\lambda\left(Q^\mu P'\right)\right)$ and the log-convexity of the moments of non-negative random variables (see Loeve 1977: 158).

$Q^{\mu}P'$, $\lambda\left(Q^{\mu}P'\right)$ goes to infinity with μ. It follows that the solution of $\ln\left(\lambda\left(Q^{\mu}P'\right)\right)=0$, $\hat{\mu}>m$. ∎

Remark 9.5 *It follows from Proposition 9.1 that if admissible solutions of (9.7) require the mean of the stationary distribution of q to exist, we can apply the assumptions of Proposition 9.1 with $m=1$; if we require both the mean and the variance to exist, we invoke the assumptions with $m=2$. Certainly if Assumption 9.1 holds for $m=1$, that is if the expectation that the Taylor rule ϕ_t is passive conditional on any ϕ_{t-1}, then the long run mean of $\{q_t\}$ exists and constitutes a stationary solution for (9.3) in addition to the MSV solution. This corresponds to indeterminacy.*

Remark 9.6 *If $P(\Phi)'>\mathbf{1}$, so that from every ϕ_{t-1} the expected value of $\phi_t>1$, then from the proof of Proposition 9.1 the stationary solutions to (9.7) for inflation other than the MSV will not have a first moment,[7] and would be inadmissible. It follows that if $P(\Phi)'>\mathbf{1}$, the only solution of (9.3) with a finite mean for $\{q_t\}$ is the MSV solution. This corresponds to determinacy.*

Remark 9.7 *However, it is possible that the overall expected value of the Taylor coefficient is passive at the stationary distribution, $E(\phi)<1$ instead of passive in expectation at any t from every state ϕ_{t-1}, that is $P\left(\Phi^{m}\right)'<\mathbf{1}$, but that $\hat{\mu}$ in Theorem 9.1 is still less than 1. In such a case even if the Taylor rule is passive on average, the stationary solution for (9.3) other than the MSV, as well as solutions converging to it, have infinite means, and can be discarded, so the MSV is the unique solution.*

The following corollary follows immediately since it implies that $\lambda\left(Q^{m}P'\right)>1$.

Corollary 9.1 *If $P\left(\Phi^{m}\right)'>\mathbf{1}$, then the stationary distribution of inflation, which exists if $\nu\ln|\Phi|<0$, has no moments of order m or higher.*

Remark 9.8 *If we have a Markov chain for ϕ_t and we want it to be i.i.d., then the rows of P must be identical: transition probabilities must be independent of the state. The dominant root $\lambda\left(Q^{\mu}P'\right)$ is simply the trace of $Q^{\mu}P'$ since the other roots are zero, and column sums $\Sigma_i\left(\bar{\phi}_i\right)^{\mu}P_{ji}$ are identical for any j.*

Remark 9.9 *Comparative statics for μ can be obtained easily since the dominant root is an increasing function of the elements of $Q^{\mu}P'$. Since $\lambda\left(Q^{\mu}P'\right)$ is a log-convex function of μ, the effect of mean preserving spreads on the random variable $\lim_{N\to\infty}\left(\prod_{n=0}^{N-1}(\phi_{-n})^{\mu}\right)^{\frac{1}{N}}$ can be studied through second-order dominance to show that they will decrease μ.*

[7] This is because if a positive μ exists it will have to be less than 1.

The results above are also consistent with Proposition 1 of Davig and Leeper (2007). First note that as long as there is a state for the Taylor coefficient, $\bar{\phi}_i > 1$ with $P_{ii} > 0$, and $\gamma_{t+1} - \varepsilon_t$ is *i.i.d.* with zero mean, then a stationary distribution of inflation that solves (9.7) will be unbounded even if $\gamma_{t+1} - \varepsilon_t$ has bounded support: there will always be a positive probability of a sufficiently long run of $\bar{\phi}_i > 1$ coupled with non-negative shocks, to reach any level of inflation. Therefore we may seek to obtain bounded solutions of (9.7) with $0 < \bar{\phi}_i < 1$, all i. In that case, the matrix given by Davig and Leeper (2007), $M = Q^{-1}P$ will have elements larger than those of P. But the dominant root of P, larger in modulus than other roots, is 1, and as is well known, an increasing function of its elements. So if M must have a root larger than 1, then the condition for determinacy given by Davig and Leeper (2007) fails. Conversely, if $\bar{\phi}_i > 1$ for all i, the dominant root, as well as other roots of $M = Q^{-1}P$, will be within the unit circle and satisfy the condition of Davig and Leeper (2007) for determinacy.

However, as shown by Farmer et al. (2009b) in an example with a two-state Markov chain, bounded sunspot solutions that satisy (9.3) may still exist. With regime switching we may allow the sunspot variable γ_{t+1} to be proportional to $\phi_t q_t$ for all transitions to the active regime, and thereby to dampen the realization of the multiplicative effect on the Taylor coefficient. This effectively transforms the system into one that behaves as if the policies were passive. The reason that this is compatible with a zero mean sunspot variable is that the dampening of the active policy can be offset by a value γ_{t+1} for all transitions to the passive regime, again proportional to the value of $\phi_t q_t$, to preserve the zero mean of γ. Therefore given transition probabilities, the random switching model makes it possible to maintain the zero mean of the sunspot variable, as long as we allow a correlation between the sunspot variable and the contemporaneous realization of the Taylor coefficient ϕ. Boundedness follows because this scheme effectively delivers a stochastic difference equation with random switching between Taylor coefficients that are below 1 in each regime. Even more generally, in a New Keynesian model, Farmer et al. (2009a) construct examples of bounded solutions without sunspots that depend not only on the fundamental shocks of the MSV solution, but also on additional autoregressive shocks driven by fundamental shocks. The coefficients of the autoregressive structure must depend on the transitions between the regimes as well as the transition probabilities in order to satisfy the analogue of (9.3). Markov switching across regimes allows the construction of such solutions. The autoregressive structure constructed in this manner, however, must also be non-explosive to allow bounded solutions. Farmer et al. (2009a) show that this can be accomplished if at least one of the regimes is passive, and would permit indeterminacy operating on its own. A key element of the construction is the dependence of the additional shocks on the transitions between states and transition probabilities.

9.4 Extensions

1. The results can be extended to the case where $\{\varepsilon_t\}_t$ is not *i.i.d.* We can define a Markov modulated process where we have a Markov chain on $\{\phi_t, \varepsilon_t, \gamma_{t+1}\}_t$ with the restriction that

$$\Pr\left(\phi_t, \varepsilon_t, \gamma_{t+1} | \phi_{t-1}, \varepsilon_{t-1}, \gamma_t\right) = \Pr\left(\phi_t, \varepsilon_t, \gamma_{t+1} | \phi_{t-1}\right).$$

   The idea is that a single Markov process, here for simplicity $\{\phi_t\}_t$, drives the distributions of ε_t and γ_t, so that the parameters of the distribution of ε_t and γ_t depend on ϕ_{t-1} but not on past realizations of ε and γ. (See Saporta 2005 in remarks following Theorem 2.) A pertinent example of such conditional independence is where the mean of interest rate deviations ε_t and the sunspot variable γ_t remain at 0 irrespective of the realizations of ϕ_{t-1}, but other parameters of their distribution may be affected by ϕ_{t-1}. With an additional technical assumption the results of the previous sections go through unchanged.[8] Furthermore, the finite state Markov chain assumptions can also be relaxed. (See Roitershtein 2007.)

2. We may also want to study higher order systems of the type $q_{t+1} = A_t q_t + b_t$, where A_t are random d-dimensional square matrices with $\Pr(A_t \geq 0) = 1$, $\Pr(A_t \text{ has a zero row}) = 0$, b_t is a d-dimensional random vector with $\Pr(b_1 = 0) < 1$, $\Pr(b_1 \geq 0) = 1$, and $\left\{A_n, b_n\right\}_n$ is a stationary *i.i.d.* Markov process. Such a structure arises for the sticky price new Keynesian models with regime-switching policies in two dimensions (as in Davig and Leeper 2007, Farmer et al. 2009a), and may be studied using the results of Kesten (1973, Theorems A and B). (See also Saporta 2004, Sections 4 and 5 and Saporta et al. 2004b.) While the results concerning power

[8] The technical assumption is

$$\Pr\left(\phi_i q + \varepsilon_i + \gamma_{i+1} = q\right) < 1 \text{ for any } i \text{ and } q.$$

This prevents a degenerate stochastic process from getting stuck at a particular value of q.

tails in the one-dimensional case generalize at least for the case of *i.i.d.* transitions,[9] the technical conditions that must be verified, although similar to the one-dimensional case, are more complex. Define $|x| = \left(\sum_{i=1}^{d} (x_i)^2\right)^{\frac{1}{2}}$ and $||A|| = \max_{|x|=1} xA$, and assume $E\ln||A_1||\ln^+||A_1|| < \infty$, $E\ln|b_1| < \infty$, $E|b_1|^{\beta} < \infty$ for some $\beta > 0$ (where $x^+ = \max(0, x)$). We must first make sure that an easy-to-check technical conditon, which holds generically and is analogous to (ii) in Theorem 9.1, holds for the higher dimensions. If $\delta(A)$ is the dominant root of A, assume that the group generated by $\{\ln\delta(\pi) : \pi = A_1 \ldots A_n \text{ for some } n \text{ and } A_i \in \text{supp}(\nu) \text{ } for\ \pi > 0\}$ is dense in R. Now we turn to the analogue of condition (i), $\nu\ln\phi_t < 0$, in Theorem 9.1: in higher dimensions we assume $\alpha = \lim_{n\to\infty}\frac{1}{n}\ln||A_1 \ldots A_n|| < 0$. This condition may seem hard to check, but an easily verified sufficient condition for it is $E\ln||A_1|| < 0$. To assure that we have $\alpha < 0$, we may also use a stronger condition, that the expected value of the dominant root of $\left(A_1 \otimes^t A_1\right)$, that is $E\delta\left(A_1 \otimes^t A_1\right) < 1$, where $\otimes$ is the Kroenecker product. However, this condition is not only strong enough to guarantee that $\alpha < 0$, but also that both the first and second moments of the stationary distribution of $\{q_t\}_t$ exist, yielding the desirable 'mean square stability' results. (See Saporta 2004 Proposition 4.1, and its proof as well as Farmer et al. 2009c.) Let us stick with the weaker condition $\alpha < 0$, guaranteed by $E\ln||A_1|| < 0$, and, following Kesten (1973), let the expected value of the minimum row sum of A_1, raised to some σ, be larger than or equal to $d^{\frac{\sigma}{2}}$, where d is the dimension of A_1. This assures that there exists $0 < \mu \leq \sigma$ such that the power law and moment results in the one-dimensional case generalize.[10] The power law will apply to xq, with x as any normalized non-negative unit row vector of the same dimension as q: $\lim_{t\to\infty}\Pr\left(xq \geq t\right) = Ct^{-\mu}$, where C is a positive constant. Note for example that if $\sigma < 1$ the stationary distribution of inflation has no mean; if $\sigma < 2$, it has no variance. If σ is not finite, all moments of $\{q_t\}_t$ will exist. It

[9] For example, when the rows of the transition matrix are identical so transition probabilities are independent of the current state.

[10] For significant extensions and relaxation of the technical assumptions, see Saporta (2004), Theorems 10, 11, 13 in Section 4 and 5.1 in Section 5. In particular in Theorem 13 Saporta (2004) also reports a condition for replacing the minimum row sum condition of Kesten (1973): If we require the expected value of smallest root of $((A^TA)^{\frac{1}{2}})^{\sigma}$ to be ≥ 1 for some σ, this can replace the minimum row sum condition to assure, as in the one-dimensional case, the existence of a finite $\mu < \sigma$ that defines the power law tails for the stationary distribution of q, provided $||A_1||$, $||B_1||$ are finite, and the column sums of A_1 are positive. If there is no finite μ, all moments of the stationary distribution of q may exist.

follows, as in the one-dimensional case, that only the moments of order $m < \mu$ of the stationary distributions of the variables of the vector q_t, as well as xq_t, will exist.[11] Note of course that these multidimensional results will immediately apply to random coefficient $AR(q)$ models transformed into matrix format.

3. To simplify matters, with some additional assumptions we can introduce a Phillips curve in a simplified model while still remaining in one dimension. Let the simple Phillips curve be given by $q_t = kx_t$, where x_t is output and q_t is inflation, and let the IS curve be $x_t = -m\left[R_t - Eq_{t+1}\right] + E_t x_{t+1}$ where R_t is the nominal interest rate. Let the Taylor rule be given by $R_t = \phi_t q_t$. Then after substitutions the system can be written as

$$Eq_{t+1} = \left(\frac{\phi_t mk + 1}{mk + 1}\right) q_t = \chi_t q_t,$$

where $\chi_t = \chi > 1$ (< 1) if $\phi_t = \phi > 1$ (< 1). There is always a bounded solution given by $q_t = 0$ where inflation is always at its target steady state. However, if ϕ_t is generated by a Markov chain, there may also be sunspot solutions given by

$$q_{t+1} = \chi_t q_t + \gamma_{t+1},$$

where γ_{t+1} is a sunspot variable. This equation may then be analysed by the same methods used above.

References

Benhabib, J., A. Bisin, and S. Zhu (2011). 'The Distribution of Wealth and Fiscal Policy in Economies with Finitely Lived Agents', *Econometrica*, 79, 123–57.

Bougerol, P., and N. Picard (1992). 'Strict Stationarity of Generalized Autoregressive Processes', *Annals of Applied Probability*, 20, 1714–30.

Brandt, A. (1986). 'The Stochastic Equation $Y_{n+1} = A_n Y_n + B_n$ with Stationary Coefficients', *Advances in Applied Probability*, 18, 211–20.

Davig, T., and E. M. Leeper (2007). 'Generalizing the Taylor Principle', *American Economic Review*, 97(3), 607–35.

[11] We may also inquire as to whether $\alpha > 0$ rules out the existence of a stationary distribution for the solution of $q_{t+1} = A_t q_t + b_t$. Bougerol and Picard (1992) prove that this is indeed the case under the assumptions that (i) $\{A_s, b_s\}$ is independent of q_n for $n < s$, and (ii) that for $\{A_0, b_0\}$ if there is an invariant affine subspace $H \in \mathbf{R}^d$ such that $\{A_0 q + b_0 | q \in H\}$ is contained in H, then H is $\mathbf{R}^d$. Condition (ii), which the authors call irreducibility, eliminates, for example, cases where $b_t = 0$ for all t, so that $q_t = 0$ is a stationary solution for all t irrespective of $\{A_s\}_s$.

Farmer, R., D. F. Waggoner, and T. Zha (2009a). 'Generalizing the Taylor Principle: A Comment', *American Economic Review.*

——,——and——(2009b). 'Indeterminacy in a Forward Looking Regime Switching Model', *International Journal of Economic Theory*, 5.

——,——and——(2009b). 'Understanding Markov-Switching Rational Expectations Models', NBER Working Paper 1470.

Kesten, H. (1973). 'Random Difference Equations and Renewal Theory for Products of Random Matrices', *Acta Mathematica*, 131, 207–48.

Loeve, M. (1977). *Probability Theory I*, 4th edn. Berlin: Springer-Verlag.

McCallum, B. T. (1983). 'On Non-Uniqueness in Rational Expectations Models: An Attempt at Perspective', *Journal of Monetary Economics*, 11, 139–68.

Roitershtein, A. (2007). 'One-Dimensional Linear Recursions with Markov-Dependent Coefficients', *Annals of Applied Probability*, 17(2), 572–608.

Saporta, B. (2004). 'Étude de la Solution Stationnaire de l'Équation $Y_{n+1} = a_{r_n} Y_n + b_n$, à Coefficients Aléatoires', thesis, available at <http://tel.archives-ouvertes.fr/docs/00/04/74/12/PDF/tel-00007666.pdf>

——(2005). 'Tail of the Stationary Solution of the Stochastic Equation $Y_{n+1} = a_{r_n} Y_n + b_n$ with Markovian coefficients', *Stochastic Processes and Application* 115(12), 1954–78.

——, Y. Guivarc'h, and E. Le Page (2004). 'On the Multidimensional Stochastic Equation $Y_{n+1} = A_n Y_n + B_n$', *C. R. Acad. Sci.* Paris, Ser. I 339 (2004), 499–502.

10

Too Many Dragons in the *Dragons' Den*

Martin Ellison and Chryssi Giannitsarou

10.1 Introduction

Dragons' Den is a reality television series in which entrepreneurs pitch their business ideas to a panel of venture capitalists in the hope of securing investment finance. The entrepreneurs are typically product designers or service providers, who need finance for what they believe is a viable business proposition. They present their idea to five rich entrepreneurs, the 'Dragons in the Den' from which the series takes its name. Before the programme begins, each entrepreneur decides on how much investment finance they need, with the rules requiring them to secure at least this level of financing from the dragons—otherwise, they receive nothing. In return for investing, the dragons negotiate an equity stake in the entrepreneur's company.[1]

The show is very popular and entertaining. Once the entrepreneur has made her presentation, the dragons ask a series of probing questions that often uncover an embarrassing lack of preparation by the entrepreneur or a series of fundamental flaws in the business proposition. Occasionally, the dragons are faced with an astute entrepreneur in possession of a sound business idea, in which case they line up to offer investment finance.

[1] *Dragons' Den* originated in Japan and was broadcast on Nippon Television from 2001 to 2004. It is syndicated in over 20 countries and was broadcast by MTV3 Finland as *Leijonan kita* in 2007. Interestingly, only one series has ever been broadcast in Finland, whereas in the UK the ninth series is currently on air. According to the European Commission Enterprise and Industry SBA Fact sheet 2010/11, small and medium-sized enterprises (SMEs) account for a smaller share of employment in Finland than the EU average. Could it be that both SMEs in Finland and *Leijonan kita* suffer from a lack of either good entrepreneurs or rich dragons?

Dragons' Den is billed as entertainment but offers plenty of food for thought for economists. Whilst only a few lucky entrepreneurs get to present their business idea in front of rich dragons on primetime television, similar presentations and negotiations are a regular feature in the lives of entrepreneurs and venture capitalists all over the world. Does watching *Dragons' Den* then provide us with new insights into how the economy works? In this chapter we contend that it does. In particular, when watching the programme we are regularly struck by how badly prepared many of the entrepreneurs are. It appears that business ideas are usually not properly thought through and the case for investing often unravels quickly once the dragons start asking questions.

Having a parade of hapless entrepreneurs on the programme is probably the conscious choice of a programme director intent on providing maximum entertainment to the television audience. It does though raise the question of how the dragons might give entrepreneurs sufficient incentives to prepare properly before presenting their business ideas. Allowing the dragons to ask probing questions usually reveals whether entrepreneurs are well prepared, but in an ideal world the dragons would presumably not waste precious time listening to badly prepared business proposals. Instead, they would prefer a system of investment financing that ensures all entrepreneurs make proper preparations before approaching the dragons.

In this chapter we explore the economics of *Dragons' Den*, by setting up a model in which an entrepreneur decides how detailed to make her preparation before pitching her business idea to a venture capitalist dragon. Students of economics will recognize our model as a principal–agent problem with possible shirking and costly state verification. If the dragon (the principal) wants to find out whether the entrepreneur (the agent) is well prepared then the dragon must spend time questioning the entrepreneur. We find that the preparation of the entrepreneur depends on both the generosity of the financing terms offered by the dragons and, crucially, on the number of dragons relative to entrepreneurs in the venture capital market. If too many dragons offer finance relative to the number of entrepreneurs who seek finance, then the incentives to make detailed preparations are weak, hence the title of our chapter suggesting that there can be too many dragons in the *Dragons' Den*.

We believe the insights from *Dragons' Den* extend beyond the world of venture capital to other situations in which a principal needs to encourage an agent to carefully prepare business propositions in advance of a meeting. An obvious example is investors wanting a financial adviser to undertake due diligence on any new investment opportunities they propose.[2] The incentives for financial advisers to do due diligence depend, as in the *Dragons' Den*, on the terms of the contract and the ratio of investors to investment opportunities. An excess of investors to investment opportunities leads to weak or no incentives to do due diligence. The lack of due diligence appears to have played a role in precipitating the financial crisis of 2007, with various contributors suggesting that incentives to do due diligence were weakened by a global lack of investment opportunities (too few entrepreneurs) and a global savings glut (too many dragons). The idea of the global savings glut weakening incentives for financial advisers to do due diligence is particularly pertinent for us. With the Chinese dragon economy widely regarded as the source of excess global savings, it could be that the financial crisis was in part caused by too many dragons in the *Dragons' Den*.

10.2 A model of the *Dragons' Den*

We assume there are more entrepreneurs than dragons in the economy, so an entrepreneur looking for investment finance will only meet a dragon with probability μ in any given period. If the entrepreneur is invited to meet a dragon then the entrepreneur must decide which of many possible business ideas she would like to present. Some of the entrepreneur's business ideas are assumed to be good projects that guarantee a normalized return of 1. The rest of the entrepreneur's business ideas are assumed to be bad projects that will never generate any return. Before deciding which idea to present, the entrepreneur has the option of doing due diligence on her projects at a fixed monetary cost of e. If the entrepreneur does due diligence then she will certainly find a good project to present to the dragon. If the entrepreneur avoids due diligence then she must randomly select a project to present, in which case a good project only gets presented with probability α. With probability $1 - \alpha$ the project is bad.

The dragon is assumed to subject the entrepreneur to probing questions with probability q. If this reveals that the entrepreneur has not done due diligence then negotiations are terminated and the entrepreneur returns empty-handed to the ranks of those looking for investment finance in the next period. If questioning shows that due diligence has been done, or the dragon does not ask probing questions,

[2] We suspect that Professor Seppo Honkapohja may, like us, have found that even Oxbridge dons managing multi-million pound endowment funds find it difficult to ensure that financial advisers always do due diligence.

then negotiations continue. They reach a successful conclusion with probability ψ. With probability $1 - \psi$ negotiations are unsuccessful due to exogenous factors beyond the control of either the entrepreneur or the dragon, in which case the entrepreneur once more returns to the ranks of those seeking investment finance in the next period. It is assumed that the dragons pay a monetary cost q each time they ask probing questions so the expected cost of questioning with probability q is q^2.

If negotiations ultimately succeed then the entrepreneur receives investment financing from the dragon. To simplify matters, we assume that the dragon takes an equity share i in the entrepreneur's company. If the entrepreneur's project turns out to be good, because the entrepreneur either did due diligence or was simply fortunate, then share i of the normalized project return accrues to the dragon and share $1 - i$ to the entrepreneur. If the entrepreneur did not do due diligence and was unlucky in choosing a bad project, then neither the dragon nor the entrepreneur receive anything and the entrepreneur is returned to the pool of those looking for investment finance next period. In our model, only successful entrepreneurs avoid a return to the ranks of entrepreneurs looking for finance in the next period. If by either design or luck the entrepreneur's project turns out to be good, then the entrepreneur and the dragon continue their relationship, albeit with the entrepreneur having to find a new project to present in the next period.

The timing of events in our model is shown in Figure 10.1. We assume that the dragon decides on the questioning probability q and the equity share $1 - i$ on offer before meeting with the entrepreneur. The entrepreneur decides whether to do due diligence once she has been invited to present a business idea to a dragon. The grey-shaded boxes show the return of the entrepreneur for each possible outcome.

10.3 The entrepreneur's problem

The entrepreneur has to decide whether to do due diligence on the business idea presented to the dragon. The choice faced is either to pay the fixed monetary cost e that guarantees a good project, or to hope for both a good project and that the dragon does not ask probing questions. The entrepreneur's decision will be influenced by the probability μ of meeting a dragon in any future period she might be looking for finance, the probability $1 - q$ that the dragon asks probing questions, the probability $1 - \psi$ that negotiations fail due to exogenous factors,

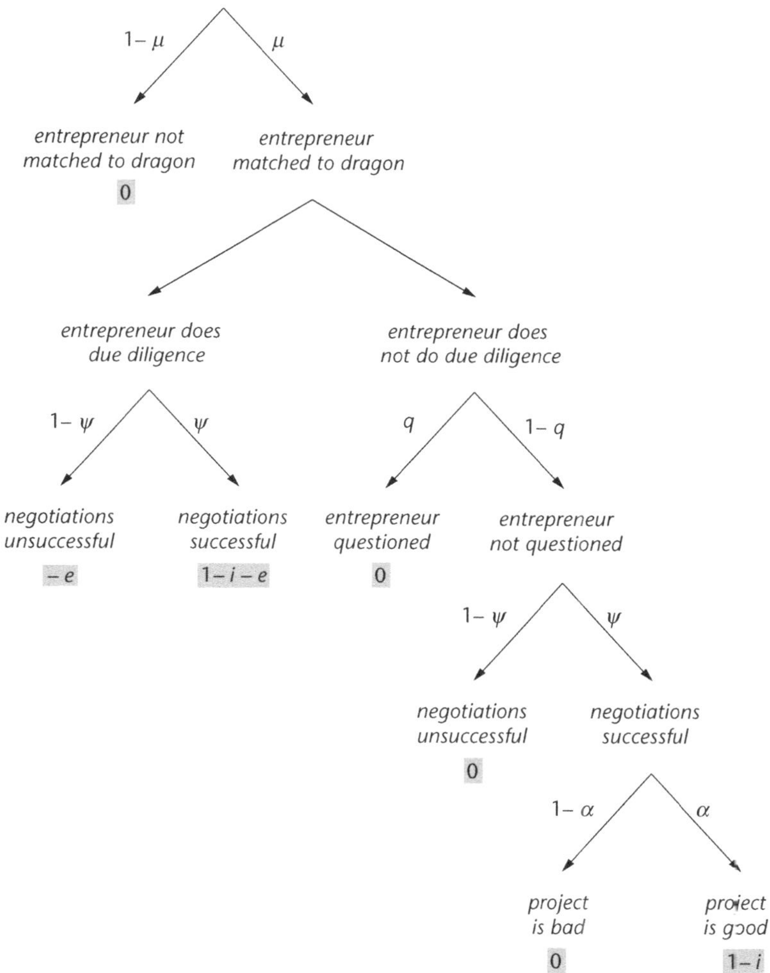

Figure 10.1 Outline of the model.

the probability α that a project is good if selected at random, and the equity share $1 - i$ offered to the entrepreneur should negotiations be ultimately successful.

We use simple finance theory to tell us whether an entrepreneur has an incentive to do due diligence. The idea is that entrepreneurs will only do due diligence if it gives them a higher expected discounted lifetime income stream. To see how this works, denote by V_E and V_N the expected discounted lifetime income streams of an entrepreneur who has just met a dragon and decides to do or not to do due diligence, respectively. We denote by V_U the expected discounted lifetime income stream of an entrepreneur who is looking for investment finance, but has not met a dragon in the current period. If the entrepreneur discounts future income at the rate r then the return to being an entrepreneur who has met a dragon and is doing due diligence rV_E has three components. Firstly, there is the entrepreneur's equity share $1 - i$ in successful projects that accrues with probability ψ. Secondly, there is the fixed cost e of due diligence which always must be paid. Thirdly, negotiations with the dragon fail due to external factors with probability $1 - \psi$, in which case the expected discounted lifetime income stream of the entrepreneur falls by $V_E - V_U$ from that of an entrepreneur who has just met a dragon and is doing due diligence to that of an entrepreneur looking for finance in the next period. The three components together imply

$$rV_E = \psi(1 - i) - e - (1 - \psi)\left(V_E - V_U\right). \tag{10.1}$$

The return rV_N to being an entrepreneur who has met a dragon but chooses not to do due diligence has only two components as there are no costs of due diligence. However, the entrepreneur's equity share $1 - i$ accrues with reduced probability $(1 - q)\psi\alpha$ as she only avoids the dragon's questioning with probability $1 - q$ and only selects a good project with probability α. There is correspondingly increased probability $1 - (1 - q)\alpha\psi$ that the entrepreneur will end up looking for finance in the next period, in which case the entrepreneur's expected discounted lifetime income stream falls by $V_N - V_U$. We have

$$rV_N = (1 - q)\alpha\psi\,(1 - i) - \left(1 - (1 - q)\alpha\psi\right)\left(V_N - V_U\right). \tag{10.2}$$

The final expression needed to solve the entrepreneur's problem is rV_U, the return to an entrepreneur who is looking for investment finance, but has not met a dragon. There are no due diligence costs or equity shares in this case but with probability μ the entrepreneur will meet a dragon, in which case her expected discounted lifetime income stream increases by either $V_E - V_U$ or $V_N - V_U$, depending on whether she plans to do due diligence,

$$rV_U = \mu\left(V_* - V_U\right), \text{ where } V_* = V_E \text{ or } V_N. \tag{10.3}$$

The entrepreneur has an incentive to do due diligence only if doing so increases the expected discounted value of her income stream, i.e., if $V_E \geq V_N$. Algebraic manipulation of this inequality and Eqs. (10.1)–(10.3) defines a **due diligence condition** (DDC), which determines the conditions under which the entrepreneur will choose to do due diligence:

$$1 - i \geq \frac{\mu + r + 1 - (1 - q)\alpha\psi}{\psi\,(\mu + r + 1)\,\big(1 - (1 - q)\alpha\big)}e. \tag{10.4}$$

The DDC has a natural interpretation in terms of the strength of the incentives an entrepreneur faces to do due diligence.[3] Simple calculations show that the dragon must increase the equity share $1 - i$ offered to the entrepreneur if the dragon wants the entrepreneur to continue doing due diligence after an increase in μ, r, α, or e, or after a decrease in either q or ψ. Increases in either μ or r weaken the incentives for due diligence, because they reduce the costs if the entrepreneur ends up looking for finance in the future. If μ increases, then future costs are reduced because the entrepreneur finds it easier to meet a dragon. If r increases, then future costs are discounted more heavily. An increase in α weakens incentives because the entrepreneur is more likely to randomly select a good project even if she does not do due diligence, whereas an increase in e has a direct effect through higher fixed monetary costs of doing due diligence. A decrease in q weakens incentives, because it implies a lower probability of the entrepreneur being questioned by the dragon. Finally, a decrease in ψ weakens incentives by increasing the role of external factors outside the control of the entrepreneur.

10.4 The dragon's problem

The dragon must decide an equity share $1 - i$ to offer to the entrepreneur and the probability q with which to ask probing questions. All choices of $1 - i \in [0, 1]$ and $q \in [0, 1]$ are feasible but only combinations that satisfy the due diligence condition will create the incentive for the entrepreneur to do due diligence on her business idea. If $1 - i$ and q are such that the DDC is *not* satisfied then the expected return to the dragon is

$$(1 - q)\alpha\psi i - q^2, \tag{10.5}$$

where $(1 - q)\alpha\psi$ is the probability that a project is ultimately successful and q^2 is the cost of questioning with probability q. The expected return is decreasing in $1 - i$ and q so it is optimal for the dragon to set $1 - i = 0$ and $q = 0$ if the dragon accepts that the entrepreneur is not

[3] The DDC also has a natural interpretation as the *Dragons' Den* condition.

doing due diligence. In other words, the dragon takes all the equity of the entrepreneur and does no questioning in an economy without due diligence. The dragon achieves an expected return of $\alpha\psi$ but is exposed to risks from bad projects and external factors.

The dragon can avoid the risk of financing bad projects by choosing a combination of $1 - i$ and q that satisfies the DDC, in which case the expected return to the dragon is

$$\psi i - q^2, \tag{10.6}$$

with ψ the probability that a project is ultimately successful and q^2 the cost of questioning with probability q. The expected return is again decreasing in $1 - i$ and q so the dragon sets $1 - i$ and q as low as possible whilst still respecting the DDC. In other words, the dragon offers the minimal equity share and minimal probability of questioning that incentivize the entrepreneur to do due diligence.

To see exactly which combination of $1 - i$ and q is optimal we plot the DDC in Figure 10.2. It is upward sloping because an increase in the probability of questioning q allows the dragon to increase her own equity share i without weakening the incentive for the entrepreneur to do due diligence. Combinations of q and i that lie on or below the DDC ensure there is due diligence in the economy.

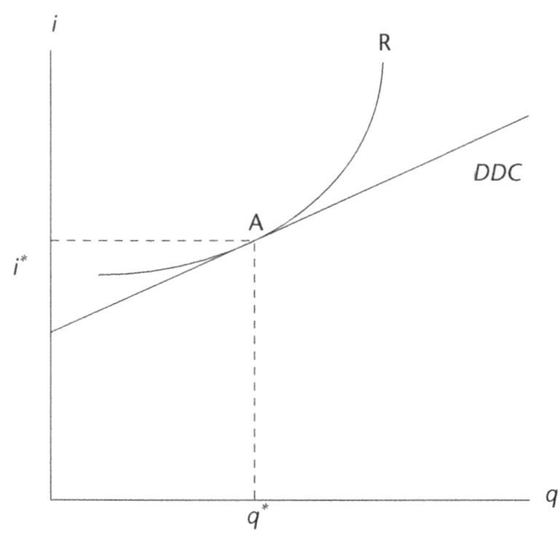

Figure 10.2 The optimal equity share i^* and probability of questioning q^* under due diligence.

To calculate the optimal combination of $1 - i$ and q we add indifference curves. From Eq. (10.6), the dragon is indifferent between combinations of $1 - i$ and q that give the same expected return $\psi i - q^2$. The dragon's indifference curves are therefore a family of quadratic functions $i = \psi^{-1}(R + q^2)$ indexed by an expected return R. The expected return to the dragon is increasing as (q, i) move north-westerly in Figure 10.2, so the optimum combination $1 - i^*$ and q^* occurs at A where the DDC is tangential to the highest possible indifference curve. At this point the dragon is only subject to risks from external factors.

Whether it is worth the dragon setting i^* and q^* to induce due diligence depends on the expected return $\psi i^* - q^{*2}$ with due diligence and the expected return $\alpha\psi$ without due diligence. The dragon chooses i^* and q^* to guarantee due diligence if

$$\psi i^* - q^{*2} \geq \alpha\psi. \tag{10.7}$$

The choice the dragon faces is between a safe but low return under due diligence and a high but risky return under no due diligence. To see which option dominates consider Figure 10.3, in which the left panel reproduces Figure 10.2 for the optimal choices of i^* and q^* under due diligence.

The right panel in Figure 10.3 uses Eq. (10.7) to delineate the region in which the optimal combination of i^* and q^* under due diligence gives an expected return that exceeds the expected return without due diligence. The way Figure 10.3 is drawn, when point A in the left panel is reproduced in the right panel, it lies in the shaded region where it is optimal for the dragon to choose i^* and q^* such that the DDC is satisfied

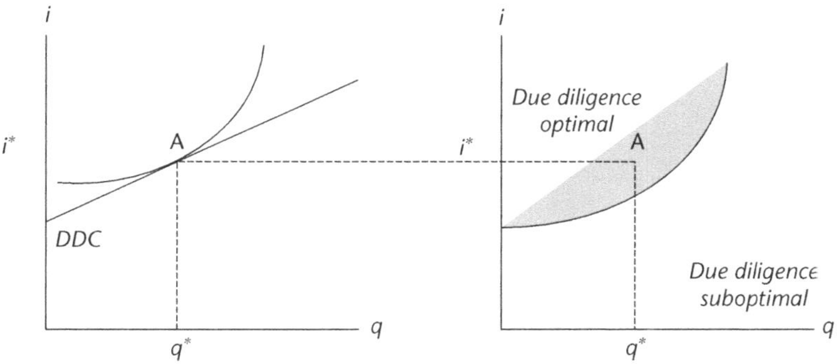

Figure 10.3 An example where it is optimal for the dragon to incentivize the entrepreneur to do due diligence.

and the entrepreneur does due diligence. In this case the expected return to the dragon under due diligence is sufficient to dominate the expected return without due diligence. However, there is no particular reason why point A could not lie in the unshaded region where it would be optimal for the dragon to give up on due diligence and set $i = 1$ and $q = 0$.

10.5 Too many dragons?

Suppose that more dragons enter the *Dragons' Den*. In this case there is an increase in the number of dragons relative to entrepreneurs, the venture capital market tightens, and an entrepreneur looking for finance is more likely to meet a dragon offering finance. The probability μ that an entrepreneur meets a dragon increases, which weakens the incentives for the entrepreneur to do due diligence and in Figure 10.4 moves the due diligence condition down from DDC_1 to DDC_2. If the dragon wants the entrepreneur to continue doing due diligence then the dragon must move to point A_2 by offering the entrepreneur an increased equity share and increasing the probability of questioning.

The impact of more dragons is potentially much more important than the incremental change from A_1 to A_2 in Figure 10.4 would suggest. This is because point A_2 in the right panel lies outside the shaded region and it is no longer optimal for the dragon to induce the entrepreneur to do due diligence. Instead, at point A_2 the dragon sets $1 - i = 0$ and $q = 0$ and accepts life as a venture capitalist in an economy without due diligence. The macroeconomic implications of this are

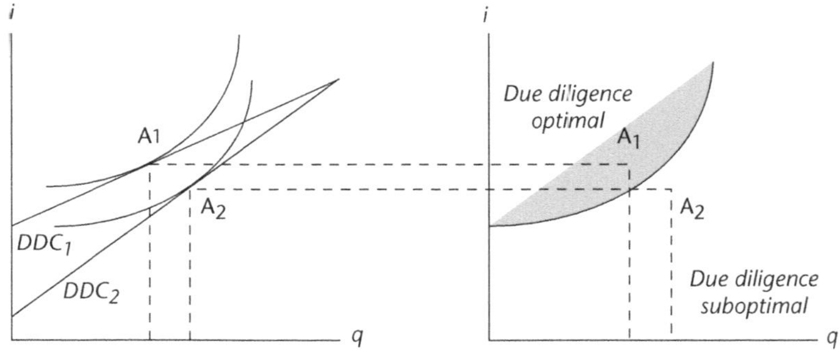

Figure 10.4 An example where too many dragons make due diligence suboptimal.

potentially serious as the economy is now characterized by increased risk, with returns to the dragon high and volatile, whereas previously they were low and safe. It is therefore unclear whether the entry of more dragons leads to an improvement in welfare. More dragons are beneficial in that more entrepreneurs receive investment financing, but there is more risk and the average quality of projects being funded is lower so it is difficult to draw firm conclusions. What is key is not the entry of dragons per se, but the way in which the entry of dragons strengthens the hand of entrepreneurs and weakens the incentives for entrepreneurs to do due diligence.

10.6 Concluding remark

The insights we obtain from the economics of *Dragons' Den* suggest that a global savings glut fuelled by new capital from Chinese dragons may be a double-edged sword. The resulting increase in credit supply is presumably beneficial since more entrepreneurs get financing, but too many dragons make it difficult for investors to ensure that their financial advisers are doing due diligence. The nature of this trade-off needs to be studied by those considering how to regulate financial markets in the wake of the crisis of 2007. As a first lesson, we recommend watching television and thinking about how many dragons to allow in the *Dragons' Den*.

11

The Impacts of Labour Taxation Reform under Domestic Heterogenous Labour Markets and Flexible Outsourcing

Erkki Koskela

11.1 Introduction

European welfare states are characterized by dual labour markets. Unskilled workers are typically unionized, while skilled workers often negotiate their wages individually, and thus face more competitive wage formation. Historically, European labour unions have been able to push for high wages for unskilled workers compared to other nations, at the cost of higher unemployment in Continental Europe than, for example, in the United States. Since the late twentieth century, globalization has put the European welfare model under increasing pressure. Wage differences across countries constitute a central explanation for the increasing dominant business practice of international outsourcing across a wide range of industries (see, e.g., Sinn 2007 for an overview and Stefanova 2006 concerning the East–West dichotomy of outsourcing).

Outsourcing can take two forms. Under strategic outsourcing, firms may write long-term contracts that fix the amount of outsourcing before the trade union sets the wage. Alternatively, firms may be flexible enough to be able to make outsourcing decisions simultaneously with employment decisions after observing domestic wages set by the trade union.

This chapter studies the effects of wage taxation under flexible international outsourcing when the domestic labour force is heterogeneous. Forces of imperfect competition enter the domestic labour market through a monopoly union which decides the wage for low-skilled workers. The wage formation of high-skilled workers, in contrast, is perfectly competitive, so that the wage adjusts to equalize supply and demand for labour. High-skilled workers optimize their labour supply by maximizing a CES-utility function of consumption and leisure. For simplicity, labour demand is determined by a representative competitive firm, which maximizes profits.[1]

We find, first, that under flexible outsourcing the competitive equilibrium wage for high-skilled labour depends negatively on the wage for low-skilled labour. In contrast, the effects of the wage tax and tax exemption on the wage for high-skilled labour depend on the elasticity of substitution between consumption and leisure of high-skilled workers. More specifically, the equilibrium wage depends (a) positively (negatively) on the wage tax and (b) negatively (positively) on tax exemption when the elasticity of substitution is higher (lower) than 1. Furthermore, the equilibrium wage for low-skilled workers increases as the wage for outsourced labour increases or as outsourcing costs rise. The reason for these effects is that the wage elasticity of the (demand for) low-skilled labour falls, thus increasing the union mark-up, which, in turn, reduces the wage for the high-skilled labour. A higher tax rate on the wage for low-skilled workers raises their wage and reduces the wage for high-skilled labour, while larger tax exemption for low-skilled workers reduces their wage and, hence, increases the wage for the high-skilled labour.

The results on the effects of labour tax reform indicate that a higher degree of tax progression of wages for the low-skilled workers, keeping their average labour tax rates constant, reduces their wage and increases the demand for their labour. The effect on the market for high-skilled workers is a fall (increase) in their employment, if the elasticity of substitution between consumption and leisure is higher (lower) than 1. On the other hand, a higher tax rate on wages or smaller tax exemption for the low-skilled workers raises their wage and reduces that for the high-skilled labour. These results hold qualitatively in the absence of outsourcing as well.

Finally, a higher degree of tax progression of wages for the high-skilled workers has no effect on their wages. Consequently, no employment effects—on either high- or low-skilled labour—emerge from an average tax rate neutral increase in progressiveness of the tax on high-skilled workers.

[1] Alternatively, we would focus on the role of firm heterogeneity to study the interaction between wage bargaining and foreign direct investment. See, e.g., Eckel and Egger (2009), which, however, abstracts from labour market policy reforms.

While there is a large literature on international outsourcing, only a few contributions have studied its implications for the economic effects of wage taxation. In the case of a monopoly trade union covering the homogenous domestic labour, Koskela and Schöb (2010) analyse the impact of labour tax policy reforms under both strategic and flexible outsourcing.

The rest of this chapter has the following structure. Section 11.2 presents the temporal sequence of decisions taken by the agents in the model. Section 11.3 solves for the equilibrium in the market for high-skilled labour and for optimal demand for both low-skilled labour and outsourcing. Section 11.3 also derives the relevant comparative statics results. Wage formation by the monopoly labour union for low-skilled workers under a linearly progressive wage tax levied on workers as well as the associated comparative statics are analysed in Section 11.4. Section 11.5 studies the impact of both high- and low-skilled wage progression on the equilibrium wage and employment of both types of workers. Finally, Section 11.6 concludes.

11.2 Basic framework

We use a model with heterogeneous domestic workers and international outsourcing to analyse the labour market effects of changes in taxation. The production combines labour services by high- and low-skilled workers. Low-skilled labour services can be either provided by domestic workers or obtained from abroad through international outsourcing. It is assumed that firms have sufficient flexibility to postpone the decision on the amount of outsourcing activity after the wage is set by the domestic labour union. Skaksen (2004) analyses the implications of both potential (non-realized) and realized international outsourcing for wage setting and employment under imperfectly competitive labour markets. He also studies flexible outsourcing, if only under homogenous domestic labour markets.

The time sequence of decisions in our model is described by Figure 11.1.

The government sets its policy at stage 1. At stage 2 conditional on policy choices by the government, the labour union determines the wage for the low-skilled workers by taking into account how this affects the demand for labour and outsourcing by firms. At stage 3, firms decide on domestic employment and international outsourcing. The wage of the high-skilled labour adjusts to equalize supply and demand

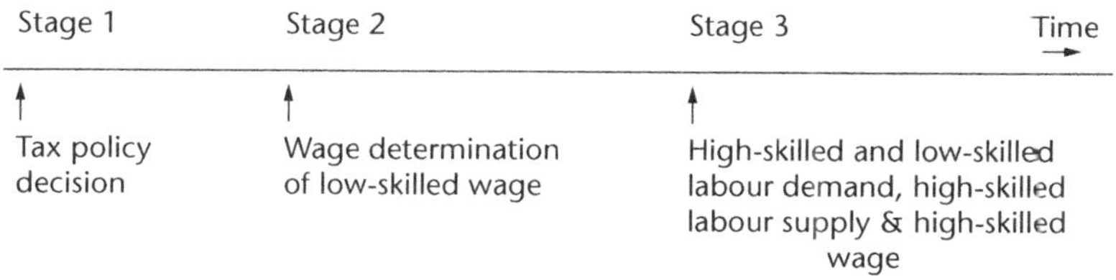

Figure 11.1 Time sequence of decisions.

for high-skilled workers. Optimal decisions at each stage are derived using backward induction.

11.3 Labour demand, outsourcing decision, and high-skilled wage formation

11.3.1 *High-skilled and low-skilled labour demand and outsourcing*

Starting from the last stage, domestic firms derive their optimal demand for high- and low-skilled labour as well as the amount of international outsourcing by maximizing their profits

$$\max_{H,L,M} \{\pi = F(H,L,M) - w_H H - w_L L - w_M M - g(M)\}, \tag{11.1}$$

where w_L, w_H, and w_M is, respectively, the wage for low-skilled, high-skilled, and outsourced labour. We assume that outsourcing is costly. More specifically, the marginal cost of outsourcing increases linearly with the amount of outsourcing. Consequently, we can formalize this assumption using the simple quadratic cost function $g(M) = 0.5cM^2$, implying that $g'(M) = cM$ and $g''(M) = c$. Outsourcing costs capture the idea that firms incur costs in the establishment of networks of suppliers in the relevant low-wage countries.

Following Koskela and Stenbacka (2010), we assume a Cobb–Douglas-type decreasing returns to scale production function in three labour inputs, i.e., $F(H,L,M) = \left[H^a (L + \gamma M)^{1-a}\right]^{\rho}$, where the parameters ρ and a are assumed to satisfy: $0 < \rho < 1$ and $\frac{1}{2} < a < 1$.[2] This latter specification means that the marginal productivity of the high-skilled

[2] Ethier (2005) has introduced a partly related Cobb–Douglas aggregate production function, in which domestic low-skilled labour and outsourcing are substitutes. In our model, domestic high-skilled labour and outsourcing are complements to analyse the effects of globalization on the skill premium as well as on the decision between international outsourcing and in-house production.

labour is higher than that of the low-skilled labour. The parameter $\gamma > 0$ captures the productivity of the outsourced low-skilled labour input relative to the domestic low-skilled labour input. The marginal products of high-skilled labour, low-skilled labour, and outsourcing are $F_H = a\rho F^{\frac{\rho-1}{\rho}} H^{a-1} (L + \gamma M)^{1-a} = a\rho F/H$, $F_L = (1-a)\,\rho F/(L+\gamma M)$, and $F_M = \gamma F_L$. The outsourced low-skilled labour input affects the marginal products of the domestic high-skilled and low-skilled labour inputs as

$$F_{HM} = \frac{a(1-a)\,\rho^2 \gamma F}{H(L+\gamma M)} = \gamma F_{HL} \text{ and } F_{LM} = -\frac{(1-a)\,\rho\gamma}{H(L+\gamma M)} F\,[1-\rho(1-a)]$$

where F_{XY} denotes $\frac{\partial F^2}{\partial X \partial Y}$ for any X and Y.

Thus, for this production function domestic high-skilled (low-skilled) labour input and outsourced labour input are complements (substitutes). Also, one can calculate from the production function that the domestic high-skilled and low-skilled labours are complements, i.e., $F_{HL} > 0$. Given the wages, the first-order conditions for optimal demand for domestic high-skilled labour, low-skilled labour, and outsourcing are

$$a\rho\left(\frac{F}{H}\right) - w_H = 0 \tag{11.2a}$$

$$(1-a)\,\rho\left(\frac{F}{L+\gamma M}\right) - w_L = 0 \tag{11.2b}$$

$$(1-a)\,\rho\gamma\left(\frac{F}{L+\gamma M}\right) - w_M - cM = 0. \tag{11.2c}$$

The first two of these first-order conditions imply the relationship between the high-skilled labour and the aggregate of low-skilled and outsourced labour:

$$H = \frac{w_L}{w_H}\frac{a}{(1-a)}(L+\gamma M). \tag{11.3}$$

Using (11.2b) and (11.2c), on the other hand, we have

$$M^* = \frac{\gamma w_L - w_M}{c}, \tag{11.4}$$

where $M^*_{w_L}, M^*_{\gamma} > 0$ and $M^*_{w_M}, M^*_c < 0$. According to (11.4) higher wages for domestic low-skilled labour and higher productivity of outsourced labour input increases outsourcing, while higher wages for outsourced labour and higher outsourcing cost decreases flexible outsourcing. In the case of production function, $F(H,L,M) = \left[H^{a}(L+\gamma M)^{1-a}\right]^{\rho}$, the following findings can be derived for the outsourcing elasticities:

$$\frac{M^{*}_{w_L} w_L}{M^{*}} = \frac{M^{*}_{\gamma}\gamma}{M^{*}} = \eta^{f}_{M} = \frac{\gamma w_L}{\gamma w_L - w_M} > 1, \; -\frac{M^{*}_{c} c}{M^{*}} = 1$$

and

$$-\frac{M^{*}_{w_M} w_M}{M^{*}} = \eta^{f}_{\widehat{M}} = \frac{w_M}{\gamma w_L - w_M} > 1.$$

Hence, the elasticity with respect to the wage for the low-skilled and outsourced labour as well as with respect to the productivity of outsourced labour are higher than 1. Higher low-skilled wage reduces these elasticities, i.e., $\frac{\partial \eta^{f}_{M}}{\partial w_L} = -\frac{\gamma w_M}{\gamma w_L - w_M} < 0$ and higher wage for outsourced labour increases them, i.e., $\frac{\partial \eta^{f}_{M}}{\partial w_M} = \frac{\gamma w_L}{(\gamma w_L - w_M)^2} > 0$. Substituting the RHS of (11.3) for H into (11.2b), $(1-a)\,\rho H^{a\rho}(L+\gamma M)^{(1-a)\rho-1} - w_L = 0$, gives

$$(1-a)\left(\frac{w_L}{w_H}\right)^{a\rho}\left(\frac{a}{1-a}\right)^{a\rho}(L+\gamma M)^{\rho-1} = \rho^{-1} w_L,$$

so that the low-skilled labour demand can be expressed as

$$L^{*} = m w_L^{-\varepsilon^{L}_{L}} w_H^{\varepsilon^{L}_{H}} - \gamma M^{*} = m w_L^{-\varepsilon^{L}_{L}} w_H^{-\varepsilon^{L}_{H}} - \gamma\left(\frac{\gamma w_L - w_M}{c}\right) \tag{11.5}$$

$$m = \left[\rho a^{a\rho}(1-a)^{1-a\rho}\right]^{\frac{1}{1-\rho}}, \; \varepsilon^{L}_{L} = \frac{1-a\rho}{1-\rho} > 1, \; \varepsilon^{L}_{H} = \frac{a\rho}{1-\rho} > 0.$$

As can be easily verified, the elasticities ε^{L}_{L} and ε^{L}_{H} are higher under weaker decreasing returns to scale, i.e., for higher ρ. According to (11.5), a more extensive outsourcing activity due to lower outsourcing cost, c, decreases the low-skilled labour demand, which is consistent with empirical evidence.[3] Moreover, higher wage for outsourced labour increases the low-skilled labour demand, i.e. $L^{*}_{w_M} = \frac{\gamma}{c} > 0$. In the presence of outsourcing the wage elasticities of the low-skilled labour

[3] For instance, Görg and Hanley (2005) have used plant-level data of the Irish electronic sector to empirically conclude that international outsourcing reduces plant-level labour demand.

$\eta_L^f = -\frac{L_{w_L}^* w_L}{L^*}\Big|_{M>0}$ and $\eta_H^f = -\frac{L_{w_H}^* w_H}{L^*}\Big|_{M>0}$, can be written as

$$\eta_L^f = \varepsilon_L^L\left(1+\gamma\frac{M^*}{L^*}\right)+\frac{\gamma}{L^*}\left(M^*+\frac{w_M}{c}\right) = \varepsilon_L^L+\frac{\gamma}{L^*}\left[M^*\left(1+\varepsilon_L^L\right)+\frac{w_M}{c}\right] \tag{11.6a}$$

where $M^* + \frac{w_M}{c} = \frac{w_L}{c}$, and

$$\eta_H^f = \varepsilon_H^L\left(1+\gamma\frac{M^*}{L^*}\right). \tag{11.6b}$$

Consequently, it is straightforward to derive the following effects of a change in outsourcing activity:

$$\begin{aligned}\frac{\partial \eta_L^f}{\partial M^*} &= \left(1+\varepsilon_L^L\right)\gamma\left[\frac{L^*-M^*L_M^*}{(L^*)^2}\right]-\frac{\gamma w_M L_M^*}{c\,(L^*)^2}\\ &= \frac{\gamma}{L^*}\left[\left(1+\varepsilon_L^L\right)\left(1+\gamma\frac{M^*}{L^*}\right)+\frac{\gamma w_M}{cL^*}\right]>0\\ \frac{\partial \eta_H^f}{\partial M^*} &= \gamma\varepsilon_H^L\left[\frac{L^*-M^*L_M^*}{(L^*)^2}\right]=\gamma\varepsilon_H^L\left(1+\gamma\frac{M^*}{L^*}\right)>0.\end{aligned}$$

These match with empirical evidence suggesting that higher outsourcing increases wage elasticities of low-skilled domestic labour demand.[4] One can also show that higher relative productivity of outsourced labour increases the own-wage elasticitiy, i.e., $\frac{\partial \eta_L^f}{\partial \gamma} > 0$.

Higher outsourcing cost and wage for outsourced labour lowers the own-wage elasticity of low-skilled labour demand

$$\frac{\partial \eta_L^f}{\partial c} = \left(1+\varepsilon_L^L\right)\gamma\left[\frac{L^*M_c^*-M^*L_c^*}{(L^*)^2}\right]-\frac{\gamma w_M}{c^2}\left[\frac{L^*+cL_c^*}{(L^*)^2}\right]<0, \tag{11.7a}$$

and

$$\frac{\partial \eta_L^f}{\partial w_M} = \left(1+\varepsilon_L^L\right)\gamma\left[\frac{L^*M_{w_M}^*-M^*L_{w_M}^*}{(L^*)^2}\right]+\frac{\gamma}{c^2}\left[\frac{L^*-w_ML_{w_M}^*}{(L^*)^2}\right]<0, \tag{11.7b}$$

[4] Slaughter (2001) and Hasan et al. (2007) have shown empirically that international trade has increased the wage elasticity of labour demand.

and it also has the same qualitative effects on the cross-wage elasticity of low-skilled labour:

$$\frac{\partial \eta_H^f}{\partial c} = \varepsilon_H^L \gamma \left[\frac{L^* M_c^* - M^* L_c^*}{(L^*)^2} \right] = \frac{\varepsilon_H^L \gamma M^*}{cL^*} \left[\frac{M_c^* c}{M^*} - \frac{L_c^* c}{L^*} \right]$$

$$= -\frac{\varepsilon_H^L \gamma M^*}{w_M L^*} \left(1 + \gamma \frac{M^*}{L^*} \right) < 0 \tag{11.7c}$$

$$\frac{\partial \eta_H^f}{\partial w_M} = \varepsilon_H^L \gamma \left[\frac{L^* M_{w_M}^* - M^* L_{w_M}^*}{(L^*)^2} \right] = \frac{\varepsilon_H^L \gamma M^*}{w_M L^*} \left[\frac{M_{w_M}^* w_M}{M^*} - \frac{L_{w_M}^* w_M}{L^*} \right]$$

$$= -\frac{\varepsilon_H^L \gamma M^*}{w_M L^*} \left(1 + \gamma \frac{M^*}{L^*} \right) \frac{w_M}{cM^*} = -\frac{\varepsilon_H^L \gamma}{cL^*} \left(1 + \gamma \frac{M^*}{L^*} \right) < 0. \tag{11.7d}$$

Finally, substituting the optimal aggregate of low-skilled and outsourced labour from Eq. (11.5) into the relationship between H and $L + \gamma M$ in Eq. (11.3) gives the demand for the high-skilled labour:

$$H^* = \frac{ma}{1-a} w_H^{-\varepsilon_H^H} w_L^{-\varepsilon_L^H}, \tag{11.8}$$

where

$$\varepsilon_H^H = -\frac{w_H H_{w_H}^*}{H^*} = \frac{1 - \rho(1-a)}{1-\rho} > 1, \ \varepsilon_L^H = -\frac{w_L H_{w_L}^*}{H^*} = \frac{\rho(1-a)}{1-\rho} > 0.$$

These elasticities are also higher with weaker decreasing returns to scale, but in this model, unlike in the case with the low-skilled labour, both the own-wage and cross-wage labour demand elasticities are independent of outsourcing. Higher own-wage and cross-wage, of course, affect negatively high-skilled labour demand.

Summarizing our findings regarding the properties of domestic labour demand in the presence of flexible outsourcing brings us to Proposition 11.1:

Proposition 11.1 *In the presence of flexible outsourcing*

(a) *The own-wage elasticity and the cross-wage elasticity for the low-skilled labour demand depend negatively on the wage for outsourced labour and outsourcing cost, whereas*

(b) *Both the own-wage and the cross-wage elasticity for the high-skilled labour demand are directly independent of the wage for outsourced labour and outsourcing cost.*

11.3.2 *Wage formation for high-skilled workers*

11.3.2.1 OPTIMAL LABOUR SUPPLY OF HIGH-SKILLED WORKERS

The market equilibrium wage for the high-skilled workers, w_H, follows from the equality of labour demand and labour supply, where, for simplicity, we use a constant elasticity of substitutuion (CES) utility function for the high-skilled worker. Labour supply is derived first and then the wage is determined from market equilibrium by taking the low-skilled wage, w_L, as given. It is assumed that the government can employ proportional wage taxes, t_H, for skilled workers, which is levied on the wage w_H net of tax exemption e_H. Thus, the total tax base in this case is $(w_H - e_H)H$, where H denotes labour supply of skilled workers. In the presence of positive tax exemption the marginal wage tax exceeds the average wage tax rate, $t_H\left(1-\frac{e_H}{w_H}\right)$, so that the system is linearly progressive.[5] The net-of-tax wage that the skilled worker receives is $\widehat{w}_H = (1-t_H)w_H + t_H e_H$. Labour supply of high-skilled workers is determined by utility maximization under the constraint $\widehat{w}_H H = C$. Using the static CES utility function in terms of consumption and leisure, the labour supply by the high-skilled worker is determined by the programme,

$$u(C,H) = \left[\alpha C^{\frac{\delta-1}{\delta}} + (1-\alpha)(1-H)^{\frac{\delta-1}{\delta}}\right]^{\frac{\delta}{\delta-1}} \quad \text{s.t. } \widehat{w}_H H = C, \qquad (11.9)$$

where $0 < \alpha < 1$ and δ describes the elasticity of substitution between consumption and leisure. Using the notation $Z = \alpha\left(\widehat{w}_H H\right)^{\frac{\delta-1}{\delta}} + (1-\alpha)(1-H)^{\frac{\delta-1}{\delta}}$, the first-order condition for labour supply can be expressed as

$$u_H(C,H) = Z^{\frac{1}{\delta-1}}\left[\alpha\left(\widehat{w}_H\right)^{\frac{\delta-1}{\delta}} H^{-\frac{1}{\delta}} - (1-\alpha)(1-H)^{-\frac{1}{\delta}}\right] = 0, \qquad (11.10)$$

so that we have the labour supply

$$H^S = \frac{(1-\alpha)^{-\delta}}{(1-\alpha)^{-\delta} + \alpha^{-\delta}\widehat{w}_H^{1-\delta}} = \frac{1}{1+\left(\frac{1-\alpha}{\alpha}\right)^{\delta}\widehat{w}_H^{1-\delta}}. \qquad (11.11)$$

[5] For a seminal paper about tax progression, see Musgrave and Thin (1948), and for another elaboration, see, e.g., Lambert (2001, Chs. 7–8).

In this case, the effects of the wage, wage tax, and tax exemption on the optimal labour supply are

$$\frac{\partial H^s}{\partial w_H} = -\frac{\left(\frac{1-\alpha}{\alpha}\right)(1-\delta)\,\widehat{w}_H^{-\delta}\,(1-t_H)}{\left[1+\left(\frac{1-\alpha}{\alpha}\right)^{\delta}\widehat{w}_H^{1-\delta}\right]^2}\left\{\begin{matrix} > \\ = \\ < \end{matrix}\right\} 0 \text{ as } \delta \left\{\begin{matrix} > \\ = \\ < \end{matrix}\right\} 1 \qquad (11.12a)$$

$$\frac{\partial H^s}{\partial t_H} = \frac{\left(\frac{1-\alpha}{\alpha}\right)(1-\delta)\,\widehat{w}_H^{-\delta}\,(w_H-e_H)}{\left[1+\left(\frac{1-\alpha}{\alpha}\right)^{\delta}\widehat{w}_H^{1-\delta}\right]^2}\left\{\begin{matrix} > \\ = \\ < \end{matrix}\right\} 0 \text{ as } \delta \left\{\begin{matrix} < \\ = \\ > \end{matrix}\right\} 1 \qquad (11.12b)$$

$$\frac{\partial H^s}{\partial e_H} = -\frac{\left(\frac{1-\alpha}{\alpha}\right)(1-\delta)\,(\widehat{w}_H)^{-\delta}\,t_H}{\left[1+\left(\frac{1-\alpha}{\alpha}\right)^{\delta}\widehat{w}_H^{1-\delta}\right]^2}\left\{\begin{matrix} > \\ = \\ < \end{matrix}\right\} 0 \text{ as } \delta \left\{\begin{matrix} > \\ = \\ < \end{matrix}\right\} 1. \qquad (11.12c)$$

Therefore, higher wage and tax exemption increases (decreases) labour supply of high-skilled workers if the elasticity of substitution δ between consumption C and leisure $1-H$ is higher (lower) than 1, while higher wage tax decreases (increases) labour supply of high-skilled worker if the elasticity of substitution δ between consumption C and leisure $1-H$ is higher (lower) than 1. In the case of Cobb–Douglas utility function, i.e., $\delta = 1$, labour supply does not depend on wage rate, w_H, wage tax, and tax exemption because $H^s|_{\delta=1} = \frac{1}{1+\frac{1-\alpha}{\alpha}} = \alpha$.

11.3.2.2 MARKET EQUILIBRIUM AND COMPARATIVE STATICS FOR HIGH-SKILLED WAGE FORMATION

Unlike in the case of low-skilled workers we assume that the high-skilled wage w_H is determined by the market equilibrium, i.e., by the equality of the demand for and supply of labour. Equating demand for labour, Eq. (11.8), and supply of labour, Eq. (11.11), gives

$$\frac{ma}{1-a} w_H^{-\varepsilon_H^H} w_L^{-\varepsilon_L^H} = \frac{1}{1+\left(\frac{1-\alpha}{\alpha}\right)^{\delta}\widehat{w}_H^{1-\delta}}, \qquad (11.13)$$

which can be expressed implicitly in terms of high-skilled and low-skilled wages as

$$w_H^{-\varepsilon_H^H} + w_H^{-\varepsilon_H^H}\left(\frac{1-\alpha}{\alpha}\right)^{\delta}\widehat{w}_H^{1-\delta} = \frac{(1-a)}{ma} w_L^{\varepsilon_L^H}. \tag{11.14}$$

Under $\delta = 1$, Eq. (11.14) can be written explicitly as

$$w_H = \left[\frac{(1-a)\,\alpha}{ma}\right]^{-\frac{1}{\varepsilon_H^H}} w_L^{-\frac{\varepsilon_L^H}{\varepsilon_H^H}}.$$

The relationship from the implicit function (11.14) between the changes in the high-skilled wage and the low-skilled wage is

$$D dw_H = \varepsilon_L^H \frac{(1-a)}{ma} w_L^{\varepsilon_L^H - 1} dw_L,$$

where

$$\begin{aligned} D \equiv & -\varepsilon_H^H w_H^{-\varepsilon_H^H - 1} + \left(\frac{1-\alpha}{\alpha}\right)^{\delta} \\ & \left[-\varepsilon_H^H w_H^{-\varepsilon_H^H - 1}\widehat{w}_H^{1-\delta} + (1-\delta)\, w_H^{-\varepsilon_H^H}\widehat{w}_H^{-\delta}(1-t_H)\right] \\ = & -\varepsilon_H^H w_H^{-\varepsilon_H^H - 1} + \left(\frac{1-\alpha}{\alpha}\right)^{\delta} \\ & \left[(1-t_H)\left(1-\delta-\varepsilon_H^H\right) - \varepsilon_H^H t_H e_H w_H^{-1}\right] w_H^{-\varepsilon_H^H}\widehat{w}_H^{-\delta} < 0 \end{aligned}$$

because $1-\varepsilon_H^H = -\varepsilon_H^L = -\frac{\rho a}{1-\rho} < 0$, making $1-\varepsilon_H^H-\delta < 0$. We can now conclude that

$$\left.\frac{dw_H}{dw_L}\right|_{\delta\neq 1} = \frac{\varepsilon_L^H \frac{(1-a)}{ma} w_L^{\varepsilon_L^H - 1}}{D} < 0. \tag{11.15a}$$

In this more general case with a CES utility function, there is a negative relationship between the high-skilled wage and the low-skilled wage, which comes via the high-skilled labour demand, where the low-skilled wage has a negative effect on the high-skilled labour demand due to complementary of H and L in production. This implies that higher outsourcing concerning domestic labour input increases the wage of high-skilled workers because it decreases the wage of low-skilled-workers, which lies in conformity with empirical evidence. It has been empirically shown that higher outsourcing decreases wages for low-skilled workers and increases those of high-skilled workers. That is, wage dispersion increases with outsourcing.[6]

The relationship from the implicit function (11.14) between the changes in the high-skilled wage and tax parameters is

$$\left.\frac{dw_H}{dt_H}\right|_{\delta\neq 1} = \frac{(1-\delta)\left(w_H - e_H\right)\left(\frac{1-\alpha}{\alpha}\right)^{\delta} w_H^{-\varepsilon_H^H} \widehat{w}_H^{-\delta}}{D} \begin{Bmatrix} > \\ = \\ < \end{Bmatrix} 0 \text{ as } \delta \begin{Bmatrix} > \\ = \\ < \end{Bmatrix} 1 \tag{11.15b}$$

and

$$\left.\frac{dw_H}{de_H}\right|_{\delta\neq 1} = \frac{-(1-\delta)\, t_H \left(\frac{1-\alpha}{\alpha}\right)^{\delta} w_H^{-\varepsilon_H^H} \widehat{w}_H^{-\delta}}{D} \begin{Bmatrix} < \\ = \\ > \end{Bmatrix} 0 \text{ as } \delta \begin{Bmatrix} > \\ = \\ < \end{Bmatrix} 1. \tag{11.15c}$$

According to these calculations, higher wage tax and lower tax exemption increase (decrease) the high-skilled wage if the elasticity of substitution δ between consumption C and leisure $1-H$ is higher (lower) than 1, because under these conditions labour supply decreases (increases) (see Eqs. (11.12b)–(11.12c) for details). In the case of $\delta = 1$, there is no effect of tax parameters on the high-skilled workers.

We can now summarize our findings regarding the comparative statics properties of the high-skilled wage determination in the presence of outsourcing:

Proposition 11.2 *In a competitive labour market equilibrium for high-skilled workers (with a CES utility function) under flexible outsourcing:*

(a) The high-skilled wage depends negatively on the low-skilled wage, whereas

(b) The high-skilled wage depends positively (negatively) on the wage tax when the elasticity of substitution between consumption and leisure is higher (lower) than 1, and

(c) The high-skilled wage depends negatively (positively) on the tax exemption when the elasticity of substitution between consumption and leisure is higher (lower) than 1, while

(d) The high-skilled wage is independent of tax parameters when the elasticity of substitution between consumption and leisure is 1.

[6] See evidence from various countries which lies in conformity with this, e.g., Braun and Scheffel (2007), Egger and Egger (2006), Feenstra and Hanson (1999), Geishecker and Görg (2008), Hijzen et al. (2005), Hijzen (2007) and Riley and Young (2007).

11.4 Wage formation by monopoly labour union for low-skilled workers

Next, we analyse wage formation of low-skilled workers assuming it takes place under labour union monopoly in anticipation of optimal labour and outsourcing decisions by the firm (see also Cahuc and Zylberberg 2004, pp. 401–3 for the case of a monopoly union). The firm, in turn, determines the wage for low-skilled workers in anticipation of the equilibrium wage for high-skilled workers w_H and of the optimal in-house low-skilled labour demand in the presence of flexible outsourcing determined simultaneously.

11.4.1 *Wage formation by the monopoly labour union*

The market equilibrium for the high-skilled wage, w_H, follows from the equality of labour demand and the supply, as presented in Section 11.3. The monopoly labour union determines the wage for low-skilled workers in anticipation of optimal domestic labour demand and high-skilled wage and outsourcing decisions by the firm. We assume that government can employ a proportional tax rate, t_L, which is levied on the wage, w_L, net of a tax exemption e_L. That is, the total tax base is $t_L (w_L - e_L) L^*$. In the presence of a positive tax exemption the marginal wage tax exceeds the average wage tax rate $t_L \left(1 - \frac{e_L}{w_L}\right)$, so that the system is linearly progressive and the net-of-tax wage is $\widehat{w}_L = (1 - t_L) w_L + t_L e_L$. The labour tax systems in all the OECD countries are progressive and show significant differences in the degree of tax progression.[7]

The objective function of the labour union is assumed to be $((1 - t_L) w_L + t_L e_L) L^* + b_L N$, where b_L is the exogenous outside option available to the unskilled workers and N is the number of labour union members. The monopoly labour union sets wage for the unskilled workers so as to maximize the surplus according to

$$\max_{w_L} \quad \left\{V = ((1 - t_L) w_L + t_L e_L) L^* + b_L N\right\}$$

$$\text{s.t. } L^* = m w_L^{-\varepsilon_L^L} w_H^{\varepsilon_H^L} - \gamma M^* = m w_L^{-\varepsilon_L^L} w_H^{-\varepsilon_H^L} - \gamma \left(\frac{\gamma w_L - w_M}{c}\right)$$

$$\text{and } H^* = H^S, \tag{11.16}$$

[7] Source: OECD (2004).

where the high-skilled labour demand and supply are, respectively,

$$H^* = \frac{ma}{1-a} w_H^{-\varepsilon_H^H} w_L^{-\varepsilon_L^H}$$

and

$$H^S = \frac{1}{1 + \left(\frac{1-\alpha}{\alpha}\right)^{\delta} \widehat{w}_H^{1-\delta}},$$

so that $H^* = H^S$ implies that

$$\frac{ma}{1-a} w_H^{-\varepsilon_H^H} w_L^{-\varepsilon_L^H} = \frac{1}{1 + \left(\frac{1-\alpha}{\alpha}\right)^{\delta} \widehat{w}_H^{1-\delta}}$$

(see Eqs. (11.8), (11.11), and (11.14)). The first-order condition associated with (11.16) can be written as (see Appendix 11.A)

$$V_{w_L} = 0 \Longleftrightarrow$$

$$(1-t_L) w_L \left[1 - \left(\eta_L^f + \eta_H^f \frac{dw_H}{dw_L} \frac{w_L}{w_H}\right)\right] + (b_L - t_L e_L) \left(\eta_L^f + \eta_H^f \frac{dw_H}{dw_L} \frac{w_L}{w_H}\right) = 0, \qquad (11.17)$$

where

$$\left.\frac{dw_H}{dw_L} \frac{w_L}{w_H}\right|_{\delta \neq 1} = \frac{\varepsilon_L^H \frac{(1-a)}{ma} w_L^{\varepsilon_L^H}}{w_H D} < 0$$

and

$$\left.\frac{dw_H}{dw_L} \frac{w_L}{w_H}\right|_{\delta = 1} = -\frac{\varepsilon_L^H}{\varepsilon_H^H} < 0.$$

Using Eq. (11.14) these can be re-expressed as

$$\left.\frac{dw_H}{dw_L} \frac{w_L}{w_H}\right|_{\delta \neq 1} = -\frac{\varepsilon_L^H}{\varepsilon_H^H} \frac{\left[1 + \left(\frac{1-\alpha}{\alpha}\right)^{\delta} \widehat{w}_H^{1-\delta}\right]}{\left[1 + \left(\frac{1-\alpha}{\alpha}\right)^{\delta} \widehat{w}_H^{1-\delta} - \left(\frac{1-\alpha}{\alpha}\right)^{\delta} w_H (1-t_H) \left(\frac{1-\delta}{\varepsilon_H^H}\right) \widehat{w}_H^{-\delta}\right]}$$

$$= -\frac{\varepsilon_L^H}{\varepsilon_H^H} \frac{T}{U} < 0 \qquad (11.18a)$$

and

$$\left.\frac{dw_H}{dw_L}\frac{w_L}{w_H}\right|_{\delta=1} = -\frac{\varepsilon_L^H}{\varepsilon_H^H} < 0 \tag{11.18b}$$

where

$$T = 1 + \left(\frac{1-\alpha}{\alpha}\right)^{\delta} \widehat{w}_H^{1-\delta} > 0$$

$$U = 1 + \left(\frac{1-\alpha}{\alpha}\right)^{\delta} \left(t_H e_H + w_H\left(1-t_H\right)\left(1 - \frac{1-\delta}{\varepsilon_H^H}\right)\right)\widehat{w}_H^{-\delta} > 0$$

Using (11.18a)–(11.18b) in Eq. (11.17) w_L^* can be presented implicitly as (see Appendix 11.A)

$$w_L^*|_{\delta\neq 1} = \left(\frac{\eta_L^f + \eta_H^f \frac{dw_H}{dw_L}\frac{w_L}{w_H}}{\eta_L^f + \eta_H^f \frac{dw_H}{dw_L}\frac{w_L}{w_H} - 1}\right)\widehat{b}_L$$

$$= \left(\frac{\eta_L^f - \eta_H^f \frac{\varepsilon_L^H}{\varepsilon_H^H}\frac{T}{U}}{\eta_L^f - \eta_H^f \frac{\varepsilon_L^H}{\varepsilon_H^H}\frac{T}{U} - 1}\right)\widehat{b}_L \tag{11.19a}$$

and

$$w_L^*|_{\delta=1} = \left(\frac{\eta_L^f - \eta_H^f \frac{\varepsilon_L^H}{\varepsilon_H^H}}{\eta_L^f - \eta_H^f \frac{\varepsilon_L^H}{\varepsilon_H^H} - 1}\right)\widehat{b}_L, \tag{11.19b}$$

where $\widehat{b}_L = \frac{b_L - t_L e_L}{1-t_L}$. The own-wage and cross-wage elasticities of the demand for low-skilled labour are $\eta_L^f = \varepsilon_L^L\left(1 + \gamma\frac{M^*}{L^*}\right) + \frac{\gamma}{L^*}\left(M^* + \frac{w_M}{c}\right)$ and $\eta_H^f = \varepsilon_H^L\left(1 + \gamma\frac{M^*}{L^*}\right)$ (see Eqs. (11.6a)–(11.6b)). These elasticities are not constant, because the demand for low-skilled labour, $L^* = mw_L^{-\varepsilon_L^L} w_H^{\varepsilon_H^L} - \gamma M^* = mw_L^{-\varepsilon_L^L} w_H^{-\varepsilon_H^L} - \gamma\left(\frac{\gamma w_L - w_M}{c}\right)$, depends negatively in a nonlinear way on the following variables: (1) the wage for high-skilled, low-skilled, and outsourced labour; (2) outsourcing cost; and (3) the productivity of the outsourced labour input relative to the domestic low-skilled labour input.

The optimal wage for low-skilled workers (11.19a)–(11.19b) in the case of a monopoly union is also given in an implicit form in the presence of outsourcing, because the wage mark-up,

$$A^f = \left(\frac{\eta_L^f - \eta_H^f \frac{\varepsilon_L^H}{\varepsilon_H^H} \frac{T}{U}}{\eta_L^f - \eta_H^f \frac{\varepsilon_L^H}{\varepsilon_H^H} \frac{T}{U} - 1} \right),$$

depends on the wage for low-skilled labour in a nonlinear way, preventing us from explicitly solving for the optimal wage for domestic low-skilled labour. Equations (11.19a)–(11.19b) can be expressed as

$$\begin{aligned} w_L^*|_{\delta \neq 1} &= \left(\frac{\overline{\eta}_L^f}{\overline{\eta}_L^f - 1} \right) \widehat{b}_L \\ &= \left[\frac{\left(\varepsilon_L^L - \varepsilon_H^L \frac{\varepsilon_L^H}{\varepsilon_H^H} \frac{T}{U}\right)\left(1 + \gamma \frac{M^*}{L^*}\right) + \frac{\gamma}{L^*}\left(M^* + \frac{w_M}{c}\right)}{\left(\varepsilon_L^L - \varepsilon_H^L \frac{\varepsilon_L^H}{\varepsilon_H^H} \frac{T}{U}\right)\left(1 + \gamma \frac{M^*}{L^*}\right) + \frac{\gamma}{L^*}\left(M^* + \frac{w_M}{c}\right) - 1} \right] \widehat{b}_L \end{aligned} \tag{11.20a}$$

and

$$\begin{aligned} w_L^*|_{\delta = 1} &= \left(\frac{\overline{\eta}_L^f}{\overline{\eta}_L^f - 1} \right) \widehat{b}_L \\ &= \left(\frac{\overline{\varepsilon}\left(1 + \gamma \frac{M^*}{L^*}\right) + \frac{\gamma}{L^*}\left(M^* + \frac{w_M}{c}\right)}{\overline{\varepsilon}\left(1 + \gamma \frac{M^*}{L^*}\right) + \frac{\gamma}{L^*}\left(M^* + \frac{w_M}{c}\right) - 1} \right) \widehat{b}_L, \end{aligned} \tag{11.20b}$$

where

$$\overline{\eta}_L^f = \left(\varepsilon_L^L - \varepsilon_H^L \frac{\varepsilon_L^H}{\varepsilon_H^H} \frac{T}{U}\right)\left(1 + \gamma \frac{M^*}{L^*}\right) + \frac{\gamma}{L^*}\left(M^* + \frac{w_M}{c}\right)$$

and, in the case of $\delta = 1$,

$$\overline{\eta}_L^f\Big|_{\delta=1} = \overline{\varepsilon}\left(1 + \gamma \frac{M^*}{L^*}\right) + \frac{\gamma}{L^*}\left(M^* + \frac{w_M}{c}\right), \; \overline{\varepsilon} = \frac{1}{1 - \rho(1 - a)} > 1.$$

11.4.2 *Comparative statics of low-skilled wage formation*

We can compute the comparative statics of the optimal wage for low-skilled workers by a straightforward application of the implicit function theorem. Starting from a marginal change in the outside option for low-skilled workers, or a change in the unemployment benefit, the solution for the optimal wage in Eq. (11.20a) implies that

$$\left[1-\frac{\left(\overline{\eta}_L^f-1\right)\frac{\partial\overline{\eta}_L^f}{\partial w_L}-\overline{\eta}_L^f\frac{\partial\overline{\eta}_L^f}{\partial w_L}}{\left(\overline{\eta}_L^f-1\right)^2}\widehat{b}_L\right]dw_L^*=\left(\frac{\overline{\eta}_L^f}{\overline{\eta}_L^f-1}\right)d\widehat{b}_L, \tag{11.21}$$

which, after using $\widehat{b}_L=\left(\frac{\overline{\eta}_L^f-1}{\overline{\eta}_L^f}\right)w_L^*$, can be expressed as

$$\frac{dw_L^*}{d\widehat{b}_L}=\left(\frac{\overline{\eta}_L^f}{\overline{\eta}_L^f-1+\frac{\partial\overline{\eta}_L^f}{\partial w_L}\frac{w_L^*}{\overline{\eta}_L^f}}\right)>0, \tag{11.22}$$

where

$$\frac{\partial\overline{\eta}_L^f}{\partial w_L}=\left(1+\varepsilon_L^L-\varepsilon_H^L\frac{\varepsilon_L^H}{\varepsilon_H^H}\frac{T}{U}\right)\frac{\gamma M^*}{L^*}\left(\frac{M_{w_L}^*w_L^*}{M^*}-\frac{L_{w_L}^*w_L^*}{L^*}\right)-\frac{\gamma w_M}{cw_L^*}\frac{L_{w_L}^*w_L^*}{L^*}$$

and $\overline{\eta}_L^f>1$. According to (11.22), the effect of the outside option on low-skilled wage formation is qualitatively the same with and without outsourcing because the wage mark-up in the case of the CES utility function is

$$A^f\Big|_{M=0,\delta\neq 1}=\left(\frac{\varepsilon_L^L-\varepsilon_H^L\frac{\varepsilon_L^H}{\varepsilon_H^H}\frac{T}{U}}{\varepsilon_L^L-\varepsilon_H^L\frac{\varepsilon_L^H}{\varepsilon_H^H}\frac{T}{U}-1}\right),$$

so that

$$\left.\frac{dw_L^*}{d\widehat{b}_L}\right|_{M=0}=A^f\Big|_{M=0,\delta\neq 1}>0.$$

On the other hand, when $\delta=1$ and there is no outsourcing the wage mark-up is

$$A^f\Big|_{M=0,\delta=1}=\left(\frac{\overline{\varepsilon}}{\overline{\varepsilon}-1}\right),$$

so that

$$\left.\frac{dw_L^*}{d\widehat{b}_L}\right|_{M=0} = A^f\Big|_{M=0,\delta=1} > 0.^8$$

The effects of the wage for outsourced labour on the wage for low-skilled labour, in contrast, can be obtained from

$$\left[1 - \frac{\left(\overline{\eta}_L^f - 1\right)\frac{\partial \overline{\eta}_L^f}{\partial w_L} - \overline{\eta}_L^f \frac{\partial \overline{\eta}_L^f}{\partial w_L}}{\left(\overline{\eta}_L^f - 1\right)^2}\widehat{b}_L\right] dw_L^* = \frac{\left[\left(\overline{\eta}_L^f - 1\right)\frac{\partial \overline{\eta}_L^f}{\partial w_M} - \overline{\eta}_L^f \frac{\partial \overline{\eta}_L^f}{\partial w_M}\right]}{\left(\overline{\eta}_L^f - 1\right)^2}\widehat{b}_L dw_M, \tag{11.23}$$

which can be expressed, using $\widehat{b}_L = \left(\frac{\overline{\eta}_L^f - 1}{\overline{\eta}_L^f}\right) w_L^*$ as

$$\frac{dw_L^*}{dw_M} = \left(\frac{\frac{\partial \overline{\eta}_L^f}{\partial w_M}\frac{w_L^*}{\overline{\eta}_L^f}}{\overline{\eta}_L^f - 1 + \frac{\partial \overline{\eta}_L^f}{\partial w_L}\frac{w_L^*}{\overline{\eta}_L^f}}\right) > 0, \tag{11.24}$$

where

$$\begin{aligned}
\frac{\partial \overline{\eta}_L^f}{\partial w_M} &= \left(1 + \varepsilon_L^L - \varepsilon_H^L \frac{\varepsilon_L^H}{\varepsilon_H^H}\frac{T}{U}\right)\gamma\left(\frac{L^* M_{w_M}^* - M^* L_{w_M}^*}{(L^*)^2}\right) + \frac{\gamma}{cL^*}\left(1 - \frac{L_{w_M}^* w_M^*}{L^*}\right) \\
&= \frac{\left(1 + \varepsilon_L^L - \varepsilon_H^L \frac{\varepsilon_L^H}{\varepsilon_H^H}\frac{T}{U}\right)\gamma M^*}{w_M L^*}\left(\frac{M_{w_M}^* w_M}{M^*} - \frac{L_{w_M}^* w_M}{L^*}\right) \\
&\quad + \frac{\gamma}{cL^*}\left(1 - \frac{L_{w_M}^* w_M^*}{L^*}\right) \qquad (11.25) \\
&= \frac{\left(1 + \varepsilon_L^L - \varepsilon_H^L \frac{\varepsilon_L^H}{\varepsilon_H^H}\frac{T}{U}\right)\gamma M^*}{w_M L^*}\left[\frac{1}{cM^*}\left(1 + \frac{\gamma M^*}{L^*}\right) + \frac{\gamma}{cL^*}\left(1 - \frac{\gamma w_M}{L^*}\right)\right] > 0
\end{aligned}$$

and $\frac{\partial \overline{\eta}_L^f}{\partial w_L} > 0$. These results hold qualitatively also in the case of $\delta = 1$, when $1 + \varepsilon_L^L - \varepsilon_H^L \frac{\varepsilon_L^H}{\varepsilon_H^H}\frac{T}{U} = 1 + \overline{\varepsilon}$. Higher outsourcing costs increase the

[8] Of course, in the absence of outsourcing the wage mark-up on the outside option $A|_{M=0} > A|_{M>0} > 1$ is higher than in the presence of outsourcing.

wage for low-skilled labour, since

$$\frac{dw_L^*}{dc} = -\left(\frac{\frac{\partial \overline{\eta}_L^f}{\partial c}\frac{w_L^*}{\overline{\eta}_L^f}}{\overline{\eta}_L^f - 1 + \frac{\partial \overline{\eta}_L^f}{\partial w_L}\frac{w_L^*}{\overline{\eta}_L^f}}\right) > 0$$

as $\frac{\partial \overline{\eta}_L^f}{\partial c} < 0$ (Eq. (11.7a)). Equation (11.15a) then implies that $\frac{dw_H^*}{dc} < 0$.

As for the effects of the tax parameters t_L and e_L, the following solutions show that the wage for the low-skilled labour increases as the wage tax increases, but falls as tax exemption increases:

$$\frac{dw_L^*}{dt_L} = \left(\frac{\overline{\eta}_L^f}{\overline{\eta}_L^f - 1 + \frac{\partial \overline{\eta}_L^f}{\partial w_L}\frac{w_L^*}{\overline{\eta}_L^f}}\right)\frac{b_L - e_L}{(1-t_L)^2} > 0 \text{ as } b_L - e_L > 0 \tag{11.26a}$$

$$\frac{dw_L^*}{de_L} = -\left(\frac{\overline{\eta}_L^f}{\overline{\eta}_L^f - 1 + \frac{\partial \overline{\eta}_L^f}{\partial w_L}\frac{w_L^*}{\overline{\eta}_L^f}}\right)\frac{t_L}{(1-t_L)} < 0. \tag{11.26b}$$

It immediately follows from (11.26a)–(11.26b) that the effects of the wage tax and tax exemption on low-skilled wages hold qualitatively also in the case of no outsourcing:

$$\left.\frac{dw_L^*}{dt_L}\right|_{M=0} = \left(\frac{\overline{\varepsilon}}{\overline{\varepsilon}-1}\right)\frac{b_L - e_L}{(1-t_L)^2} > 0$$

and

$$\left.\frac{dw_L^*}{de_L}\right|_{M=0} = -\left(\frac{\overline{\varepsilon}}{\overline{\varepsilon}-1}\right)\frac{t_L}{(1-t_L)^2} < 0.$$

This is because the tax parameters do not affect the wage mark-up but have an effect only via the outside option. Of course, in the absence of outsourcing the mark-up between outside option and wage formation $A|_{M=0} = \left(\frac{\overline{\varepsilon}}{\overline{\varepsilon}-1}\right) = \frac{1}{\rho(1-a)} > 1$ is higher than in the presence of outsourcing. Moreover, Eqs. (11.26a)–(11.26b) jointly with Eq. (11.15a) imply that $\frac{dw_H^*}{dt_L} < 0$ and $\frac{dw_H^*}{de_L} > 0$. Consequently, together with Eq. (11.22), these results in turn imply that a higher outside option for and higher wage tax on low-skilled workers reduces the wage for skilled labour, while higher tax exemption for low-skilled labour increases the wage for the skilled labour.

We can now summarize these findings concerning the comparative statics behaviour of the optimal wage for low-skilled workers and its implied effect on the wage for high-skilled workers in the presence of flexible outsourcing:

Proposition 11.3 *In a competitive labour market equilibrium for high-skilled workers with a monopoly union-based wage for low-skilled workers:*

(a) *Higher outside option for low-skilled workers in the presence of outsourcing increases their wage and therefore decreases the wage for the high-skilled labour;*

(b) *Higher wage for outsourced domestic low-skilled labour and higher outsourcing cost, in the presence of outsourcing, increases the wage for the low-skilled labour (because the wage elasticity of the demand for low-skilled labour decreases) and these decrease the wage for the high-skilled labour; and*

(c) *The above results hold qualitatively also in the absence of outsourcing.*

11.5 Effects of labour tax policy under imperfectly and perfectly competitive domestic labour markets

We next analyse the effect of labour wage tax progression on equilibrium wages and employment of the workers in each skill set.

11.5.1 *Effects of low-skilled wage tax progression on wage and employment*

In what follows, we assume that the tax reform keeps the relative tax burden per low-skilled worker constant, which implies that the average tax rate on low-skilled labour,

$$t_L\left(1-\frac{e_L}{w_L}\right)=R^L, \tag{11.27}$$

is kept constant.

The government can raise the degree of wage tax progression by increasing t_L and e_L, taking into account changes in equilibrium w_L

under the condition $dR^L = 0$.[9] Formally, we have

$$\left.\frac{de_L}{dt_L}\right|_{dR^L=0} = \frac{\left(w_L^* - e_L + \frac{t_L e_L}{w_L^*}\frac{\partial w_L^*}{\partial t_L}\right)}{\left(t_L - \frac{t_L e_L}{w_L^*}\frac{\partial w_L^*}{\partial e_L}\right)} > 0. \tag{11.28}$$

To capture the effect of this reform on the equilbrium wage for low-skilled workers we use the fact that $dw_L^* = \frac{\partial w_L^*}{\partial t_L}dt_L + \frac{\partial w_L^*}{\partial e_L}de_L$. Dividing through by dt_L and substituting the RHS of (11.28) for $\frac{de_L}{dt_L}$ gives (see Appendix 11.B)

$$\left.\frac{dw_L^*}{dt_L}\right|_{dR^L=0} = \frac{\left[\frac{\partial w_L^*}{\partial t_L} + \left(\frac{w_L - e_L}{t_L}\right)\frac{\partial w_L^*}{\partial e_L}\right]}{\left(1 - \frac{e_L}{w_L^*}\frac{\partial w_L^*}{\partial e_L}\right)} < 0, \tag{11.29}$$

so that a higher degree of wage tax progression, keeping the relative tax burden per low-skilled worker constant, decreases the low-skilled wage rate. In the absence of outsourcing the qualitative effect is similar, i.e. $\left.\frac{dw_L^*}{dt_L}\right|_{dR=0,M=0} < 0$, but it is quantitatively different (see Appendix 11.B).

Next, the effect of the tax reform on the equilibrium employment of the low-skilled workers can be obtained from the decomposition

$$dL^* = \left[L_{w_L}^* + L_{w_H}^*\frac{\partial w_H}{\partial w_L}\right]\left[\frac{\partial w_L^*}{\partial t_L}dt_L + \frac{\partial w_L^*}{\partial e_L}de_L\right].$$

Dividing this through by dt_L and substituting the RHS of (11.28) for $\frac{de_L}{dt_L}$ gives

$$\left.\frac{dL^*}{dt_L}\right|_{dR=0} = \left(L_{w_L}^* + L_{w_H}^*\frac{\partial w_H}{\partial w_L}\right)\left.\frac{dw_L^*}{dt_L}\right|_{dR^L=0} \tag{11.30}$$

$$= -\frac{L^*}{w_L^*}\left(\bar{\varepsilon}\left(1 + \frac{\gamma M^*}{L^*}\right) + \gamma\frac{\gamma w_L^*}{cL^*}\right)\underbrace{\left.\frac{dw_L^*}{dt_L}\right|_{dR^L=0}}_{-} > 0,$$

[9] A way to define tax progression is to look at APR (the average tax progression), which is given by the difference between the marginal tax rate t_L and the average tax rate $\text{APR} = t_L - R$. Tax system is progressive if APR is positive and the progression increases if the difference increases.

so that a higher degree of wage tax progression under a constant average tax rate on wages of the low-skilled workers increases the demand for low-skilled labour. As shown by Koskela and Schöb (2010), the results in (11.29) and (11.30) hold qualitatively also in the case of homogeneous domestic labour markets with outsourcing. The qualitative effect is also similar in the absence of outsourcing, because a higher degree of tax progression does not affect the wage mark-up.[10,11]

Proposition 11.4 *The tax reform also affects the equilibrium for high-skilled workers. The effect, however, depends on the elasticity of substitution between consumption and leisure in the CES utility function of the high-skilled workers, as:*

$$\begin{aligned}\left.\frac{dH^*}{dw_L}\right|_{\delta\neq 1} &= H^*_{w_L} + H^*_{w_H}\frac{\partial w_H}{\partial w_L} \\ &= \frac{H^*}{w^*_L}\left(-\varepsilon^H_L + \varepsilon^H_H\frac{\varepsilon^H_L}{\varepsilon^H_H}\frac{T}{U}\right) \\ &= \underbrace{-\frac{\varepsilon^H_L H^*}{U w^*_L}}_{-}(U-T) \qquad (11.31) \\ &= \underbrace{-\frac{\varepsilon^H_L H^*}{U w^*_L}}_{-} w_H(1-t_H)\left(\frac{\delta-1}{\varepsilon^H_H}\right)\begin{Bmatrix} < \\ = \\ > \end{Bmatrix} 0 \text{ as } \delta \begin{Bmatrix} > \\ = \\ < \end{Bmatrix} 1\end{aligned}$$

Consequently, we can summarize the labour market effects of changing the progressivity of taxation for wages for low-skilled workers under a constant average tax rate.

Proposition 11.5 *Given a constant average tax rate, a higher degree of tax progression of wages for low-skilled workers*

1. *In the presence of flexible outsourcing*
   (a) *Decreases the wage and increases labour demand of low-skilled workers;*
   (b) *Increases (reduces) employment of high-skilled workers when the elasticity of substitution between consumption and leisure in the utility function of high-skilled workers is higher (lower) than 1; and*

[10] The wage mark-up, however, is affected by the presence of outsourcing.

[11] This has been analysed in the absence of outsourcing under imperfectly competitive homogeneous domestic labour markets in, e.g., Koskela and Vilmunen (1996) and Koskela and Schöb (2002).

(c) *Has no effect on employment of high-skilled workers when the elasticity of substitution is 1; and*

2. *Has the same qualitative effects as above in the absence of outsourcing.*

11.5.2 *Effects of high-skilled wage tax progression on wage and employment*

Assume now that the tax reform keeps the relative tax burden per high-skilled worker constant, which implies that the average tax rate on high-skilled labour,

$$t_H\left(1-\frac{e_H}{w_H}\right)=R^H, \tag{11.32}$$

is kept constant.

As in the previous case for low-skilled workers, the government can raise the degree of wage tax progression of high-skilled wages by increasing t_H and e_H and allowing change in w_H under the condition $dR^H=0$. Formally, we have

$$\left.\frac{de_H}{dt_H}\right|_{dR^H=0}=\frac{\left(w_H^*-e_H+\frac{t_He_H}{w_H^*}\frac{\partial w_H^*}{\partial t_H}\right)}{\left(t_H-\frac{t_He_H}{w_H^*}\frac{\partial w_H^*}{\partial e_H}\right)}>0. \tag{11.33}$$

To derive the effect of this tax reform on high-skilled wages, start with the decomposition of the change in high-skilled wages into the change in the marginal tax rate and tax exemption, $dw_H^*=\frac{\partial w_H^*}{\partial t_H}dt_H+\frac{\partial w_H^*}{\partial e_H}de_H$. Dividing by dt_H and substituting the RHS of (11.33) for $\frac{de_H}{dt_H}$ gives

$$\left.\frac{dw_H^*}{dt_H}\right|_{dR^H=0}=\frac{\left[\frac{\partial w_H^*}{\partial t_H}+\left(\frac{w_H-e_H}{t_H}\right)\frac{\partial w_H^*}{\partial e_H}\right]}{\left(1-\frac{e_H}{w_H^*}\frac{\partial w_H^*}{\partial e_H}\right)}=0, \tag{11.34}$$

because the numerator is 0 (see Appendix 11.C). This says that a higher degree of wage tax progression, keeping the relative tax burden per high-skilled worker constant, has no effect on the high-skilled wage in the case of the CES utility function. By implication, then, there are no employment effects arising from the tax reform whereby the marginal tax rate on high-skilled wages increases, while at the same time tax exemption also increases to keep the average tax rate on high-skilled wages constant. This leads to the following proposition summarizing the main findings from the current comparative statics exercise

Proposition 11.6 *In the presence of flexible outsourcing and a CES utility function*

(a) *A higher degree of wage tax progression for the high-skilled worker, keeping the relative tax burden per high-skilled worker constant, has no effect on the high-skilled wage; and, consequently,*

(b) *The higher-degree of tax progression has no employment effects.*

11.6 Conclusions

Most western European countries are characterized by dual labour markets, in which wages of some workers are set by labour unions, while other wages are determined competitively. In this chapter, we have studied an economy in which low-skilled workers form a monopoly labour union while the market for skilled workers is competitive. We have analysed how the presence of flexible outsourcing affects the labour market equilibrium in such an economy, when flexible outsourcing is decided only after the low-skilled wage is set by the monopoly labour union.

The chapter has shown in the competitive labour market equilibrium for high-skilled workers under flexible outsourcing: (a) the high-skilled wage depends negatively on the low-skilled wage, whereas (b) the high-skilled wage depends positively (negatively) on the wage tax when the elasticity of substitution between consumption and leisure of the high-skilled workers is higher (lower) than 1, whereas (c) the high-skilled wage depends negatively (positively) on the tax exemption when the elasticity of substitution is higher (lower) than 1. On the other hand, the high-skilled wage is independent of tax parameters under the relevant Cobb–Douglas utility function—when the elasticity of substitution between high-skilled workers' consumption and leisure is 1. Moreover, under both the general CES utility function and the special case of a Cobb–Douglas utility function higher outsourcing cost increases the wage for the low-skilled labour, because the wage elasticity of the demand for low-skilled labour falls. That is, the wage mark-up increases. The increase in the low-skilled wage, in turn, reduces the equilibrium wage for high-skilled labour.

A higher low-skilled wage tax rate increases the wage for the low-skilled labour and decreases the wage for high-skilled labour. Increasing the tax exemption for low-skilled workers reduces the wage for the low-skilled labour and, consequently, increases the wage for the high-skilled labour. Similar qualitative effects arise in the absence of outsourcing. In terms of labour tax reform a higher degree of tax progression, meaning higher marginal wage tax and higher tax exemption to keep the average tax rate for the low-skilled workers constant, decreases the wage rate and increases labour demand of low-skilled workers. In the implied labour market equilibrium for high-skilled workers this tax reform, in turn, reduces (increases) employment of high-skilled workers when the elasticity of substitution between their consumption and leisure is higher (lower) than 1. No employment or wage effects for high-skilled workers arise in the case of the associated Cobb–Douglas utility function.

Finally, it has been shown that a higher degree of wage tax progression for high-skilled workers, keeping their per head tax burden constant, has no effects, under either the general CES or the associated Cobb–Douglas utility function, on the labour market equilibrium for high-skilled workers. Consequently, the equilibrium for low-skilled workers also remains intact after the tax reform for high-skilled workers.

This framework suggests avenues for further research. For one, the resources that domestic firms spend on outsourcing give rise to welfare effects in other countries. This suggests that uncoordinated policies might be inefficient from the perspective of society as a whole, and that outsourcing may provide an argument for policy coordination across countries. This has been studied by Aronsson and Sjögren (2004) in the absence of outsourcing. In addition, it would also be very useful to study the implications of optimal monetary policy under heterogeneous labour markets and outsourcing when product markets are imperfectly competitive, such as due to monopolistic or oligopolistic competition.

Appendix 11.A Optimal low-skilled wage setting under linearly progressive wage taxation

The first-order condition associated with

$$\max_{w_L} \left\{ V = \left((1 - t_L)\, w_L + t_L e_L \right) L^* \right\}$$

$$\text{s.t. } \pi_L = 0$$

$$\text{and } H^* = H^S$$

can be written as $V_{w_L} = 0 \Longleftrightarrow$

$$\frac{L^*}{w_L}\left[(1-t_L)w_L + (w_L(1-t_L)+t_Le_L-b_L)\right]$$
$$\left[\frac{L^*_{w_L}w_L}{L^*} + \frac{L^*_{w_H}w_H}{L^*}\frac{dw_H}{dw_L}\frac{w_L}{w_H}\right] = 0, \tag{11.A1}$$

where the own-wage elasticity of the low-skilled labour demand is $\eta_L^f = \varepsilon_L^L\left(1+\gamma\frac{M^*}{L^*}\right)+\frac{\gamma}{L^*}\left(M^*+\frac{w_M}{c}\right)$, the cross-wage elasticity is $\eta_H^f = \varepsilon_H^L\left(1+\gamma\frac{M^*}{L^*}\right)$, and the low-skilled labour demand is $L^* = mw_L^{-\varepsilon_L^L}w_H^{\varepsilon_H^L} - \gamma M^* = mw_L^{-\varepsilon_L^L}w_H^{-\varepsilon_H^L} - \gamma\left(\frac{\gamma w_L - w_M}{c}\right)$. Equation (11.A1) can be expressed as Eq. (11.17) in the text:

$$w_L^* = \left(\frac{\eta_L^f + \eta_H^f\frac{dw_H}{dw_L}\frac{w_L}{w_H}}{\eta_L^f + \eta_H^f\frac{dw_H}{dw_L}\frac{w_L}{w_H} - 1}\right)\widehat{b}_L. \tag{11.A2}$$

In the case of the CES utility function we have

$$w_H^{-\varepsilon_H^H} + \left(\frac{1-\alpha}{\alpha}\right)^{\delta}\widehat{w}_H^{1-\varepsilon_H^H-\delta} = \frac{ma}{1-a}w_L^{\varepsilon_L^H} \tag{11.A3}$$

so that

$$\frac{dw_H}{dw_L} = \tag{11.A4}$$

$$-\frac{\varepsilon_L^H\frac{(1-a)}{ma}w_L^{\varepsilon_L^H-1}}{\left[-\varepsilon_H^H w_H^{-\varepsilon_H^H-1} + \left(\frac{1-\alpha}{\alpha}\right)^{\delta}\left((1-t_H)\left(1-\delta-\varepsilon_H^H\right)-\varepsilon_H^H t_H e_H w_H^{-1}\right)w_H^{-\varepsilon_H^H}\widehat{w}_H^{-\delta}\right]} < 0,$$

where $1-\delta-\varepsilon_H^H < 0$. Using (11.A3) and (11.A4) gives

$$\left.\frac{dw_H}{dw_L}\frac{w_L}{w_H}\right|_{\delta\neq 1}$$

$$= \frac{\varepsilon_L^H\frac{(1-a)}{ma}w_L^{\varepsilon_L^H}}{\left[-\varepsilon_H^H w_H^{-\varepsilon_H^H} + \left(\frac{1-\alpha}{\alpha}\right)^{\delta}\left(w_H(1-t_H)\left(1-\delta-\varepsilon_H^H\right)-\varepsilon_H^H t_H e_H\right)w_H^{-\varepsilon_H^H}\widehat{w}_H^{-\delta}\right]}$$

$$= -\frac{w_H^{-\varepsilon_H^H}\varepsilon_L^H\left[1+\left(\frac{1-\alpha}{\alpha}\right)^{\delta}\widehat{w}_H^{1-\delta}\right]}{w_H^{-\varepsilon_H^H}\varepsilon_H^H\left[1+\left(\frac{1-\alpha}{\alpha}\right)^{\delta}\widehat{w}_H^{1-\delta}-\left(\frac{1-\alpha}{\alpha}\right)^{\delta}w_H\left(1-t_H\right)\left(\frac{1-\delta}{\varepsilon_H^H}\right)\widehat{w}_H^{-\delta}\right]} \tag{11.A5}$$

$$= -\frac{\varepsilon_L^H}{\varepsilon_H^H}\frac{T}{U} < 0$$

where $T = 1+\left(\frac{1-\alpha}{\alpha}\right)^{\delta}\widehat{w}_H^{1-\delta}$ and $U = 1+\left(\frac{1-\alpha}{\alpha}\right)^{\delta}\widehat{w}_H^{1-\delta}-\left(\frac{1-\alpha}{\alpha}\right)^{\delta}w_H\left(1-t_H\right)\left(\frac{1-\delta}{\varepsilon_H^H}\right)\widehat{w}_H^{-\delta}$. Therefore, given the CES utility function for the high-skilled workers, the monopoly union sets the equilibrium wage for low-skilled workers according to

$$w_L^*|_{\delta\neq 1} = \left(\frac{\eta_L^f-\eta_H^f\frac{\varepsilon_L^H}{\varepsilon_H^H}\frac{T}{U}}{\eta_L^f-\eta_H^f\frac{\varepsilon_L^H}{\varepsilon_H^H}\frac{T}{U}-1}\right)\widehat{b}_L$$

$$w_L^*|_{\delta=1} = \left(\frac{\eta_L^f-\eta_H^f\frac{\varepsilon_L^H}{\varepsilon_H^H}}{\eta_L^f-\eta_H^f\frac{\varepsilon_L^H}{\varepsilon_H^H}-1}\right)\widehat{b}_L, \tag{11.A6}$$

where $\left.\frac{dw_H}{dw_L}\frac{w_L}{w_H}\right|_{\delta=1} = -\frac{\varepsilon_L^H}{\varepsilon_H^H}$.

Appendix 11.B Tax progression and low-skilled labour demand

Substituting the RHS of (11.28) into $dw_L^* = \frac{\partial w_L^*}{\partial t_L}dt_L + \frac{\partial w_L^*}{\partial e_L}de_L$ implies that

$$\left.\frac{dw_L^*}{dt_L}\right|_{dR^L=0} = \frac{\left(\frac{\partial w_L^*}{\partial t_L}t_L\left(1-\frac{e_L}{w_L^*}\frac{\partial w_L^*}{\partial e_L}\right)+\frac{\partial w_L^*}{\partial e_L}\left(w_L^*-e_L\right)+\frac{\partial w_L^*}{\partial e_L}\frac{t_Le_L}{w_L^*}\frac{\partial w_L^*}{\partial t_L}\right)}{t_L\left(1-\frac{e_L}{w_L^*}\frac{\partial w_L^*}{\partial e_L}\right)}, \tag{11.B1}$$

which gives (11.29), where the denominator is positive. However, the numerator $\frac{\partial w_L^*}{\partial t_L}+\frac{\partial w_L^*}{\partial e_L}\frac{(w_L^*-e_L)}{t_L}$ in (11.29) is negative, as

$$\frac{\partial w_L^*}{\partial t_L}+\frac{\partial w_L^*}{\partial e_L}\frac{\left(w_L^*-e_L\right)}{t_L} = \frac{B}{\left(1-t_L\right)^2}\left(b_L-\widehat{w}_L\right) < 0, \tag{11.B2}$$

where $B = \frac{\bar{\eta}_L^f}{\bar{\eta}_L^f - 1 + \frac{\partial \bar{\eta}_L^f}{\partial w_L} \frac{w_L^*}{\bar{\eta}_L^f}}$ and $b_L - \widehat{w}_L = b_L - ((1-t_L)\, w_H + t_L e_L) < 0.$

Without outsourcing we have the same qualitative, but quantitatively different result:

$$\left.\frac{dw_L^*}{dt_L}\right|_{dR^L=0,\, M=0} = \left[\frac{\partial w_L^*}{\partial t_L} + \frac{\partial w_L^*}{\partial e_L}\frac{(w_L^* - e_L)}{t_L}\right]_{M=0}$$
$$= \frac{\bar{\varepsilon}}{(\bar{\varepsilon}-1)(1-t_L)}\,(b_L - \widehat{w}_L) < 0. \qquad (11.B3)$$

Appendix 11.C Tax progression and high-skilled labour demand

Using Eqs. (11.15b)–(11.15c) and denoting the denominator as

$$-\varepsilon_H^H w_H^{-\varepsilon_H^H - 1} + \left(\frac{1-\alpha}{\alpha}\right)^{\delta}$$
$$\left[(1-t_H)\left(1-\delta-\varepsilon_H^H\right) - \varepsilon_H^H t_H e_H w_H^{-1}\right] w_H^{-\varepsilon_H^H}\, \widehat{w}_H^{-\delta} = X < 0 \qquad (11.C1)$$

allows us to conclude that

$$\frac{\partial w_H^*}{\partial t_H} + \frac{\partial w_H^*}{\partial e_H}\frac{(w_H^* - e_H)}{t_H}$$
$$= X^{-1}\left[(1-\delta)\left(w_H^* - e_H\right)\left(\frac{1-\alpha}{\alpha}\right)^{\delta} w_H^{-\varepsilon_H^H}\, \widehat{w}_H^{-\delta}\left(\frac{t_H - t_H}{t_H}\right)\right] = 0. \qquad (11.C2)$$

References

Aronsson, T., and T. Sjögren (2004). 'Efficient Taxation, Wage Bargaining and Policy Coordination', *Journal of Public Economics,* 88, 2711–25.

Braun, S., and J. Scheffel (2007). 'Does International Outsourcing Depress Union Wages?', SFB 649 Discussion Papers SFB649DP2007–033, Sonderforschungsbereich 649, Humboldt University, Berlin, Germany.

Cahuc, P., and A. Zylberberg (2004). *Labor Economics*. Cambridge, MA: MIT Press.

Eckel, C., and H. Egger (2009). 'Wage Bargaining and Multinational Firms', *Journal of International Economics*, 77, 206–14.

Egger, H., and P. Egger (2006). 'International Outsourcing and the Productivity of Low-Skilled Labor in the EU', *Economic Inquiry*, 44, 98–108.

Ethier, W. J. (2005). 'Globalization, Globalisation: Trade, Technology and Wages', *International Review of Economics and Finance* 14, 237–58.

Feenstra, R. C., and G. H. Hanson (1999). 'The Impact of Outsourcing and High-Technology Capital on Wages: Estimates for the United States, 1979–1990', *Quarterly Journal of Economics*, 114, 907–40.

Geischecker, I., and H. Görg (2008). 'Winners and Losers: A Micro-level Analysis of International Outsourcing and Wages', *Canadian Journal of Economics*, 41, 243–70.

Görg, H. and A. Hanley (2005). 'Labor Demand Effects of International Outsourcing: Evidence from Plant-Level Data', *International Review of Economics and Finance*, 14, 365–76.

Hasan, R., D. Mitra, and R. V. Ramaswamy (2007). 'Trade Reforms, Labor Regulations, and Labor-Demand Elasticities: Empirical Evidence from India', *Review of Economics and Statistics*, 89(3), 466–81.

Hijzen, A. (2007). 'International Outsourcing, Technological Change, and Wage Inequality'. *Review of International Economics*, 15, 188–205.

——, H. Görg, and R. C. Hine (2005). 'International Outsourcing and the Skill Structure of Labor Demand in the United Kingdom', *Economic Journal*, 115, 860–78.

Koskela, E., and R. Schöb (2002). 'Optimal Factor Income Taxation in the Presence of Unemployment', *Journal of Public Economic Theory*, 4, 387–404.

—— and —— (2010). 'Outsourcing of Unionized Firms and the Impact of Labour Market Policy Reforms', *Review of International Economics*, 18(4), 682–95.

——and R. Stenbacka (2010). 'Equilibrium Unemployment with Outsourcing and Wage Solidarity under Labour Market Imperfections', *European Economic Review*, 54, 376–92.

——and J. Vilmunen (1996). 'Tax Progression is Good for Employment in Popular Models of Trade Union Behaviour', *Labour Economics*, 3, 65–80.

Lambert, P. J. (2001). *The Distribution and Redistribution of Income*, 3rd edn. Manchester: Manchester University Press.

Musgrave, R. A., and T. Thin (1948). 'Income Tax Progression, 1929–1948', *Journal of Political Economy*, 56, 498–514.

OECD (2004). *Taxing Wages: 2004–2005*, Centre for Tax Policy and Administration, <http://www.oecd.org/ctp/taxingwages>

Riley, R., and G. Young (2007). 'Skill Heterogeneity and Equilibrium Unemployment', *Oxford Economic Papers*, 59, 702–25.

Sinn, H.-W. (2007). 'The Welfare State and the Forces of Globalization', CESifo Working Paper 1925.

Skaksen, J. R. (2004). 'International Outsourcing When Labor Markets Are Unionized', *Canadian Journal of Economics*, 37(1), 78–94.

Slaughter, M. J. (2001). 'International Trade and Labor-Demand Elasticities', *Journal of International Economics*, 54, 27–56.

Stefanova, B. M. (2006). 'The Political Economy of Outsourcing in the European Union and the East-European Enlargement', *Business and Politics* 8(2), 3.

Index

Introductory Note: References such as '178–9' indicate (not necessarily continuous) discussion of a topic across a range of pages. Wherever possible in the case of topics with many references, these have been divided into sub-topics and/or only the most significant discussions of the topic are listed. Because the entire volume is about 'macroeconomics' and 'public policy', the use of these terms (and certain others which occur throughout) as entry points has been minimized. Information will be found under the corresponding detailed topics.

The manufacturer's authorised representative in the EU for product safety is Oxford University Press España S.A. of El Parque Empresarial San Fernando de Henares, Avenida de Castilla, 2 - 28830 Madrid (www.oup.es/en or product.safety@oup.com). OUP España S.A. also acts as importer into Spain of products made by the manufacturer.
Printed and bound by CPI Group (UK) Ltd, Croydon, CR0 4YY
13/08/2025
01935906-0005